D1034252

an **ITC** *publication in*
FINANCE

READINGS IN
INVESTMENT ANALYSIS

READINGS IN
INVESTMENT ANALYSIS

edited by

DAVID A. WEST

University of Missouri

INTERNATIONAL TEXTBOOK COMPANY
Scranton, Pennsylvania

Randall Library   UNC-W

Standard Book Number 7002 2228 6

Copyright ©, 1969, by International Textbook Company

All rights reserved. No part of the material protected by this copyright notice may be reproduced or utilized in any form or by any means, electronic or mechanical, including photocopying, recording, or by any informational storage and retrieval system, without written permission from the copyright owner. Printed in the United States of America by The Haddon Craftsmen, Inc., Scranton, Pennsylvania. Library of Congress Catalog Card Number: 70-76411.

HG4921
.W45

67415

For J., T., and L.

PREFACE

This book is designed to supplement a basic understanding of investments. It includes articles by a number of well-known authors in the field of investments who represent different and occasionally somewhat conflicting viewpoints and who utilize various analytical tools in accomplishing their various investment objectives. Several articles deal with some of the developing problem areas in investments; some with problems that have been around for a long time. Both the individual investor and the institutional investor viewpoints are discussed; both the conservative and the aggressive investment attitudes are considered. Various analytical approaches are represented and various analytical problems are discussed.

These essays have been selected with the primary thought of providing numerous divergent investment viewpoints that will provide the student of investments with a greater appreciation for the variety of opinion in the field of investments. Most of the selections are very readable, although a few are more difficult. A few are more specialized, but most are of general interest to anyone who wishes to be a more successful investor himself or who wishes to be of greater service as a security analyst, an investment advisor, or a professional investment manager.

Acknowledgment is due to my teachers and colleagues for nurturing my interest in the area of investments; to my students who have helped me to define those topics which need further explanation and to identify the readings that are more helpful in providing such explanation; to F.L. Stubbs, my department chairman at Missouri, for his continuous encouragement; to Phillip H. Clervi, my graduate assistant, for his invaluable research aid; to Roy Beck and Mrs. Mary Grace Robertson for their efficient secretarial services; and to my family for their patience and understanding. I am especially grateful to the authors of the essays and to their publishers for their earlier efforts and for granting me permission to include the essays in this volume. It is my sincerest hope that these readings will stimulate a greater interest in the field of investments for some readers and will facilitate the efforts of all who are seriously trying to attain a higher level of economic and financial understanding.

DAVID A. WEST

Columbia, Missouri
March 1969

CONTENTS

Part IV INVESTMENT ANALYSIS

CROSS-INDEX OF READINGS

Readings	A	B	G	D	E	F
1	Pt. I	Pt. I	Pt. I	Ch. 1	Ch. 1 & 28	Ch. 1
2	Pt. VII	Pt. I	Pt. IV	Ch. 7 & 21	Ch. 2, 4, & 28	Ch. 1
3	Pt. VII	Pt. I	Pt. IV	Ch. 7	Ch. 4 & 28	Ch. 1
4	Pt. IV & VII	Pt. I	Pt. I	Ch. 1 & 7	Ch. 2	Ch. 2
5	Pt. VII	Pt. I	Pt. I	Ch. 21	Ch. 28	Ch. 2 & 15
6	Pt. IV & V	Pt. I	Pt. I	Ch. 10 & 11	Ch. 2 & 13	Ch. 2 & 13
7	Pt. II & VII	Pt. I	Pt. I & IV	Ch. 7 & 21	Ch. 28	Ch. 16
8	Pt. II & VII	Pt. I	Pt. IV	Ch. 7	Ch. 28	Ch. 16
9	Pt. II & VII	Pt. I	Pt. IV	Ch. 7	Ch. 28	Ch. 16
10	Pt. VII	Pt. I	Pt. I	Ch. 21	Ch. 4 & 28	Ch. 5 - 9
11	Pt. VII	Pt. I	Pt. I	Ch. 21	Ch. 4 & 28	Ch. 5 - 9
12	Pt. VII	Pt. I	Pt. I	Ch. 21	Ch. 19	Ch. 17
13	Pt. VII	Pt. III	Pt. III	Ch. 16 & 17	Ch. 19	Ch. 19
14	Pt. VII	Pt. III	Pt. III	Ch. 16 & 17	Ch. 19	Ch. 18
15	Pt. VII	Pt. III	Pt. III	Ch. 17	Ch. 19	Ch. 17
16	Pt. VII	Pt. III	Pr. III	Ch. 17	Ch. 19	Ch. 17
17	Pt. VII	Pt. III	Pt. III	Ch. 17	Ch. 19	Ch. 17 - 19
18	Pt. III	Pt. III	Pt. I	Ch. 9	Ch. 8 - 12	Ch. 2
19	Pt. IV & V	Pt. II	Pt. III	Ch. 10	Ch. 13	Ch. 4 & 5
20	Pt. V	Pt. II	Pt. I & IV	Ch. 10 & 21	Ch. 4	Ch. 5 - 9
21	Pt. V	Pt. II	Pt. III	Ch. 10	Ch. 13	Ch. 4 - 9
22	Pt. V	Pt. II	Pt. III	Ch. 10	Ch. 13 - 20	Ch. 4 - 9
23	Pt. VI	Pt. II	Pt. I	Ch. 10 & 20	Ch. 9 & 10	Ch. 14 & 15
24	Pt. IV & V	Pt. II	Pt. I	Ch. 3 & 10	Ch. 2	Ch. 10, 11 & 13
25	Pt. V	Pt. II	Pt. I	Ch. 10 - 13	Ch. 2 & 13	Ch. 8 & 10
26	Pt. V	Pt. II	Pt. III	Ch. 12 - 15	Ch. 13 - 17	Ch. 5 - 9

KEY:
A. Amling, Frederick, *Investments An Introduction to Analysis and Management,* Englewood Cliffs, N. J.: Prentice-Hall, Inc., 1965.
B. Badger, Ralph E., Harold W. Torgerson, and Harry G. Guthmann, *Investment Principles and Practices,* Englewood Cliffs, N. J.: Prentice-Hall, Inc., 1961.
C. Bellemore, Douglas H., *Investments Principles, Practices and Analysis,* Cincinnati: South-Western Publishing Company, 1966.
D. Bowyer, John W. Jr., *Investment Analysis and Management,* Homewood, Ill.: Richard D. Irwin, Inc., 1966.
E. Clendenin, John C., *Introduction to Investments,* New York: McGraw-Hill Book Company, 1964.
F. Cohen, Jerome B., and Edward D. Zinbarg, *Investment Analysis and Portfolio Management,* Homewood, Ill.: Richard D. Irwin, Inc., 1967.

TO INVESTMENTS TEXTBOOKS

G	H	I	J	K	L
Pt. 1	Pt. I	Pt. I	Ch. 1	Pt. III	Pt. I & II
Pt. IV	Pt. I	Pt. III	Ch. 8	Pt. II	Pt. I & II
Pt. IV	Pt. I	Pt. I	Ch. 8	Pt. III	Pt. I & II
Pt. I	Pt. I	Pt. II	Ch. 8	Pt. II	Pt. I & II
Pt. IV	Pt. I	Pt. VII	Ch. 8	Pt. IV	Pt. I, II & V
Pt. V	Pt. I	Pt. II	Ch. 8	Pt. II	Pt. I & II
Pt. IV	Ch. 5 - 9 & 13	Pt. VII	Ch. 8	Pt. IV	Pt. I & II
Pt. IV	Ch. 5 - 9 & 13	Pt. VII	Ch. 8	Pt. IV	Pt. I & II
Pt. IV	Ch. 5 - 9 & 13	Pt. VII	Ch 8	Pt. IV	Pt. I & II
Pt. IV	Ch. 5 - 9 & 13	Pt. VII	Ch. 8	Pt. IV	Pt. I & II
Pt. IV	Ch. 5 - 9 & 13	Pt. VII	Ch. 8	Pt. IV	Pt. I & II
Pt. IV	Ch. 10 - 12	Pt. VII	Ch. 8 & 9	Pt. IV	Pt. I & II
Pt. IV	Ch. 10 - 12	Pt. V	Ch. 1 & 9	Pt. V	Pt. V
Pt. IV	Ch. 10 - 12	Pt. V	Ch. 9	Pt. V	Pt. V
Pt. IV	Ch. 10 - 12	Pt. V	Ch. 9	Pt. V	Pt. V
Pt. IV	Ch. 10 - 12	Pt. V	Ch. 9	Pt. V	Pt. V
Pt. III	Ch. 10 12	Pt. I	Ch. 4 & 5	Pt. I	Pt. V
Pt. V	Pt. III	Pt. II	Ch. 1	Pt. IV	Pt. III & IV
Pt. V	Pt. III	Pt. II	Ch. 8	Pt. IV	Pt. III & IV
Pt. V	Pt. III	Pt. II	Ch. 8	Pt. IV	Pt. III & IV
Pt. V	Pt. III	Pt. II	Ch. 1	Pt. II & III	Pt. III & IV
Pt. V	Pt. III	Pt. II	Ch. 8	Pt. IV & V	Pt. III & IV
Pt. V	Pt. III	Pt. II	Ch. 2, 11, & 12	Pt. II	Pt. III & IV
Pt. V	Pt. III	Pt. II	Ch. 8	Pt. II	Pt. III & IV
Pt. V	Pt. III	Pt. II	Ch. 13 - 17	Pt. II	Pt. III & IV

G. Dougall, Herbert E., *Investments*, Englewood Cliffs, N. J.: Prentice-Hall, Inc., 1968.
H. Dowrie, George W., Douglas R. Fuller, and Francis J. Calkins, *Investments*, New York: John Wiley and Sons, Inc., 1961.
I. Hayes, Douglas A., *Investments: Analysis and Management*, New York: The Macmillan Company, 1966.
J. Prime, John H., *Investment Analysis*, Englewood Cliffs, N. J.: Prentice-Hall, Inc., 1967.
K. Sauvain, Harry, *Investment Management*, Englewood Cliffs, N. J.: Prentice-Hall, Inc., 1967.
L. Vaughn, Donald E., *Survey of Investments*, New York: Holt, Rinehart and Winston, Inc., 1967.

READINGS IN

INVESTMENT ANALYSIS

PART I

BASIC
INVESTMENT
CONCEPTS

INTRODUCTION TO PART I

The concepts of growth, market psychology, speculation, capital appreciation, and risk taking are only a few of the concepts that every investor wants to understand. In the following six essays all of these concepts and others are discussed by the various authors. In some cases these authors are in rather violent disagreement; in some cases they hold the same approximate viewpoint but approach the concepts from different angles. Regardless of the authors' agreement with each other or the reader's agreement with the authors, the important thing is to understand the concepts and their relationships to investment planning, investment analysis, and investment portfolio policy.

In the first essay Tracy Herrick suggests that the optimism prevalent today is unfounded and that the economy cannot be expected to expand without periodic setbacks. He examines three areas: the stock market, the balance of payments and gold problem, and land speculation. Examples and parallel trends from the past are examined. Looking at the anti-depression weapons of today, Herrick suggests that they are untried and may not be as useful as some believe. He goes on to suggest the development of a deflationary business plan.

In the second essay Benjamin Graham examines two past periods of the stock market (1949-1961 and 1871-1961) and tries to answer the question of what type of market the future will bring, particularly as to how it will effect such savings plans as CREF and variable annuities. He answers these questions by examining the three major differences between the economic realities of the 1920's and the present. He concludes by picturing the current stock market as an institution cut adrift from old standards of value without having found dependable new standards.

In the third essay Gerald M. Loeb, the best-known advocate of the investment philosophy "Put all your eggs in one basket and watch the basket" presents his basic philosophy on capital appreciation, namely, that you must invest for price appreciation. He develops a "Plan of Learning" to help the new investor gain experience in the market. "Learn by doing" is the keynote.

In the fourth selection Edmund Mennis discusses economic analysis as a tool of the financial analyst, noting particularly the major problems involved in applying economic theory. The functions and contributions of the economist and his discipline are reported, and an effort is made to bring the flow of data in economic analysis to bear on the formulation of policy decisions in security analysis and selection. Mennis emphasizes the fact that investment decision must be made within an economic and political environment with the aid of all the analytical tools available.

In the fifth essay Leonard Ascher suggests that dollar averaging is the high road to financial success, and this thesis is put to the test through a theoretic model and in the application of historic data. Both the systematic saver and the single commitment plan are examined. Although maximum results are impossible with dollar averaging, Ascher emphasizes that it is also impossible to miss the market completely.

In the sixth selection the author emphasizes the increased significance of inflation risk and interest-rate risk compared to financial risk in the management of investment portfolios in periods of stimulated economic growth. Emphasis is placed upon an increased need for protection against inflation risk and interest-rate risk, noting the increased inflation in the mid-1960's and the extremely high interest rates of 1966, with the resulting greater risk of loss that the portfolio manager assumes in such a growth environment. Also noted is the risk that the authorities might act to reduce inflation, with a likely prospect that equity prices will fall in response to tighter money. The author uses mutual fund data to indicate that increasing numbers of portfolio managers have acted in response to such changing risk patterns as they have recognized that a stimulated growth economy has become a reality.

1

CAN 1929 HAPPEN AGAIN?*

TRACY G. HERRICK, formerly an economist with the Federal Reserve Bank of Cleveland, is currently coordinator of planning for a worldwide corporation.

Thursday, Oct. 24, 1929, is recognized as a symbol of financial catastrophe. The depression in business activity during the following decade is remembered even more clearly. A concerned public is anxiously asking: Can those days happen again?

Most leading economists, financial experts, and government officials offer assurances that the crash of 1929 represents the result of a special case of speculation that is not comparable to the present financial state. They assert that the U.S. economy is strong and that the stock market is moving within a sustainable range. Speculation, furthermore, is notably absent in all sectors of the economy; these experts take a broad view to declare that the economy will climb to new heights for as long as can be foreseen. Further doubt is assuaged by assurances that, should a depression ever again appear imminent, the U.S. government is prepared to use an arsenal of defenses to bolster the economy.

This optimism is unfounded. Indications are that, once again, major areas of the U.S. economy are supported by speculative activities, and that three great markets—the stock market, the balance of international payments, and land-may be vulnerable to prolonged and disruptive declines. Moreover, it is not known that the arsenal of antidepression weapons would be as effective as is often claimed, if the time ever arrived that they had to be used in earnest.

The three areas of the economy mentioned above that are considered particularly vulnerable were selected from a much longer list for two reasons. First, wholly on the basis of current information and using strictly objective measures, it is possible to show speculative activity in these areas of the economy. Second, where data are available, parallel trends can be shown

*From *Business Horizons,* Vol. 9, No. 1 (Spring 1966), pp. 53-62. Reprinted by permission.

between the present period and the late 1920's—and in one case a parallel trend shows an even earlier similar period of speculation.

Speculation is the purchase of items (or holdings, in the case of securities) at a price that does not justify their immediate use. The buyer believes that the price will increase substantially in the future. To some extent, speculative buying and building have always been a necessary part of the U.S. economy, making economic growth possible. Nevertheless, during most periods speculative ventures have been limited in scope. The present concern is that speculative activities are unrecognized and widespread, and that they represent a threat to the economy. Two of the categories selected for review, the stock market and land, account for nearly one-half of the total stock of assets in the United States.[1] Any major change in the valuation of these assets is important to holders of the assets. In addition, a change in the valuation of these assets may be very important to commodity price levels, the investment climate, and general business activity.

THE STOCK MARKET

Speculation

As all investors know, the broad average of common stock prices has increased substantially in the past fifteen years. Short periods of decline in stock prices have occurred, and during a six-week period in May and June, 1965 the Dow Jones average of stock prices dropped 10 per cent. But this drop has not been regarded as a reflection of a basic weakness of stock prices, nor have other declines, and most observers expect stock prices to continue their upward trend for years to come.

However, a disturbing set of statistics may indicate that stock market levels are, at this writing, unsustainably high. During the postwar period prior to 1958, as well as most of the recorded earlier period, stocks showed a higher yield than bonds, because stocks represented an investment of greater risk than bonds in the event that a corporation ever faced a liquidation. During the last eight years the average yield of common stocks, as measured by Moody's series, has been substantially lower than the yield of corporate bonds. The average yield from Moody's Aaa corporate bonds in 1964 was 4.57 per cent and from the composite common stock series, 3.00 per cent; in 1965 that gap in yields has widened further. Today, this pattern has been interpreted as reflecting buyers' expectations of a continued long-run business expansion and fears of continued

---

[1] This calculation is based on the estimated value of commercial mining and industrial buildings, inventories and producer durable equipment, and the estimated value of all land in the United States, excluding parks, Indian reservations, and other public land.

erosion of buying power by inflation. It is considered an indication that a new era of investment guidelines has arrived. Apparently, the eventuality of corporate liquidation has diminished in the eyes of the buying public.

Parallel Trends

The useful historical record for observation of modern economic development extends to the past ninety-three years, and the search for parallel trends will be confined to this period. A comparable ratio of bond yields to stock yields has occurred twice during these years, lasting more than a year each time. Contemporary reports from both periods show other similar features, such as the feeling that a new era was imminent, and the widespread belief that there was a need for new values to judge the wisdom of investing. In the perspective of history, each period is regarded as an era of speculation.

During the period 1871-73 the yield from utility stocks, as measured by Moody's series, was significantly lower than the yield from railroad bonds, as measured by the series of the National Bureau for Economic Research. Following the failure of Jay Cooke & Company on Sept. 18, 1873, stock prices dropped, and the U.S. economy slipped into one of the three major depressions in U.S. history. From 1879 (the end of that depression) to 1914, utility stock yields were higher than railroad bond yields in all except three years. (During these years the gap was small and probably reflected differences between the markets of the two types of securities rather than differences in investment patterns.)[2]

The late 1920's showed a similar pattern. From 1922 to 1927 (except 1925), industrial stock yields, as measured by Moody's industrial stock series, were higher than corporate bond yields, as measured by Moody's Aaa corporate bonds series. In 1928 the average of industrial stocks showed a yield of 3.82 per cent, while bonds showed a yield of 4.55 per cent. The gap in yields widened further in 1929.[3]

---

[2]Comparisons of stock and bond yields prior to 1914 need special consideration. From 1871 to World War I, the industrial base of the country was less developed than during the most recent period. Similarly, stock and bond markets were less developed. Yields from railroad bonds may be used to represent over-all bond yields during the earlier period because railroads were the only major large-scale corporations. Railroad stock yields should not be compared with railroad bond yields because of the widespread use of railroad stock issues as a device in campaigns of various management groups to gain control of railroads. Instead, stock yields of utilities may be used as a comparison with railroad bond yields. Issues of utility stocks were not widely used in management struggles, and utilities represented a type of investment which, along with railroads, served large segments of the population.

[3]The series of corporate bonds includes some firms that are not included in the series of industrial stocks, although for the broad purposes of this study the two series may be compared. Industrial stocks are used because both this series and the corporate bond series are available on a continuous basis from 1922 to 1964.

The present policies of the U.S. government may have sustained higher bond yields longer than one would expect, in comparison to earlier periods.

THE BALANCE OF PAYMENTS AND GOLD

Speculation

Gold speculators believe that the government will eventually run out of gold, and that it will not be able to honor its promise to redeem dollars or federal short-term liabilities in gold. Private citizens in many foreign countries may buy gold from their central banks, and, in order to replenish their own supplies, central banks of all nations may buy gold from the United States. However, U.S. citizens may not buy gold or legally hold gold for speculative purposes. A revaluation upward in the price of gold by the federal government would represent a windfall profit to holders of gold.

Gold speculators believe that the gold supply will dwindle because they fear that the government will not be able to eliminate persistent deficits in the capital account of the balance of payments. This inability, they feel, will exist even after allowance for more drastic currency controls than the recent tax on foreign securities flotations in U.S. money markets, and the program of voluntary restraint by U.S. lenders and manufacturers urged by the President in the spring and fall of 1965.

The trend of gold losses and the accompanying rise in short-term liabilities held abroad suggest that the speculators may be right. At the end of October, 1965, the U.S. gold supply totaled $13.9 billion, and at that time it is estimated that U.S. government short-term liabilities to foreign countries and international organizations amounted to over $29.1 billion, leaving a gap of $15.2 billion. As recently as 1957 the United States had a surplus of $4.4 billion in gold over foreign holdings of U.S. short-term liabilities.

Parallel Trends

A close similarity exists between the position of Great Britain in the 1920's and the position of the United States today. The principal international banker in the 1920's, Great Britain spread liquidity throughout the world by running a continuous balance of payments deficit of considerable magnitude from 1927 to 1930. When financial difficulties developed, sufficient gold and acceptable short-term funds were not available to back up the obligations that had been issued to underwrite the accumulation of payments deficits.[4] Similarly, in each of the past seven years, the United States has run a deficit in the capital account of its balance of payments, and is spreading liquidity in the form of short-term claims throughout the world.

Once more the stage is set for a titanic financial struggle, and speculators are again putting their money behind their convictions. From 1958 to 1963, gold absorbed by industry, the arts, and private hoards (which probably accumulated most of it) totalled nearly $6 billion in noncommunist nations. At the same time, only $3.5 billion of gold was added to central bank reserves of non-Communist nations. That trend presumably has continued to date.

Remedial Action

The concern to the economy is not that these speculators in gold will win or lose, but that, in an effort to cope with them, the government may be forced to make decisions which have serious consequences to the economy. Four kinds of action would be open to the government. Two kinds do not appear likely in the framework of political institutions that we have today, and either of the other two would probably bring about side effects to international trade that would be more serious than the gold problem.

International Depository. According to one proposed solution, all national governments would turn over their gold supplies to an international organization and would receive borrowing rights in return. The suggestion has formed the basis of many plans that have received considerable publicity, particularly from the recent International Monetary Fund meetings. However, this course of action is not likely to be favored by the U.S. banking community that is engaged in foreign business, because the proposal would reduce the demand for the dollar, and an important source of U.S. banking profits would suffer. Nor would it be supported by some staff government sectors, because the government's ability to extend political pressure to foreign governments would also be reduced. Finally, it is doubtful whether Congress would give to an international currency organization the power to intervene in domestic economic life that it would need to enforce sanctions, especially if the policies of the organization run counter to the views of Congress. Thus, this course of action appears unlikely.

---

[4]In 1925 the British pound was returned to its pre-World War I gold valuation. During the following year evidence shows there was a moderate surplus of £15 million in the capital account of the balance of payments of Great Britain. In 1927, there was a small deficit in the balance of payments; in 1928 the deficit grew to an estimated £135 million, and in 1929 the deficit was £120 million. Although the deficit was reduced in 1929, and subsequently measures were taken to protect the pound, speculators forced Great Britain to unpeg the pound to gold in 1931.

Sharing the Cost. Another course of action would be to try to eliminate the U.S. balance of payments deficit by sharing with other industrial countries the cost and responsibility of policing the world and lending to the underdeveloped countries. While this approach sounds equitable to the United States, it would require the countries of Western Europe and Japan to accept a very significant burden. To fill expanded manpower needs of armies and navies of these countries might require reinstituting a military draft. The need for additional military equipment would increase taxes in these countries.

These changes would involve many unpopular political choices for nations that have been enjoying freedom from the costs and problems of a large military establishment and of underwriting the security of the world. As long as the United States provides satisfactory military and financial insurance, it does not seem likely that Western European countries and Japan will voluntarily share these burdens.

Revaluation of Gold. In the third course of action, unilateral revaluation of gold by the United States, the U.S. government would set the price of gold higher than $35 an ounce. Such a move would have far-reaching consequences.

Governments throughout the world now hold dollars rather than gold to back their currency. A sudden rise in the value of gold would cause these foreign governments to feel defrauded: had they held gold, they would have gained a windfall profit. Fear of further upgrading in the value of gold and political pressures within their country might lead them to convert part or all of their dollar holdings into gold. Further trust in U.S. financial policy would be increasingly difficult. Most important, international financial transactions would be disrupted by gold speculation.

Currency Controls. A fourth approach appears to be the current direction of U.S. policy. Currency controls whereby dollars are rationed to the rest of the world could be voluntary on the part of lenders or could be directives from the U.S. government. One problem, however, would be difficult to correct. If currency controls of any kind were applied with severity, they would appear as a financial shock to a large number of firms that have traditionally, in the postwar years, relied on short-term financing.

The firms that use this type of financing are often small unrecognized trading and manufacturing firms that cater to international markets, although some large firms have also relied on this method. Many of these firms cannot find adequate long-term financing because of their size or lack of history, and until recently they have had no need to secure the protection against short-term swings in money markets that long-term lending provides.

While no precise figures show the magnitude of borrowing by these traders and manufacturers, they are generally regarded as a key factor in international trade, and as a group they are important customers of banks that are active in international trade, including many New York banks. If, in order to protect the U.S. dollar against gold speculators, large numbers of these traders should fail, a major part of the pyramid of international credit would be weakened, and the demand for dollar liquidity could spread to other firms and lending institutions.

It has been suggested that the accounting procedures used to present the balance of payments negatively bias the U.S. position in that these procedures do not consider the tremendous strength of our long-term investment position. A strong long-term position, however, would be of little help in case funds were needed to bolster the short-term position, because long-term investments are held primarily by private concerns, while short-term obligations are mainly federal. It would be difficult to conceive of a domestic steel firm being asked to liquidate a major million-dollar holding in Asia within a week's notice in order to make a short-term loan to the government.

Thus, the trend of international financial policy appears to be forcing the United States either to capitulate to the gold speculators or to apply severe constraints to international liquidity. Either choice will probably disrupt international currency transactions and depress international trade.

LAND

Speculation

Every recent survey and report on the subject indicates that land prices have increased sharply in the past few years. Federal Housing Administration figures show that the average cost of land used for house building rose from $2,363 in 1959 to $3,113 in 1964, an increase of nearly one-third. At the same time, home construction, the major use of land, declined; the number of one-family housing starts dropped more than one-quarter, declining from 1.25 million units in 1959 to 0.98 million units in 1964.

These figures presumably reflect the effect of land speculation on general land prices. Direct measures of land speculation, although not backed by the statistical authority of a government agency, show a much sharper rise in land prices. According to one nationwide survey prepared by an architectural service, increases in the price of usable land over the past ten years ranged from 100 per cent in slowly growing areas such as Pittsburgh, to 2,000 per cent for choice land in fast growing areas such as Los Angeles and Houston. Another survey, which was prepared by a large land development firm, showed that the average price of land at the edges of twenty-five major U.S. cities has increased tenfold in the past eight years. These price increases should be considered in light of the decline in the residential use of land. Other uses of land, including highway, slum clearance, and commercial and industrial building, have not increased enough to offset the decline in home building or otherwise account for such spectacular price rises.

Parallel Trends

The Florida land boom and bust of 1926 is sometimes used as a model example of land speculation. Less extreme speculation in land can be cause for concern if it is more widespread. Although data about prices and use of land are throughout the country sketchy for the late 1920's, some evidence exists that during that period land prices rose to speculatively high levels. This view is supported by the fact that a number of firms that developed properties failed even prior to the 1929 stock market decline, because of inability to sell, without a loss, land purchased at very high prices.

For example, a major real estate developer in Cleveland, S. Ulmer and Sons, Inc., failed in 1928 because, in words of a company spokesman, "We find ourselves, for the first time in our long history, with a large amount of real estate on our hands . . . with no possibility of selling it in the present real estate market without substantial sacrifice."[5] That story was repeated many times in Cleveland and elsewhere during the next five years.

Once again a number of major real estate developers are in trouble, largely because certain land prices have outpaced their usefulness. In Cleveland, a major developer has attemped to reorganize a vast holding of properties under bankruptcy law, and a number of other local developers are facing foreclosure proceedings.[6] More spectacular examples may be cited, including the fall of Lous Glickman in 1962 and the recent fall of Webb and Knapp Associates in New York City. This information supports the view that large developers have speculated extensively in real estate. The extent of this speculation by small investors—the suburban hardware retailer and local police chief—cannot be estimated; if it is widespread, it may be a matter of even greater concern.

Many observers do not consider this recent sharp increase in the price of land to be speculative, despite the decline in the use of land, because there is widespread belief that the demand for housing will increase substantially over the next ten years. One forecast points to an increase of nearly 14 million in the 18-44 age group by 1974, and some interpret this as a large enough increase to support present prices for land.

On the contrary, the record shows that an increase of nearly 14 million persons in the 18-44 age group during the coming ten years should not be interpreted as a guarantee of business prosperity in general, or of brisk building

---

5"Memories of Failures in 1920's Still Haunting Builders Here," (Cleveland) *Plain Dealer,* June 13, 1965, pp. 1,8.
6"Plush Apartments in Trouble, " *Plain Dealer,* June 14, 1965, pp. 1,8.

activity in particular. From 1929 to 1939 the number of persons in the 18-44 year old group increased 5.4 million. Compared with other periods of the past thirty years, this increase was large. However, during this period, building activity contracted sharply from earlier levels and economic activity lagged. In fact, the increase in population of that age group from 1929 to 1939 may have aggravated the unemployment problem that prevailed in all industries during that period.

TEMPORARY OR LONG-TERM DECLINE?

The possibility of a sharp drop in stock prices, a decline in land prices, or an upsurge in demand for gold has been considered here in light of the immediate financial problems of each of these markets separately. Nevertheless, if one or more of these situations developed, a more important question to the economy would be whether such a break in the market (or markets) represented a temporary financial debacle or the prelude to a depression in general business activity. For example, in 1907 the drop in stock values foreshadowed only a temporary drop in business activity, which regained strength by 1908. However, as is well known, the drop in stock values in 1929 preceded a much more drastic decline.

Apparently, the important differential between these two situations may be the behavior of commodity price levels, which held firm following the drops in stock prices in 1907, 1946, and 1962, as well as after the 1926 drop in Florida land prices, but fell sharply following the stock price drop in 1873 and 1929. In 1873-79 the level of commodity prices dropped 20 per cent, and in 1929-33 nearly 25 per cent—sharp drops in comparison with the behavior of commodity prices during other periods.

A sharp and prolonged decline in commodity prices would act as a severe damper to the long-term financing in the private sector of the economy, which is a major user of funds for plant and equipment investment. Debts that were made during a high price level would have to be repaid with scarce dollars—dollars that are more valuable in terms of buying power and probably much more difficult to obtain from profit. Defaulting of bonds would occur, further depressing the incentive for new private investment. Under these conditions, corporations may be expected to find desirable a policy of buying distressed firms at bargain prices, rather than a policy of new investment in the economy.

The opinion of most economists is that commodity price levels currently show basic strength. From 1959 to 1964 commodity price levels in the United States, as measured by the wholesale price index, remained steady. As further support to this view, it can be noted that prices for commodities moved up moderately in 1965. Moreover, it is claimed that the upward drift of consumer prices represents a built-in buoyancy factor for commodity prices, since wage rates of many firms that produce these commodites are tied to increases in consumer price levels.

It would be a mistake, however, to construe the recent strength of commodity price averages as a certain indication of future price stability. Commodity prices were steady preceding their 1873-79 decline, and followed a slightly upward trend prior to their 1929-33 drop. Moreover, a number of areas of current price weakness in internationally traded commodities could intensify and spread in case of a sharp downturn in stock or land prices. Prices for food and fibers from agricultural countries have fallen in the past year, following two earlier years of strength in these markets, and prices of a number of basic steel products from Japan, including cold rolled sheets, bars, and angles, have weakened in international markets in the past year.

In addition, certain speculative factors within the domestic economy, which may be masked by the broad measures of domestic price levels, should not be considered as representing basic strength of prices in commodity markets. For example, advances in land prices, which may be speculative in many cases, helped push up the rent category in the consumer price index in recent years. Moreover, nearly all of the recent increase in nonagricultural commodity prices of the wholesale price index has been due to increased prices of nonferrous metals, which rose 12 per cent from June, 1964 to June, 1965. An important factor in this rise was the increase in precious and semiprecious metals, including mercury (which more than doubled in price during the period), tin, and platinum. This sharp rise cannot be completely explained by an increase in their industrial use; part of the explanation may be that these metals are held by speculators who anticipate a rise in value of all precious and semiprecious metals if gold and silver are revalued. If, as some observers believe, the prices of these metals have been overbid, a decline may be expected at some future date.

Thus, it is not certain that commodity price levels will continue strong in the event of a decline in prices of stock or land. Moreover, basic weaknesses may be present in the structure of commodity prices that could represent a serious threat to the strength of the over-all economy, if the economy suffers a financial jolt.

ANTIDEPRESSION WEAPONS

Many prominent public officials assert that the U.S. government has the ability, the obligation, and the desire to prevent another depression. If stock prices spiraled downward for several years, or if a major crisis occurred in internationally traded currencies, the government, they claim, would cushion the shock, and in no case would these crises lead to a catastrophe similar to the 1929-33 period.

Even these assurances, however, leave considerable room for doubt.

Without question, the government's intention would be to make every attempt to prevent such a recurrence. Yet no one has presented a convincing case that the antidepression measures now available will work without a full-scale revamping of the U.S. economy.

Price Level Support

In the event of a cutback in demand, unemployment compensation and welfare payments would be used to support price levels. Nevertheless, it is hard to believe that these relatively meager payments would provide much of a prop to prices in contrast to the earlier period of health when economic growth needed massive personal and corporate spending, and the general commodity price level was steady or rose slightly.

It is proposed that the government could directly stimulate price levels; the only U.S. experience that appears relevant occurred in 1933, when, in order to stimulate a rise in commodity prices, the gold content of the dollar was reduced 41 per cent. True, commodity price levels did rise, but the rise was slow throughout the 1930's and did not act as much of a stimulus to investment. In fact, the wholesale price index did not make up the difference until 1946, obviously as a result of war shortages, not of the devaluation.

Support can also be effected by a price freeze, but the record indicates that price controls are difficult to enforce without accompanying government control in varying degrees in all other sectors of the economy.

Federal Spending Program

A huge public works program, or some other program of massive buying, is commonly viewed as an effective antidote to depression. The experience of the 1930's, however, indicates that even a moderate volume of government investment and purchases in peacetime may widely discourage, rather than encourage, private investment. Although these programs may have helped cure the unemployment problem, they cannot be accepted as successful restorers of confidence to the private sector of the economy.

Of course, a much faster, more inclusive program of direct investment by the government could be undertaken to restore prosperity, but the political changes in the roles of government and business would be enormous. It is not likely that these changes would be made without a prolonged political siege and a profound change in the attitudes of most people in regard to the role of government in the life of the nation.

This brief review of the problem is noted here to point out that one is no more likely to find an instant cure for a depression than one is to find an instant cure for any other economic problem. Moreover, recent evidence indicates that long swings in economic activity may be outcomes of major shocks to the economy, such as a war or a financial debacle, and that attempts to nudge the economy out of a possible depression through the use of moderately stimulative measures may be futile.[7] A possible future depression would involve new and difficult economic and moral decisions. Of course, certain government actions could help people endure the period without the deprivation of the last depression, but, these measures would really be palliatives, and they should not be looked upon as basic remedies.

A DEFLATIONARY BUSINESS PLAN

Most businessmen and economists do not share this view of the likelihood of a speculative boom and subsequent crash. Their expectations are more optimistic. Nevertheless, if the managing group of a corporation seriously believes that this course of affairs is possible, then it has a need and a financial responsibility to develop a business plan for a depression. Properly guided, such a course of corporate action could represent a growth opportunity for a firm. For example, Chyrsler automobiles reached their highest level of consumer acceptance as the 1929-33 depression worsened.

The art of charting corporate policy, in its broadest scope, consists of knowing how to use the policies that are based on a period of business expansion as long as they are most profitable, and then knowing when and how fast to turn to policies that are based on a different economic climate. The objective is to utilize every chance of profitmaking. A business plan in three parts, designed to promote that goal and yet cope with the future financial reversal, is presented here.

The first part of the plan would be the development of an early warning reconnaissance, so that corporate policies would be timed right. In order to be as objective as possible about problems of timing, working models of various types of economic climates are needed, because the question of the future of the economy in the early period of a changing economic climate is difficult to assess without a coherent set of alternatives. In fact, no other consideration of management is likely to be fraught with so much confusion and disagreement. When policies that have been profitable for a number of years are changed on the basis of incomplete information, the move represents nothing less than an act of fool's courage, with final comment reserved for many years.

A second part of the business plan would be the development of the program that would be needed to keep the corporation's capital structure intact.

---

[7]Irma Adelman, "Long Cycles—Fact or Artifact?" *American Economic Review*, LV (June 1965), pp. 444-63.

A deflation in over-all price levels would make repayments of corporate debt difficult and represent a potential threat to corporate solvency. Moreover, a lowered sales volume and a severe profit squeeze would reduce the flow of dollars that could be used for debt repayment.

A final part of the business plan would consist of measures designed to provide for the corporation's long-run growth. In its broadest scope, the growth policy of a corporation would look at the basic changes in investment patterns that would probably accompany a depression, including changes in basic beliefs underlying political and economic thought. Two brief examples follow.

In the depression that began in 1873, investment in basic metal manufacturing in the United States moved up strongly, as compared with the earlier years. By 1879, the final year of that depression, the mills first produced one million tons of steel. During that depression, substantial changes in government policy encouraged this new direction of investment. A protective tariff kept many foreign products from our markets, and a government generally favorable to manufacturing and farming interests was largely deaf to the demands from labor groups.

In the 1930's the United States needed adequate consumer credit in order to match the domestic market with productive capabilities. During this period the banking community, considering consumer loan companies as close cousins to the pawn brokers, did not favor consumer loans. By supplying to the public the consumer credit needed in order to buy many of the costly durable goods, consumer loan companies showed one of their best growth periods during the 1930's. Government policies also aided the development of consumer lending. Through measures such as subsidies to farmers, the WPA, social security, labor legislation, and many others, the risks associated with a complete cutoff to income were minimized, and farmers and workers could borrow with some assurance that they could repay their loans.

Relating the broad sweep of a new investment era of a depression to profit-making opportunities for a specific corporation is not an easy task. It is not likely that the methods that corporations have relied on to promote growth during prosperous times will be useful during a period of hard times. Nevertheless, the record shows that some corporations had their best growth period during a depression. The future may again test the resourcefulness and inventiveness of corporations and show that the only secret to prosperity is an agile mind.

The first date marked is October 1929, the month in which the bull market crashed. Though stock prices had reached their peak on September 7, when Standard and Poor's composite price index of 90 common stocks stood at 254, the decline in the following four weeks was orderly and produced no panic. In fact, after falling to 228 on October 4, the index rose to 245 on October 10. The decline thereafter degenerated into a panic on October 23. The next day, blocks of securites were dumped on the market and nearly 13 million shares were traded. On October 29, when the index fell to 162, nearly 16½ million shares were traded, compared to the daily average during September of little more than 4 million shares.

> *Milton Friedman*
> *and Anna Jacabson Schwartz*
> *The Great Contraction, 1929-1933*

2

SOME INVESTMENT ASPECTS OF ACCUMULATION THROUGH EQUITIES*

BENJAMIN GRAHAM, author, lecturer, and university professor, lives in Beverly Hills, California.

I

The terms of reference for this paper relate to systematic plans for saving or accumulation through common stocks. Such plans might include (*a*) a pension plan concentrating on equities, such as the CREF arrangement for college professors; (*b*) the very similar mechanics of the newly developing variable annuities; (*c*) systematic purchases of mutual-fund or closed-end investment company shares; and (*d*) an individual dollar-averaging plan, such as the monthly-purchase program of the New York Stock Exchange.

The chairman has asked me to consider investment aspects of such plans in longer perspective and to give my views on the following questions: What results can be expected from them in the future as compared with the results either of the shorter term past—i.e., since 1949—or of the longer-term past, going back

*From *Journal of Finance*, Vol. XVII, No. 2 (May 1962), pp. 203-14. Reprinted by permission.

into the last century and farther? How good will common stocks be as an inflation hedge in the future? Can dollar-averaging be counted on infallibly to produce satisfactory results? More specifically, can the much better performance of common stocks as against bonds be counted on to repeat itself in the next fifteen years?

I shall leave the chances and the effects of atomic war out of the following discussion, except for some observations regarding the indefinite continuance of the Cold War. Which of the two past periods will the future stock market resemble more closely—that of 1949-61 or that of, say, 1871-1961?

The latter comprises the 90 years for which we have common-stock indexes of earnings, dividends, and prices, as compiled first by the Cowles Commission and then continued by Standard & Poor's. In discussing equity experience in terms of the future behavior of these indexes, we are assuming that the various equity-accumulation plans within our purview are likely to show results, in the aggregate, approximating those of the S-P Composite or 500-Stock Index. It would seem easy enough to equal these average results; all that is needed is a representative diversification "across the board" and without that selectivity which is a watchword of today. But, paradoxically, if it is easy to equal the averages, it seems almost impossible for the average skilled investor to beat them.

We have very full information regarding the operations and achievements of the investment funds. For the 1949-60 period, as in the earlier years, they have not managed as a group to outperform the S-P 500 Stock Composite. It may be that professionally managed funds are too large a part of the total picture to be able to outperform the market as a whole; it may also be true, as I suspect, that certain weaknesses in their basic principles of stock selection tend to offset the superior training, intelligence, and effort that they bring to this task. But our main point is to establish that what happens to the stock market in general is going to happen to the typical or average accumulator of equities by any plan or under any auspices.

Let us attempt to summarize briefly the chief characteristics of the two market periods to which we are turning for clues to the future and among which we may have to choose. Table 1 gives some data covering the three salient factors of earnings, dividends, and price behavior. We bring down the 1949-61 period into two 6-year halves. The longer span can be handled in a variety of ways; we have decided to supply average computations for each of the nine decades between 1871 and 1961.

A cursory study of our table shows a number of striking differences between the exhibits of the two periods. Molodovsky has demonstrated that the over-all gain to investors for the 88 years, 1871-1959, has averaged about 5 per cent per annum in dividend return and 2½ per cent per annum in price appreciation—both taken against annual market prices. The 2½ per cent annual

A Picture of Stock-Market Performance, 1871–1960 and 1947–61*

Period	Average Price	Average Earnings	Average P/E Ratio	Average Dividend	Average Yield (Per Cent)	Average Payout (Per Cent)	Annual Growth Rate† Earnings (Per Cent)	Annual Growth Rate† Dividends (Per Cent)
1871–80	3.58	0.32	11.3x	0.21	6.0	67	....	....
1881–90	5.00	0.32	15.6	0.24	4.7	75	−0.64	−0.66
1891–1900	4.65	0.30	15.5	0.19	4.0	64	−1.04	−2.23
1901–10	8.32	0.63	13.1	0.35	4.2	58	+6.91	+5.33
1911–20	8.62	0.86	10.0	0.50	5.8	58	+3.85	+3.94
1921–30	13.89	1.05	13.3	0.71	5.1	68	+2.84	+2.29
1931–40	11.55	0.68	17.0	0.78	5.1	85	−2.15	−0.23
1941–50	13.90	1.46	9.5	0.87	6.3	60	+10.60	+3.25
1951–60	39.20	3.00	13.1	1.63	4.2	54	+6.74	+5.90
1951	22.34	2.45	9.1	1.41	6.3	58	....	....
1961(H)	72.20	3.10	23.2	1.97	2.7	64	+2.5	+3.5
1947–49	15.71	2.18	7.1	0.97	6.4	45	....	....
1953–55	31.64	3.02	10.1	1.51	4.8	50	+5.7	+7.8
1959–61	59.70	3.24	18.3	1.91	3.2	58	+3.5	+5.9

*The data are based largely on figures appearing in N. Molodovsky's article "Stock Values and Stock Prices," *Financial Analysts Journal,* May 1960. These, in turn are taken from the Cowles Commission book *Common Stock Indexes* for years before 1926 and from the spliced-on Standard-Poor's 500-Stock Composite Index for 1926 to date.

†The annual growth-rate figures are Molodovsky compilations covering successive 21-year periods ending in 1890, 1900, etc. The lower growth-rate figures cover the 10 years ended 1961, the 6 years ended 1953–55, and the 12 years ended 1959–61. The 1961 price is the high to December 7.

increase, compounded, in market price was closely paralleled by the annual rate of growth in both earnings and dividends.[1]

But between 1947-49 and 1959-61 the growth rates for the various components have been quite diverse, and they have also varied sharply between the first and the second halves of the period. Thus we get very different indications of recent performance if we consider earnings rather than market price and if we consider the last 6 years rather than the last 12.

The behavior of the stock market itself has been significantly different in the last 12 years from any previous period of equal length covered by our

1See N. Molodovsky, "Stock Values and Stock Prices," *Financial Analysts Journal,* March 1960.

records. We have experienced what appears to be a single bull market, beginning at 13.55 for the composite index and rising to a current high of 72. The advance has been interrupted by three recessions, each on the order of some 20 per cent. Under the usual terminology, these would be characterized as corrections or setbacks within a bull market.

As is well known, the long-term history of the stock market has been completely different. The picture, shown in Table 2, is one of a succession of bull and bear markets of varying duration and amplitude. Between 1899 and 1949 there were ten such well-defined cycles, thus averaging 5 years in length. (The longest period between peaks was 10 years, from 1919 to 1929, and the

Table 2.   *Major Stock–Market Swings between 1871 and 1949*

	Cowles–Standard 500–Composite			*Dow–Jones Industrial Average*		
Year	*High*	*Low*	*Per Cent Decline*	*High*	*Low*	*Per Cent Decline*
1871		4.74				
1881	6.58					
1885		4.24	28			
1887	5.90					
1893		4.08	31			
1897					38.85	
1899				77.6		
1900					53.5	31
1901	8.50			78.3		
1903		6.26	26		43.2	45
1906	10.03			103		
1907		6.25	38		53	48
1909	10.30			100.5		
1914		7.35	29		53.2	47
1916	10.21			110.2		
1917/8		6.80	33		73.4	33
1919	9.51			119.6		
1921		6.45	32		63.9	47
1929	31.92			381		
1932		4.40	86		41.2	89
1937	18.68			197.4		
1938		8.50	55		99	50
1939	13.23			158		
1942		7.47	44		92.9	41
1946	19.25			212.5		
1949		13.55	30		161.2	24

shortest was 2 years, from 1899 to 1901 and from 1937 to 1939.) Most of the declines in the industrial averages were in the range of 40-50 per cent; in the earlier years the composite average had somewhat smaller losses. The largest, of course, was the shocking fall of the Composite Index from 31.92 in 1929 to a low of only 4.40 in 1932, a loss of 86 per cent. About the same proportionate decline was shown by the Dow-Jones Industrial Average.

It should be pointed out also that the gyrations of past stock markets may not properly be viewed as taking place around a well defined and persistent upward trend line, sloped at 2½ per cent per annum. Both the price record and the earnings record disclose an irregular, rather than a regular, trend line. This should be evident from an inspection of our successive 10-year average figures between 1871 and 1950 and the Molodovsky growth rates appended thereto.

The price-earnings ratio has also shown wide fluctuations. Since earnings have been even more unstable than prices—because of the recurrent business cycles—there has been a clear-cut tendency for the highest earnings multipliers to be established in years of depression, when profits tended toward the vanishing point. Our average figures by decades smooth out this type of variation; but they do not show the upward trend in price-earnings ratios that we might have expected to accompany improvement in the underlying strength of our corporations and in the dependability of published earnings figures. Actually, the ratio of 6.2 times for 1949-50, at the beginning of the present bull market, was the lowest for any 2-year period in our 90-year history of stock prices and earnings. A devotee of the pendulum-swing theory of economic phenomena might well explain the current record-high multiplier as a reaction to the opposite extreme from the 1949-50 depreciation of the earnings dollar.

II

With these two quite diverse stock-market pictures before us, let us now inquire what are the respective arguments for considering the 1949-61 period as an integral continuation of the 1871-1949 span or for recognizing it as a new dispensation which will determine the character of the markets of the future. It is not too difficult for the student to fit the pattern of the recent market into that of the longer past. True, both the duration and the extent of its rise are already greater than those of any other.[2] But that a pattern of many decades should establish new records of various kinds from time to time is only to be expected. A new record does not create a new pattern or character.

Is it possible, then, that we are living through a modified, but not essentially different, version of the experience of the 1920's? That there must be impressive differences goes without saying; for otherwise all of us would have

---

[2]These statements refer to the S-P Composite Index. The percentage rise in the industrials was somewhat larger from 1921 to 1929 than from 1949 to date because it started from a relatively lower level.

been so struck by the incipient similarity as to make its continuation impossible. What may be more likely-speaking in abstract terms—is that the original differences have convinced us that the 1929 experience is irrelevant but that the similarities have been developing later, gradually, and so insidiously as to find us psychologically incapable of recognizing them. Let us attempt an enumeration of the major differences and resemblances between the current market and that of the 1920's, as they appear to this observer.

The two major internal differences relate to financial manipulation of various sorts and to excessive borrowing for speculation. The bull-market heights of 1929 were made possible by a huge wave of buying on thinner margins than are now permitted. Brokers' loans rose from $2.769 million in 1926 to $8.549 million in 1929, at which time they constituted about half of total member-bank loans. By contrast, the corresponding rise to date has been relatively much smaller. (Borrowings on smaller margins through other sources are no doubt significant at present but not sufficiently so to change the broad picture.) In the field of financial practices, the major abuses of the 1920's consisted of crass manipulation of stock prices by speculative pools and of corporate pyramiding through successive tiers of holding companies of various types. Both stock-market manipulation and corporate-structure manipulation have been greatly restricted by the SEC legislation and by tighter stock-exchange supervision. The amount that escapes detection is comparatively small, in my view. Although the various investigations now under way produce some startling exposés, whatever abuses now exist will not be found to have permeated the whole fabric of finance as was the case 30 years ago.

An exception to the above reassuring statement may have to be made in the field of new offerings of common stocks. Here I think a set of at least semi-manipulative practices has developed in handling so-called "hot issues." The number of such offerings has been increasing steadily in the last 2 years, and their quality has been retrogressing at an equal rate. It is in this speculative area that I sense the closest parallel between the internal market conditions of the late 1920's (and particularly of 1919) and those of today. Whether the new-issue financing of dubious merit will prove to be so heavy in aggregate dollars as ultimately to turn the market scales definitely downward, I shall not venture to guess. It is not impossible.

The widespread belief that we are in a new stock-market era, differing in its essential character from the bull-and-bear sequences of the past, rests on a number of claimed differences between then and now. These go well beyond the reforms in stock trading and in corporate financial practices. The case to justify the present unprecedented level of stock prices and earnings multipliers is essentially that which would justify the concept of a permanently changed character and future for the stock market. The safety and attractiveness of common-stock investment today is thought to be solidly grounded on a complex of favorable factors. Among the are (*a*) assured growth of population and GNP; (*b*) a rate of expansion more rapid than formerly, created by technological progress and the rivalry with Russia; (c) an assurance against major depressions provided by the government's new responsibility to prevent or quickly terminate them; (d) the public's recognition that common-stock investment is a necessary protection against continued inflation; and (e) the emergence of mutual funds, pension trusts, and other institutional investors as the chief source of demand and continuous support for common stocks.

Those who study the record of the 1920's will find that reasons similar to most, but not all, of the above were advanced to justify the ill-fated market rise of those years. The doctrine of "Common Stocks as (the Best) Long-Term Investments" emerged in 1924 and was made the cornerstone of the market's philosophy and its excesses. There was the same optimism about the future growth of the country and perhaps a better-founded confidence in the share of common-stock earnings in that growth. (The rate of return on invested capital was better maintained between 1922 and 1929 than between 1950 and 1961.) Old standards of value—particularly the once normal relationship between bond yields and common-stock yields—were thrown aside then as now, on the grounds that they had no relevance to the new economic climate. There was great confidence, also, in the future stability of business and its immunity from severe depressions. This was founded on the idea that scientific management, careful control of inventories, the absence of inflation, and other factors would help our business leaders avoid the costly mistakes of the past.

In my view, there are three major differences between the economic realities of the 1920's and the present. The first relates to the inflation factor, the second to the Cold War, and the third to the role of government in business. The bull market of the 1920's ran its course without the aid of commodity-price inflation; the market rise since 1949 has been accompanied by an irregular, but virtually continuous, advance in wholesale and consumer prices. It is difficult to say whether the investor's current emphasis on future inflation possibilities should be considered primarily as a recognition on his part of objective fact or rather as a strong *subjective* reaction to an element that is by no means new to the financial scene. We had more inflation in wholesale prices from 1900 to 1910 than from 1950 to 1960; the rise from 1900 to 1920 also exceeded that from 1940 to 1960 (the equivalent of from 36 to 100 versus from 51 to 120). Most of us believe that inflation is the path of least resistance for governments, labor leaders, and business heads and that hence it will be followed. But the record of the past will not help us much to determine what the amount of inflation will be over future decades, whether its course will be regular or interspersed with sharp deflations, as in 1921 and 1932, and whether investors will remain as inflation-conscious in the future as they are today. The reaction to inflation, like almost every other investment and speculative attitude, seems to be more the result of the stock market's behavior than the cause of it.

My view of the effects of the Cold War on common-stock values is quite a personal one, not shared by many, I am sure. In the first place, I think that it has contributed a good deal to the business expansion and relative stability of the past decade. But, in a contrary sense, I cannot see how the kind of Cold War we are now living through can continue throughout "our lifetime and that of our children." Sometime within the present decade a way will have to be found to terminate the Cold War, or it will be transformed into large-scale hostilities with all their nuclear implications. If our prosperity since 1949 has, in fact, rested rather heavily on our defense expenditures and if, in truth, we must fairly soon have either no war or nuclear war in place of Cold War, then today's international situation cannot be termed more favorable for common stocks than the cloudless one of 1929.

The government's commitment to prevent large-scale unemployment and serious depressions is both a new factor and one of major importance. The most logical reason for expecting a different kind of stock-market cycle in the future than in the long-term past would appear to be by analogy with the business cycle. The record since 1949 strongly supports this thesis. The new material on "Business Cycle Developments," now available monthly, shows four periods of business contraction since 1948—in 1949, 1953-54, 1957-58, and 1960. All these were very moderate, as compared with the sharp recession of 1937-38 and the major depressions after 1919 and 1929. The three declines of about 20 per cent each in the stock averages since 1950 appear to correspond fairly well to the three setbacks of about 10 per cent in the index of industrial production. If we have now entered a new era that excludes old-time business depressions, it seems reasonable to deduce that we are also in a new era that precludes old-fashioned bear markets.

III

Both my analysis and my instinct warn me that there may be a catch in this plausible and reassuring parallel. If the recent picture had been one of the stock market's advancing in step with the national product and in close proportion with it also, then the observer might conclude—somewhat to his amazement—that not only has the economy been reformed but human nature as well. But here the facts part company with the hypothesis. The stock-market level has not been governed primarily by the level of business but rather by the development of new investment theories and attitudes and by a typical growth of speculative interest and activity. Some of the old financial abuses that characterized former bull markets have, indeed, been virtually eliminated. But some have again raised their heads, and some new ones have appeared and are spreading apace. These are in the areas of corporate reporting, corporate financing, the quality of the enterprises offered for public sale, and the ways in which new issues of common stocks are offered and subsequently traded.

Equally important and dangerous, in my eyes, is the ready acceptance by security analysts of the going market levels and earnings-multipliers as the proper standard of value and of camparison for any issue under study. The new analytical concepts of growth-stock valuation, of "cash flow," of desirability of tax-free dividends from companies which are triumphantly able to report earnings *deficits*—all have enough plausibility and lack of inner discipline to lead both investors and speculators far astray. In sum, the new investment theories and techniques remind me very much of 1928-29, and the outpouring of common-stock issues of secondary and lower-degree enterprises reminds me equally of 1919. If the relative stability of general business and corporate profits produces an unlimited enthusiasm and demand for common stocks, then it must eventually produce *instability* in stock prices. We have already seen the working of this paradox in the area of growth stocks. The price of a successful and promising concern such as Texas Instruments can be driven up so high by speculative emphasis on its prospects that the ensuing reaction has cut the price in half—with no change in the underlying worth of the business. Examples of this sort are now numerous. Conceivably, this behavior of issues in the growth-stock class may give us a preview of the ultimate behavior of the general market—as represented by comprehensive averages—if common-stock investment becomes essentially identical with common-stock speculation. In that case the stock market will have a life-cycle of its own, quite independent of the business cycle. The market cycle will once more prove to be the human-nature cycle; its economic background will have changed but not its basic character or the consequences of its character.

These arguments against a new character for the stock market are not necessarily arguments that the present levels are too high, although they certainly would be adjudged so by older standards. Conceivably and even probably, new factors in the economic figure have moved upward the central value of the average dollar of corporate earnings and justify a more favorable relationship than heretofore between stock yields and bond yields. This would certainly be true if the general business picture can be counted on to continue indefinitely the relative immunity to depression it has shown since as far back as 1941. What we are concerned with here is not the future central value of the stock market but rather the amplitude and the consequences of possible future variations around this value.

To soften a possible charge of old-fogyism and prejudice against new standards of value, may I take this paragraph to show how the recent record level of stock prices may be justified by some not implausible calculations. Let us assume that the investor wants an over-all return of 7½ per cent annually, as a composite of dividend income and average market appreciation. (This 7½ per cent target is itself taken from the long-term record of dividend yields and price advances; it seems reasonable as a guide to the future.) Assume, next, that earnings and dividends will grow in the indefinite future at the annual rate of 4½ per cent, which appears to be the projection for this decade. Then the investor should be satisfied with a 3 per cent dividend return. This would justify a current level of 65 for the S-P Composite, only 10 per cent below the recent high. A small adjustment here or there would put us over the top.

It is by no means impossible to assume a permanent growth rate of 4½ per cent; we have been told that we must increase our GNP faster than this or lose out in the race with Russia. The basic objection is that it is only an assumption, that the experience of the longer past puts the figure rather at 2½ per cent and that the difference between 4½ and 2½ per cent in this calculation means the difference between 65 and 39 for the value of the S-P Composite. My experience leads me to predict that the action of the market will govern the investor's choice as to probable future growth rates rather than vice versa.

This completes my case for and against a new era and character for the stock market. If the market since 1949 foreshadows the stock markets of the future, the investment aspects of equity accumulation are unbelievably favorable. All that will be needed will be the funds to buy a representative assortment of common stocks and a little patience to sit through periods of mild reaction. The annually compounded rate of over-all return from the 500-Stock Composite has been about 13 per cent—curiously enough, this has been about the same as the average from a selected list of growth stocks.[3] A much lower annual rate, without severe interruptions, will prove amply rewarding.

IV

But if, as I deem more likely, the fundamental character of the stock market must be as unchanging as that of human nature, then the accumulator of equities who starts today is faced with quite a different prospect. The new appearance of the variable annuity suggests a broad analogy with the 1920's. It was during that bull market that investment trusts had their first important development in this country. Most of the arguments in their favor were the same as those now used for the sale of mutual-fund shares and for equity accumulation in general. The collapse of 1929 resulted in a severe and protracted setback for the investment-trust movement, as part of a widespread loss of faith in common stocks generally. It is true that many—although perhaps less than half—managed to survive the bitter subsequent experience and to re-establish themselves more firmly than before in public esteem. Furthermore, the principle of dollar-cost-averaging—which is the most systematic of the equity-accumulation techniques—was able to vindicate itself in the end, after perhaps 20 years of unsatisfactory-to-mediocre results.[4]

---

[3] See, for example, J.F. Bohmfalk, Jr., "The Growth Stock Philosophy," *Financial Analysts Journal,* November 1960, Table A.

[4] For calculated results of dollar-cost-averaging results for 10-year period ending from 1929 through 1952, see Lucile Tomlinson, *Practical Formulas for Successful Investing* (New York: Wilfred Funk, 1953), Table 3, p.62.

The computations made of theoretical dollar-averaging experience in the past embolden us to predict that such a policy will pay off ultimately, regardless of when it is begun, *provided* that it is adhered to conscientiously and courageously under all intervening conditions. This is by no means a minor proviso. It presupposes that the dollar-cost-averager will be a different sort of person from the rest of us, that he will not be subject to the alternations of exhilaration and deep gloom that have accompanied the gyrations of the stock market for generations past. This I greatly doubt—particularly because most of the dollar-cost-averagers we are speaking of will be typical members of the public who have been persuaded to embark on an equity-accumulation program by the arts of salesmanship now so highly developed in the mutual-fund field.

Let me return once again to the problem of the proper perspective for viewing the character of the stock market and the investment aspects of equity accumulation. At the outset I presented a statistical comparison of the market's behavior over the last 12 years and over the last 90 years. But our knowledge of stock-market behavior goes back a good deal more than 90 years—a full two centuries and a half, in fact, to the inception of the South Sea Company in 1711. In our first edition of *Security Analysis* published in 1934, we characterized the stock-market madness of the 1920's as a repetition or rerun of the famous South Sea Bubble. By comparison, the behavior of our present market appears more rational, dignified, and reassuring, No one today, not even ingrained conservatives (like this speaker), expects consequences to this market and the economy even faintly resembling the catastrophe of 1929-32. Yet I have a feeling that the financial world has become too complacent about the future, too confident of the invulnerability of common stocks as a whole to a drastic change in their fortunes.

A great corporation can withstand great vicissitudes; the same is true of great institutions, among which not the least important is common-stock investment and equity accumulation over a span of time. But a bull market has never become a financial institution, and I have great doubts whether this attractive development is an admissible possibility, when the frailty of human nature is taken into account.

My own inward picture of the present stock market is that of an institution cut adrift from old standards of value without having found dependable new standards. (In this respect present-day investment may be in somewhat the same position as present-day painting.) The market may either return to the old measures of central value or—as is perhaps more probable—eventually establish a new and more liberal basis for evaluating equities. If the first happens, common stocks will prove highly disappointing over a long period for many accumulators of equities. If the newer and higher value levels are to be established on a sound basis, I envisage this working out by a process of trial and error, covering an unpredictable period of time and a number of pendulum swings of unforeseeable magnitude. I do not know whether bonds will do better than stocks over the next 15 years, but I do know that the people behind College Retirement Equity Fund (CREF) are eminently wise in insisting that its beneficiaries have at least an equal dollar stake in bond as in stock investment.

3

HOW TO INVEST FOR CAPITAL APPRECIATION*

Gerald M. Loeb is a financial analyst for E. F. Hutton and Company.

Having decided to invest only in the more active, listed issues for the start at least, the next point is to learn to "invest for appreciation." Every purchase must be considered almost solely on the basis of what it will return in income and appreciation added together and treated as one. Looked at in this light, a thousand dollars invested in a stock with an assured dividend of say $50 a year on the purchase price but not likely to advance more than a point or two in the coming 12 months suggests an expected profit-return of $60 or $70, whereas another issue paying no dividend, but likely to double in price, would promise a profit-return of $1,000.

It is absolutely futile to try to get results except by buying into anticipated large gains. It is far better to let cash lie idle than to buy just to "keep invested" or for "income." In fact, it is really vital,—and just this one point, in my opinion, represents one of the widest differences between the successful professional and the loss-taking amateur. One often is kept out of a dangerous market by this rule. Obviously, the possibilities of decline must also be carefully weighed and the largest positions taken when it seems as if the odds are in one's favor. Actual income needed for living expenses need cause no problem as withdrawals at predetermined percentages can safely be made against

---

*From *The Battle for Investment Survival* (New York: Simon and Schuster, 1957), pp. 31-36, copyright © by G. M. Loeb. Reprinted by permission of the publisher.

one's purchases. At times it may happen that enough "income" exists to cover one's needs. At other times the debit will be against realized or unrealized appreciation. Occasionally it will be against capital. Even so, in my view it is usually much safer than buying for "income."

The only way to begin is to learn by doing. Here lies the greatest handicap of most investors. They have had no experience. And, unfortunately, most of them go for advice to others who either have had no experience or have had enough to induce them to leave markets alone and concentrate on brokerage or advisory or statistical work.

Experience, as I see it, means every sort in every kind of market. Hence the purchase of one issue and its successful or unsuccessful retention over a period of years proves nothing. Years ago, in wondering how one could gain such invaluable market knowledge and yet not pay a prohibitive cost in tuition, I thought of the plan of learning by always maintaining a position not in excess of a hundred shares of an average-priced stock, yet always striving to be long or short the most suitable issue of the moment. This plan takes a minimum of capital. It also results in a minimum of risk, as the beginner is forced to close one commitment before he opens the next. Ordinarily, new investors buy one stock after another, and should the market go down, they lose on the whole position before they realize their inexperience. A purchaser of a single stock under this plan, is forced to a decision whether to keep it, take a loss or a profit, or exchange it for another. It is quite different, and many times more valuable in teaching market technique, than the imaginary "paper transactions" in which many tyros indulge. The latter are completely lacking in testing the investors' psychological reactions stemming from such important factors as fear of loss, or greed for more gain. This method also teaches that if there is no one outstanding purchase or sale at the moment, one should strive to be out of the picture entirely.

This means frequent swapping, and I guarantee that in no time at all most people who think these discussions too pessimistic as to the difficulties involved will change their minds. Furthermore, this method tends to stress and teach the paramount importance of timing. It is not enough to buy something cheap if it stays cheap. One must buy it just as it starts to get dearer. One must decide between 100 shares of an average-priced issue, or 50 of a high-price one, or 200 of a low-priced, or 10 of 10 different issues. In each and every case the advantages and disadvantages will become very clear in a reasonably short time, where no amount of reading would be a satisfactory substitute for experience.

All this, of course, means that one must devote some time every day to the subject of investment. Nothing is more logical, yet nothing more suprising to most people. They must devote months to earn a net savable profit, after living and running expenses and taxes, and then in a few moments often toss a large part of it to the winds because they look on investing very much as buying seats for a theater. One *must* devote time to investment, and, in doing so, one's surplus savings become, instead of a doubtful asset for the future, in many cases a more powerful factor in increasing one's wealth than the original way of gaining one's living.

This initial experience fund should be quite small, preferably not over 10 per cent of one's assets; $5,000 is a useful amount, and in no event need it exceed that figure. This period of learning by trial and error is obviously going to take time. In the meanwhile, it is going to take some self-control to let the balance of one's funds lie idle. It may even prove costly if we happen to be in a period of rapidly depreciating purchasing power for money. But it is not as apt to prove so costly as experimenting with one's total funds. A 10 per cent ratio would seem to limit or exclude a large number of readers. This will not prove to be the case in practice, because there always will be some venturesome people who will take the risks that are necessary to achieve greater success. Probably in most cases they will feel that at least they have had a chance, which should give them a good deal of satisfaction.

There is the question also whether many of the readers of these memos are going to find the time to trade at all. Naturally it is going to take time daily from one's business. However, as pointed out before, in many cases one will earn far more with the time applied to keeping what he has made or increasing it than by 100 per cent devotion to his regular occupation. In any event, if a person is sure he cannot take the time or "interfere" with his regular pursuits, (if conserving one's surplus is "interfering") then he must delegate the whole thing rather than dabble at it. A reading of these chapters should be helpful in making up one's mind whether to handle one's own affairs or turn them over to a professional, and if the latter, what to look for in a professional adviser. Another point is that, after experimenting with trading, many may convince themselves that they are not cut out for it and that they are better off devoting all their time to their own particular business. I think a great deal has been gained if one determines that once and for all, because, in my view, one should devote either a generous amount of time, or no time at all. Halfway measures are impossible.

All this suggests the question—are we learning to trade for the quick turn or to invest for the long pull? We are investing for appreciation, and the length of time one holds a position has nothing to do with it. I lean towards rather short turns for many reasons. To begin with, experience is gained much more rapidly that way.

Short-term investing, once mastered, has very much more the elements of dependable business than the windfalls or calamities of the long pull. One simply can't continue to buy and sell successfully without being "good." Without a succession of varying trades one can never be sure of one's ability and consequent safety. There is much more peace of mind in frequent turns. One can take a fresh view often. Long worrying declines, without apparent reason until near the bottom, are avoided. There are many other advantages. The majority, perhaps, claim that there is much more peace of mind in the long-pull but if my observation of thousands of accounts since 1921 means anything, this is a popular fallacy.

By "short-term," however, I do not mean to imply one must close a trade quickly just because one is thinking of the short term. Trades should never be closed unless a good reason is at hand. But many "long-pull" traders ignore a sign of a change of trend because they feel it is temporary. Often they are right, but eventually they are wrong, and usually at great cost. The short-term method requires the closing of the trade for a reason, and if later the situation changes, then one can re-establish the position. It sometimes can be done at a profit, and sometimes only at a loss in which case one has in effect paid for insurance.

Once in a while the long-pull buyer stumbles on some good thing and imagines himself a great speculator. More often than not he later gets a rude awakening, though occasionally he is fortunate enough to retain what he has.

However, the long-pull position has its uses, and in these days taxes often compel it. However, opening the trade must be done on what I might term short-turn principles. There is nothing I am going to write here that applies exclusively to any policy. Some of the best long-pull buys grew out of a continuing series of bullish short-term indications. Some of the really vital last-chance selling points first look like minor temporary tops.

4
ECONOMICS AND INVESTMENT MANAGEMENT*

EDMUND A. MENNIS, C.F.A., is a senior vice president and chairman of the Trust Investment Committee of the Republic National Bank of Dallas. He is also an associate editor of the Financial Analysts Journal, and a member of the Council of the National Association of Business Economists.

A significant development in the postwar period has been the growing use of economic analysis and the increased employment of professional economists in government and business. Certainly this trend has been helped by

*From *Financial Analysts Journal,* Vol. 22, No. 6 (November-December 1966), pp. 17-23. Reprinted by permission.

the greater availability of economic data and the improved analytical tools at the economist's disposal. Moreover, the increased role of the Federal Government in economic policy-making as well as a better understanding by both the professional economist and the businessman of how the economy operates have focused increasing attention on economic analysis as a guide to policy formulation and decision-making.

Economic analysis has been used in the investment field as well, particularly in the banking community, where interest rates and the money market require constant attention. However, more recently a marked increase has occurred in the use of economic analysis in common-stock investment. A good part of this application of economics undoubtedly stems from the growth in the number and size of institutional investment portfolios and the development of institutional research staffs in the financial community to serve these important clients.

It would be an overstatement, however, to claim that economic analysis has received widespread acceptance as a tool in common-stock investment. In the United States, the abundance of financial data on individual companies and the increasing willingness of corporate management to speak with financial analysts have made industry and company analysis the area of major concentration for financial analysts. A further difficulty facing the economist in the investment field is the characteristic lead of the turning points in stock prices ahead of the turning points in business. If the market leads business, what is the advantage of following business trends? Moreover, yesterday's stock prices are known and will not change. Business data, however, are invariably reported several weeks or months after the fact, with the perennial hazard of subsequent revision and adjustment, so that it is difficult to determine where the economy has been recently, let alone where it is now and where it is going. For promptness in obtaining economic data, precision is sacrificed; for precision, revision is inevitable.

More important than all of these difficulties, in my opinion, is the problem of linking economic analysis to investment decisions. This problem might be compared to an hour glass, with a vast quantity of economic data on top and an equally vast array of corporate data on the bottom, and only a narrow channel of communication in between. It is frustrating, for example, to find that the traditional classification of industries used by the government in reporting economic information does not particularly match the conventional industry classifications of stock prices. The wealth of industry information provided by various Federal Government agencies, not to mention the gems that occasionally come to light in Congressional hearings, are not used nearly enough by the financial analyst. The lack of familiarity with economic data and with the new methods of economic analysis, particularly among the older members of the financial analysts profession, also has prevented full utilization of the tools available. But the major obstacle lies not in the data but in the failure to find common ground where both the economist and the financial analyst can meet.

To reach this common ground, it is necessary to recognize that an investment is the purchase of future economic performance. The economist can provide information about the current or probable future economic environment, the analysis and projection of monetary and fiscal trends, international developments, and a variety of other economic information that can assist the investment manager and the financial analyst. However, unless this information is directed toward the goal of determining the profitability of the economy, a particular industry, or a company, the economist will not satisfy the needs of the financial analyst.

ECONOMICS IN THE INVESTMENT PROCESS

Let me see if I can summarize briefly the position of the economist in the investment decision process, using the accompanying chart. The first step is the determination of investment objectives, which will vary in risk-reward ratio depending on the objectives selected. Other factors enter into the selection of investment objectives, including the need for current income, the desire to realize capital gains and the investor's tax position. This determination of objectives is independent of the investment environment in which decisions are made and will change seldom, and only as the circumstances of the investor change. The investment environment is the broad background of domestic and international economic and political factors that will influence the investment decision; this environment is in a constant state of flux. The environment must be analyzed, evaluated and interpreted. This function is performed jointly by the economist and the financial analyst, each working in his particular area of competence. The information generated by both the economist and the analyst is provided to the investment manager, who makes decisions affecting asset distribution and individual security selection. These decisions then are executed by the trading operation. Finally, and again independent of the investment environment, an evaluation of performance is necessary in order to determine whether the objectives have effectively been met.

In the remaining sections of this paper I should like to discuss the various functions the economist can perform in an investment organization. Then I will describe how this information can be combined in a logical way so that you can see how economic analysis can be integrated into investment management.

THE BUSINESS FORECAST

Analysis of current economic developments and forecasting the future usually are considered the primary contribution of the economist in the

Development of the Investment Decision

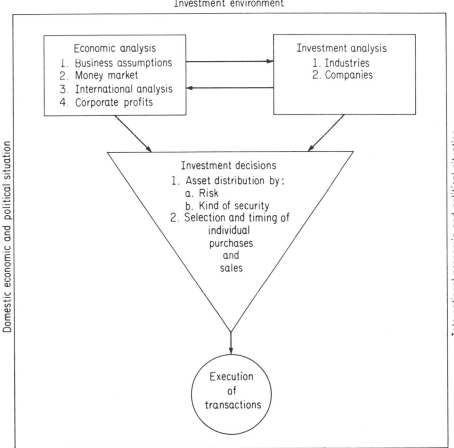

investment field; sometimes this is his only function. The stock market may lead current business developments, but if you can forecast business accurately and sufficiently far ahead, presumably you can get a lead on the stock market.

In performing his forecasting function, the economist ordinarily provides quarterly estimates, usually for the succeeding year, of economic data such as Gross National Product and its components, industrial production, personal income, and aggregate corporate profits. These forecasts are presented in neat, tabular form, usually accompanied by a description of where the economy is, with perhaps a statement of the assumptions that underlie the projected figures These forecasts most frequently are made toward the end of each calendar year. They may be revised at regular intervals, or they may be used until the next forecasting season rolls around, regardless of how they age in the interval. This approach assumes that the function of the economist is "to win the numbers game," that is, to provide in advance a set of numbers that will accurately project the future.

This practice does not seem to me to be the most advantageous use of the economist's talents. I consider it an unwarranted expectation that an economist or anyone else can provide even a reasonably precise numerical forecast four quarters or more in advance of what future business statistics will be. Periodic revisions of data, which, although necessary and desirable, place the economist in the difficult position of standing on a most shaky and uncertain platform as he launches into the future. Another reason for lack of enthusiasm for this approach is my belief that there is nothing magic in numbers. These neat, tabular presentations of economic data are no more than the quantifying of a large number of qualitative assumptions and evaluations that often change, sometimes quite suddenly. A perfect example of how abruptly business conditions can change materially was the sharp drop in automobile sales in the spring of 1966, when sales fell from a seasonally adjusted annual rate of 9.3 million domestically produced cars in the first quarter to an 8.0 million rate in April and a 7.5 million rate in May. Such an unexpected decline clearly calls for a reassessment not only of automobile demand but also of consumer buying attitudes generally. A forecast, therefore, is not something done by the calendar; rather it should be a daily reappraisal of the future as new information becomes available. In addition, many factors besides economic developments affect stock prices, so that even the best economic forecast may not provide the clue to stock price performance. The unusually sharp drop in stock prices in 1962, unaccompanied by a business contraction, is a good illustration.

How, then, do I believe economic forecasts should be used in the investment field? One suggestion, and not an insignificant one, would be to stop labeling such exercises "forecasts." The word "forecast" implies a prediction of what the future will be. Personally, I much prefer the word "assumption," which clearly announces that the economic information provided is not a prediction but rather an assessment of the most probable outcome based on what we know now and where we are today. Assumptions can be changed, but forecasts are expected to come true.

But if assumptions are not useful to predict stock prices, for they can at best be only part of the factors influencing stock prices, what purpose can they serve? In the first place, they describe the probable business environment in which investments will be made. Aided by this information, the investment manager is better able to appraise the investment climate; that is, in what kinds of investments is he most likely to make money? Should he be moving from bonds to stocks? Should he be more or less conservative in his equity selections? What industries should he favor? How should he balance his portfolio to take advantage of the most probable developments and also retain some hedges in case the assumptions have to be changed? In addition, the financial analyst is given guidelines to assess the profitability of the industries and companies he follows.

The nature of the assumptions is important also. The economist can provide a perspective far broader and for a longer time period than either the investment manager or the analyst is likely to have in his preoccupation with daily events. The economist's assumptions provide not only an overview but also can extend horizons out three to five years, indicating the trends as well as the dimensions of possible downturns during that period. With this background, the investment manager is better equipped to meet the challenge of sudden market movements or the distortions caused by overemphasis on near-term developments. For the large institutional investor, where the accumulation or sale of large positions takes time, the longer-term view obviously is most important.

Flexibility and willingness to change are vital if the economist is to perform his function effectively. His usefulness is enhanced if he avoids the temptation to substitute his ideas of what should be for his best appraisal of what probably will be. The latter obviously is of greater importance. Moreover, a purely economic analysis is not nearly so effective as one which includes the political climate as well. Political decisions are often not economically based, but they can have an important influence on economic activity. Consumer attitudes also may not be economically rational, but they have an important impact on spending and investment. A properly trained and experienced economist will be aware of these requirements, all of which are necessary to make him a useful member of the investment team.

How should business assumptions be prepared? My own experience suggests that business assumptions should be prepared initially in the late summer to cover the remaining quarters of the current year and the four quarters of the succeeding year. In addition, it is extremely useful to have an estimate of the economy for a good business year about five years away as well as an estimate of the probable dimensions of any downturn in that period. This procedure provides not only a fairly detailed analysis of the year ahead but also the trend for the next several years and some measure of the possible pitfalls in between. The starting point for this work is a review of where the economy is believed to be and a qualitative evaluation of such critical areas as expected consumer durable demand, plant and equipment spending trends, the residential construction outlook, probable inventory developments and Federal Government monetary and fiscal actions. With these essentials determined, a numerical forecast then can be prepared.

The data contained in these assumptions should include the details of Gross National Product and its components; the Federal Reserve Index of Industrial Production; plant and equipment spending; automobile sales, production and inventories; housing starts; personal income and personal disposable income; and aggregate profits. The economic assumptions, together with assumptions about the money market and the stock market, summarize the most probable future investment environment and form the basis for investment policy. In addition, the results should be used uniformly by all of the industry analysts in preparing their company earnings estimates. This approach provides a consistent framework for investment decisions and avoids the internal conflict and confusion that might result if, for example, the steel analyst anticipated production of 130 million tons of steel, and the automobile analyst expected production of only 7 million cars.

Having prepared the detailed business assumptions, the monitoring process begins. Current economic information, both published and unpublished, should be gathered daily and analyzed in order to determine if the assumptions still are valid. When necessary, rather than at stated intervals, a new set of numbers should be prepared. While assumptions should not be changed unnecessarily, whenever substantial economic shifts occur the assumptions should be adjusted rapidly.

To summarize, then, economic assumptions may not be the best guide to future stock price movements. However, they should provide the broad perspective of the environment in which investments will be made and the fundamental ingredients to determine the relative profitability of particular industries and companies. Effective use of these services of the economist can, I believe, make a vital contribution to successful investment performance.

MONEY MARKET TRENDS

In addition to providing business analysis and assumptions about the future, there are other areas in which the economist can be effective. Although frequently considered a part of general economic analysis, the financial sector really deserves separate treatment, particularly where investment in fixed-income obligations is important. Money market trends must be followed because of their impact on the business picture, because of their impact on the timing and selection of bond purchases and sales, because of their influence on shifts in the equity ratio of a balanced investment portfolio and, finally, because of their influence on investment in financial institutions, the earnings of which depend fundamentally on the difference between the interest rates they must pay and the rates that they can earn.

In addition, money market analysis provides an important feedback to business analysis. The recent effect of high interest rates and tight money in the economy is a reminder that fiscal policy has not completely displaced monetary policy as an economic regulator. Tight money may cause a slowing of economic expansion and raise questions about future profits stability and growth. Tight money has an influence on investment attitudes and alters the yield relationships and relative attractiveness of bonds and stocks. The trend of commercial loans gives an indication of business demand. The pattern of institutional investors' forward investment commitments provides a clue to the willingness of businessmen to make future investments and to the strength of the housing market. Thus you can see that the contribution of monetary analysis to business analysis is significant.

The specialized nature of the research in the money market area can be touched on only briefly. Fundamentally, this work requires an analysis of the supply and demand for funds. It includes a detailed evaluation of savings flows and the demand for funds by the business sector, the mortgage market, and the Government sector—Federal and state and local. An essential part of this research is an analysis of the attitudes, objectives, and actions of the Federal Reserve System and the U.S. Treasury, both of whom are critical forces in the money market. Federal, state, and local budgets and projected financing plans are other essential ingredients in effective money-market analysis. Not to be overlooked is the balance of payments, which in recent years has acted as an important inhibiting factor on the money managers from taking action that might otherwise have been indicated, were only domestic considerations important. The result is not only an evaluation of the future course of interest rates, both long- and short-term, but also additional evidence from the financial side of current and prospective business activity and the investment climate.

INTERNATIONAL DEVELOPMENTS

A good economics staff in the investment field also must be aware of what is happening in the world outside of a country. Analysis of foreign developments is essential for a variety of reasons. Money rates are affected by changes in the balance of payments and competitive interest rates abroad. Developments in the balance of payments can lead to restrictions on direct investment, such as the voluntary restraints on corporate investing abroad or indirect restrictions such as the interest equalization tax. Devaluation losses in foreign currencies can have a significant impact on the earnings of American corporations, sometimes eliminating one or two years growth in earnings. Devaluation of the dollar or the pound, whether actual or feared, will have important repercussions on domestic companies as well as an impact on security values, both short- and long-term. Foreign companies provide competition for American companies, which must be assessed. Wage and price developments abroad influence both the effectiveness of this competition and the operation of foreign subsidiaries of American companies. Finally, in spite of temporary inhibitions such as the interest equalization tax, investment is becoming more international, and securities of foreign companies will continue to find a place in the portfolios of American investors.

Obviously, the kind of research done in the international field is different and may not be as thorough as that done on the U.S. economy. Distance and the lack of available data make this type of analysis less comprehensive. Nevertheless, at a minimum economic and political developments abroad, foreign and the U.S. balance of payments, trends in prices and wages, and major industry and company developments should be followed. Foreign periodicals and statistical reports can be helpful, but much useful information also can be provided by reports from and personal contacts with research organizations and banks, both in the United States and abroad. This information should be integrated into the preparation of the economic assumptions and also be reported to the research staff to assist them in the evaluation of their industries and companies.

CORPORATE PROFITS RESEARCH

Although all of the information the economist can provide may be helpful, the most valuable contribution he can make is to focus and interpret this information as it bears on the outlook for corporate profits. The remaining section of this paper will indicate an approach for accomplishing this task of fully integrating economic analysis and investment management.

The detailed set of business assumptions described earlier can be used to outline for the analysts the probable business environment in which particular companies and industries will operate. These business assumptions are therefore a very helpful guide in making estimates of sales volume for the period ahead. Some industry sales are closely related to cyclical factors, others to aggregate activity, others are influenced by population and income trends, still others by financial forces. A skilled analyst will know which inputs are most useful.

In addition to help in estimating sales trends, the economist can also assist in estimating changes in factors affecting costs and prices and therefore profit margins. Aggregate data are available on trends in labor costs and productivity not only in broad areas of the economy but also in many specific industries. In addition, the economist has available a wide variety of data on price trends that cover the economy generally as well as many particular areas and products. More importantly, with his broader perspective he can evaluate the economic and political forces affecting prices and give valuable clues to future price trends. His perspective may help the analyst to determine whether a price change is in the offing or whether a given price change will stick.

An economist who is aware of the changing trends in the business scene and the political forces at work also can advise whether changes in the tax structure should be considered in making estimates. Economic assumptions have definite implications for the Federal budget and the flow of funds into and out of the Treasury. This information, combined with knowledge of the political attitude of the Administration and of Congress, can be important determinants of fiscal policy, an area most financial analysts usually are willing to leave to someone well acquainted with this field.

With this information to guide him, coupled with his knowledge and experience and the additional benefit of contacts with companies, the analyst can now prepare earnings estimates for individual companies. However, this ordinarily is not the ultimate objective of an investment organization; from these individual earnings estimates an investment policy and program must emerge. Most institutional investment is done with some concept of relative investment values in mind rather than concentrating on the earnings and market value of individual securities taken in isolation. Consequently some procedure must be used to obtain benchmarks against which any particular company can be compared.

Many analysts use the Dow-Jones Industrial Average as a yardstick, although the composition of this average does not make it particularly suitable for this purpose, in my opinion. The Standard and Poor's average would seem more useful, particularly since historical data are available covering a large number of industries. However, using the Standard and Poor's average requires making a great many individual company earnings estimates. My own experience suggests that earnings of the Standard and Poor's average can be approximated by a smaller sample of 125-150 companies. Individual earnings estimates can be aggregated by industry, by economic groupings and in total, in order to determine general earnings trends as well as trends in specific investment areas.

Here is another place the economist can be helpful. These earnings estimates can be compared with the economic assumptions in order to see if the estimates seem reasonable. They can also be compared with estimates of other broad aggregates of corporate profits that the economist can prepare, such as the Department of Commerce profits figures or those of the Federal Trade Commission-Securities and Exchange Commission in the manufacturing area.[1] Differences in the expectations for some of these broad profit aggregates and any sample of large, successful companies should not be surprising, because the profits performance of companies that are of primary investment interest usually is better than that of companies generally. However, comparison of trends and turning points is useful.

Two further steps can be taken. The first would be to aggregate data for particular industries into groups, the earnings of which are affected differently by changing economic conditions. A possible division might be cyclical, cyclical growth, growth and defensive industries. Others will occur to the sophisticated analyst. In this way, broad divergences in earnings trends can be ascertained that may indicate shifts in investment emphasis.

A second step would be to add data on prices in order to compute price-earning ratios and yields. This step provides a basis for relative value comparisons, because a stock can be compared with its industry, with the group of which it is a part and also with a broad measure of the market in terms of the two fundamentals of security analysis, earnings and their valuation. This comparison can be made at a point in time, and, if the historical data are available, a comparison may also be made with past relationships over time. This perspective provides invaluable insight for investment selection.[2] Admittedly, the historical data are not easily prepared, although the computer has simplified the task materially.

These last two steps are not necessarily the function of the economist. They have been described, however, in order to indicate the logical steps in investment decision making and to show the flow from the broad economic assumptions to earnings to their valuation. Such a logical, step-by-step approach will give the framework in which investment policy is set. It also will assist in the investment program, that is, the selection and timing of individual security purchases and sales. At each point, critical judgments must be made, and a constant review is necessary in the light of the flow of new information. The economist, with his background and perspective, can play a key role in interpreting the information and assisting in making better investment decisions. I am convinced that more rather than less use of this kind of analysis will occur in the years ahead.

---

[1]Such comparisons must be made with care, for these broad profit aggregates may be conceptually as well as statistically different from aggregates of shareholder profits. For a further discussion of this point, see Edmund A. Mennis, "Forecasting Corporate Profits" in *"How Business Economists Forecast,"* edited by William Butler and Robert Kavesh, Prentice-Hall, 1966.

[2]For an outline of how such an analysis can be done, see Edmund A. Mennis, "Profit Trends and Values in Mid-1965," *Financial Analysts Journal* (July-August 1965), pp. 63 ff.

5

DOLLAR AVERAGING IN THEORY AND PRACTICE*

LEONARD W. ASCHER is professor of economics and business at San Francisco State College. During World War II, he served with the War Production Board and the Foreign Economic Administration.

Among the beliefs strongly held in financial circles today is that dollar averaging is a high road to financial success.

Investors are advised to put a constant dollar sum into common stocks at regular intervals, regardless of price. Not only will such a program overrule the emotional urges to plunge into stocks when the market is booming, and to dump stocks at ruinous low prices, but it will automatically provide investors with stocks at bargain prices. Dollar averaging is offered as a technical device, a mathematical principle, that "unfailingly produces superior results."

The program is simplicity itself: buy a constant amount of common stocks, say, $600 every quarter year. Some purchases will be made at high prices, some at middle prices, and some at low prices; but at high prices few shares will be obtained, and at low prices many will be gotten for the constant dollar sum. The result will be a portfolio purchased not at average prices, but at weighted average prices, the majority of shares bought at low prices.

The process may be illustrated by a hypothetical investment program. Assume that at the beginning of each period a fixed sum, $600, is committed to an average common stock portfolio (for this we will invent a mutual company and call it the Average Fund). In this example stock prices will fluctuate between $10 and $30 in a regular cycle. To give the system a fair test, asking neither too much nor too little of it, let us start and end with the middle price for stocks, carrying operations through a complete cycle of fluctuations.

In the first period, see Table 1 the $600 programmed will buy 30 shares at $20 per share. Thereafter the market starts to rise, so at the end of the period

*From *Financial Analysts Journal,* Vol. 16, No. 5 (September-October 1960), pp. 51-53. Reprinted by permission.

(and beginning of the second) price per share is $25, giving the 30 shares in the portfolio a value of $750. Following the plan, however, another $600 is "invested" in 24 shares of stock at $25 per share, increasing holdings to 54 shares. The market continues to rise, so the 54 shares are worth $1,620 at the end of the period, and we buy $600 more at $30 per share, getting only 20 shares for our money this time. Dollar averaging restrains any enthusiasm we may have acquired from heady experience with a booming market.

At this point the market turns down from its high—a development to test the stoutest heart—because at the end of the third period our 74 shares are worth only $25 per share or a total of $1,850, and we are ahead only $50 despite the recent boom. But dollar averaging demands unwavering faith of its devotees, so another $600 is tossed into the market at $25 per share, adding 24 shares to the portfolio. Thereafter, prices decline even more, hitting a low of $10 per share at the beginning of the seventh period, bringing a loss of almost $2,000 on the $3,600 invested in the six preceding periods.

Here is the crucial point. Assuming that the investor still has $600 despite the depression, and the courage to invest it, he will get 60 shares for his money. Now comes the pay-off. The market starts up, hitting first $15 per share and then $20, the price at which the program was started. The dollar averager has laid out a total of $4,800 in eight periods, for 268 shares of stock worth, at $20 per share, $5,360. His average price comes to $17.91 per share, a saving of $2.09 per share over the market average of $20 (about enough to pay the average fund-load).

Dollar averaging will always result in an average cost per share, less than the simple average of market prices, because it is a weighted average of prices in which weights are inversely proportional to prices, the higher prices receiving less weight than the lower. Dollar averaging may also be viewed as a harmonic mean of stock prices, and the formula can be written as a harmonic mean:

$$\text{D.A.} = \frac{ns}{\dfrac{s}{p_0} + \dfrac{s}{p_1} + \dfrac{s}{p_2} + \cdots + \dfrac{s}{p_n}}$$

where s is the dollar sum periodically invested.

A harmonic mean of a series of values will always be smaller than a simple arithmetic average of the same series.

Although it is true that dollar averaging does accumulate stocks, at less than the average of market prices, it is not true that the program will lead inevitably to profit. Stock must be sold, or be saleable, above cost to bring success, and in a fluctuating market there will be times when the portfolio will show a capital loss.

Indeed, if a program is started at the bottom (instead of the middle) price and carried through a complete market cycle, the portfolio will be accumulated

Chart 1. Dollar Averaging in Theory, Starting at Middle Price

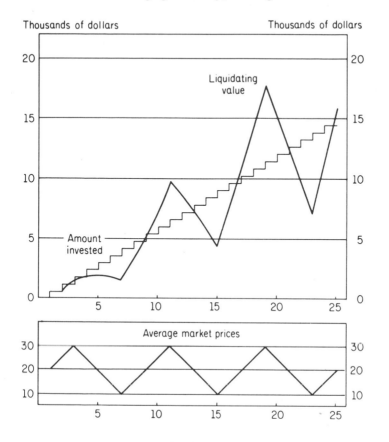

Thousands of dollars   Thousands of dollars

Liquidating value

Amount invested

Average market prices

Table 1.

Period	Market Price per Share	Number of Shares Bought	Number of Shares Accumulated	Value at End of Period	Total Amount Invested
1	$20	30	30	$ 750	$ 600
2	25	24	54	1,620	1,200
3	30	20	74	1,850	1,800
4	25	24	98	1,960	2,400
5	20	30	128	1,920	3,000
6	15	40	168	1,680	3,600
7	10	60	228	3,420	4,200
8	15	40	268	5,360	4,800
9	20				

*Table 2.   Experience with Dollar Averaging Programs Started
at Various Times*

Year Started	Number of Shares Accumulated Through 1958*	Average Cost per Share*	Average of Market Prices	Amount Invested	Liquidating Value 1959 Price*
1929	2,010	$14.94	$19.35	$30,000	$115,300
1939	1,183	16.90	22.05	20,000	67,900
1944	705	21.27	2587	15,000	40,500
1949	370	27.03	31.26	10,000	21,200
1954	124	40.32	41.48	5,000	7,100

*Slide rule accuracy.

at a dollar average price less than the market average, but the liquidating price at the bottom of the cycle will bring a capital loss. Thus, with prices fluctuating between $10 and $30, with $600 invested each period over eight periods, the program will accumulate 268 shares of stock at a cost of $4,800 with a liquidating value of $2,680. An investor has to know when to get out or dollar averaging may bring him loss instead of gain.

So much for *theory*. What could have been the *experience* of those who got into the stock market at various times during the past three decades? To answer this question, programs have been worked out for selected years, using annual commitments of $1,000 and Standard and Poor's combined index of 500 stocks. A dollar averaging program started in 1929 when average stock prices were $26.02 per share (1941-43 = 10) and continued through 1958 would have accumulated 2,010 shares worth, at 1959 prices of $57.38, approximately $115,000. The $30,000 put into the program has resulted in a (paper) profit of $85,000. Dollar average cost was $14.94 and average of market prices over 30 years was $19.35 per share, an advantage of $4.41 per share for dollar averaging, or about $8,800 on the 2,010 shares acquired.

Nor is success confined to a program started in 1929. Portfolios initiated in 1939, 1944, 1949 and 1954 also produced gains for the dollar averager. Table 2 and Chart 2 show the results of programs started in these years.

A skeptic may next ask, what would have been the consequence had each investor committed his entire capital to the market at the beginning instead of spreading his purchases over the years? This question has practical importance for the person suddenly in possession of a substantial sum of cash. The answer is found in Table 3.

Except for the 1929 programs, plunging into the market has produced better results than dollar averaging, and hindsight suggests that anyone with money should have committed it immediately to the stock market for maximum capital gains (as well as dividend income).

Chart 2. Dollar Averaging Experience
Assuming Annual Commitments of $1,000 at Average Prices

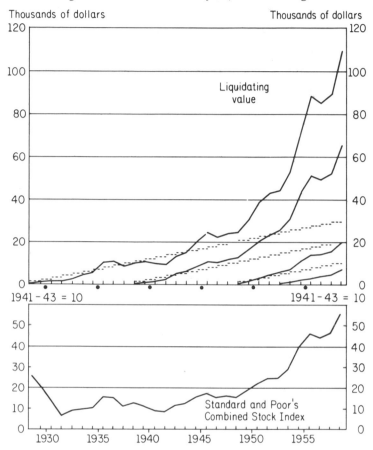

Table 3. Experience with Single
Commitment Programs Undertaken at Various Times

Year Committed	Sum Committed	Price at Time of Commitment	Number of Shares Acquired*	Liquidating Value (at $57.38)*	Dollar Averaging Results*
1929	$30,000	$26.02	1,153	$66,200	$115,300
1939	20,000	12.06	1,658	95,100	67,900
1944	15,000	12.47	1,203	69,000	40,500
1949	10,000	15.23	657	37,700	21,200
1954	5,000	29.69	168	9,650	7,100

*Slide rule accuracy.

The systematic saver who can manage at best to accumulate only a certain amount each year has little choice but to dollar average, making a virtue of necessity, getting into the market as he can in the faith that a rising market will carry his accumulating portfolio to progressively higher values. Should the stock market falter, he may expect his dollar averaging program to yield losses, not gains.

In conclusion, dollar averaging has the merit of lower average cost for the systematic investor, and experience in the market suggests that it forces the investor to buy—even though he go behind—so that if the market goes up, the investor is with it, and has not missed his chance. The same outcome might be realized by following the uncritical motto of the 1920's: "Never sell America short!"

6

RISK ANALYSIS IN THE SIXTIES*

DAVID A. WEST is associate professor of finance, School of Business and Public Administration, University of Missouri.

During the 1960's investment portfolio managers have faced a twist in financial analysis due to the increased significance of interest-rate risk and inflation risk as compared to financial risk (or business or credit risk). With interest rates reaching forty-year highs in 1966, the significance of interest-rate risk was greater than any time since at least 1957. Furthermore, with inflation occurring at almost 4 per cent in 1966, inflation risk increased to a degree more significant than it had been for at least the last ten years.

Of course financial risk always exists, and selectivity always is essential to successful portfolio management. However, during periods of stimulated economic growth, the risk of across-the-board financial difficulties must be recognized as significantly less than during periods of economic decline, whereas

*From *Financial Analysts Journal,* Vol. 23, No. 6 (November-December 1967), pp. 124-6. Reprinted by permission.

the risk of portfolio loss due to interest-rate increases and inflation is significantly greater.

Sensitivity to these factors is being intensified by the increasing pressures placed on portfolio managers for comparatively favorable market performance. As a result, more consideration is being given the intermediate-term market risks, i.e., the risk of loss due to declines in market prices which may be quite apart from any immediate change in the rate of economic growth or any reduction in inflation risk or interest-rate risk. That mutual fund portfolio managers have tended to act as though they recognized these risks, is indicated by the quarterly data shown in Figure 1.[1]

In earlier studies, conclusions are conflicting regarding the success of this group in responding to these divergent risks. Donald Farrar concluded that investment company portfolio management had been fairly efficient in minimizing variances for various levels of expected return, noting particularly that the balanced funds had been successful in minimizing variance for their somewhat lower required expected return.[2] In contrast, Jack Treynor's studies led him to conclude that mutual fund portfolio managers had not been successful in experiencing more than average success.[3] Nevertheless, in analyzing the aggregate data and certain individual funds included in it, five specific points became apparent.

CONCLUSIONS

First, over the last ten years, there has been a tendency toward including larger percentages of common stocks in the portfolios. From a high in excess of 21 per cent allocated to non-common stock holdings to a low of 14 per cent, the portfolio managers have tended toward less involvement in fixed-dollar instruments. Although this trend has been irregular, and although the fluctuations in the aggregate data are less indicative of changes in policy than might be expected since many fund restrictions prohibit free substitution of instruments, the trend is evident and marked. As the economy has continued to expand, the fund managers have tended to reduce their holdings of fixed-income instruments despite the higher yields and lower prices.

Second, analysis of specific portfolios indicates the same tendency in the stock funds in the form of less involvement in what may be considered defensive

[1]Investment Company Institute, *Mutual Fund Fact Book 1967* (New York: Investment Company Institute, 1967).
[2]Donald E. Farrar, *The Investment Decisions Under Uncertainty* (Englewood Cliffs, New Jersey: Prentice-Hall, Inc., 1962).
[3]Jack L. Treynor, "How to Rate Management of Investment Funds," *Harvard Business Review*, Vol. 43, No. 1 January-February 1965), and Jack L. Treynor and Kay K. Mazuy, "Can Mutual Funds Outguess the Market?" *Harvard Business Review*, Vol. 44, No. 4 (July-August 1966). Both articles appear in this book.

*Figure 1.   Non-Common Stock Portfolio
Holdings of Mutual Funds* (Source: *Mutual Fund Fact Book 1967)*

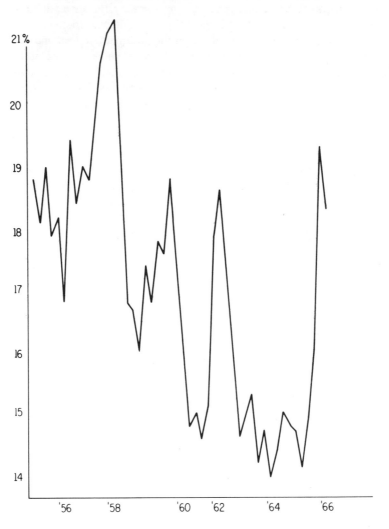

stocks, i.e., those that respond less than average to growth conditions.[4] While partially debatable in that there is some disagreement about what is a defensive equity, substantial agreement should be reached that the stock fund managers emphasized growth issues. This tendency is greater in the case of the stock funds

---

[4]Arthur Wiesenberger, *Investment Companies 1966* (New York: Arthur Wiesenberger and Co., 1966).

than for balanced funds, since the stock funds are restricted to holding stock positions; the tendency exists for both groups, however.

Third, the fluctuations around the downward trend in non-common stock holdings indicate that mutual fund managers are aware of the intermediate-term market risk due to declines in stock prices. Any 25 per cent decline in stock prices, for example, must be considered more immediately important than a 50 per cent loss in real value over ten years due to inflation or a 10 per cent loss in dollar value of fixed-payment instruments over five years due to interest-rate risk. In addition, stock price declines are not always unrelated to changes in economic conditions, and on occasion may mean that inflation risk and interest-rate risk will become less significant. During periods of reduced growth or decline, financial risk assumes greater importance. Inflation risk can disappear and interest-rate changes can become positive attractions. The fluctuations around the trend over the past ten years indicate that the fund managers as a group are aware of the changing importance of risks through time.

Fourth, the impact of counter-inflationary monetary and fiscal policies has been a major financial force, most recently in 1966. At some level of economic expansion, the inflation will reach a rate considered unacceptable by the monetary and fiscal authorities. As the counter-inflationary tools are applied, corporate profit expectations may very well decline. To the extent that they do, the common stocks in the portfolio that are affected will decline in price and thereby reduce the value of the entire portfolio. This risk cannot be ignored as a possibility; indeed, it was the most significant factor in portfolio policy in 1966, as is indicated in Figure 1.

Fifth, there is considerable variation in investment policy—even among funds with similarly stated objective restrictions. Despite the decline in total mutual fund industry holdings of non-common stock instruments in the 1960's, some balanced funds and even one so-called performance fund have expanded their holdings in non-common stock issues. In at least one case, a fund's cash and equivalent holdings went from a temporary low of zero per cent to a temporary high of almost 40 per cent.[5]

FUTURE RISK ANALYSIS

In the years ahead, portfolio managers will gain experience with economic developments in an economy with a strong, stimulated growth bias. As they do, their investment policies must increasingly reflect their efforts to

---

[5]Four of these five conclusions were initially presented in a paper at the Southern Finance Association meetings in Atlanta, Georgia, in November 1966, and they have been modified in response to the comments of Professor Donald E. Vaughn. This earlier paper entitled, "Investment Policy in a Growth Economy," was published in the *Southern Journal of Business*, Vol. II, No. 3 (July 1967.)

protect against the increased inflation risk and interest-rate risk associated with a managed growth economy. Whether one is concerned more with personal or with institutional investments, one is forced to consider the possibility that inflation risk and interest-rate risk may be more significant than financial risk. In the case of personal funds, ordinarily a larger proportion is placed in fixed-dollar instruments of one kind or another (e.g., insurance, pension programs, savings deposits, and savings bonds). To the extent that this is true, inflation risk will have greater relative impact upon personal investment results.

In the case of an institutional portfolio, the proportion placed in fixed-income instruments depends upon the institution handling the funds (e.g., mutual fund, pension fund, bank trust department, or insurance company). The manager is placed in the difficult position of a fiduciary charged with the responsibility of preserving his clients' funds while simultaneously being regulated as to investment opportunities and being judged by investors on the basis of his performance in competition with unregulated accounts. Historically, a trustee has been considered more conservative when he has invested to effectively avoid financial risk and conserve the original dollars in the trust. In a growth economy, however, a fiduciary investor is in the dilemma of whether or not to follow traditional policy and to conserve the dollars in the trust fund by avoiding financial risk when he knows that by so doing, he guarantees that the value of those dollars will decline as the purchasing power of the dollar continues to decline.

In order to meet his responsibilities in a growth economy, the fiduciary investor must recognize that inflation risk may be greater than financial risk for some or all instruments included in his assets. He must attempt to include equity instruments that will increase in value in approximate response to the inflationary bias in the economy. By this action, he is not being speculative or even aggressive; he is being conservative.

In the computation of comparative yields, fixed returns can be deflated by an anticipated rate of inflation to arrive at a real yield figure. This figure may be especially helpful to the investment manager faced with the necessity of requesting a change in portfolio restrictions. In comparing real yields on bonds with expected returns on common stocks, however, the latter must be reduced to real values. To the extent that stock price appreciation is included in the computation of expected return, the expected yield must be deflated both for the anticipated inflationary bias and for an estimated price reaction to the restraints of the monetary and fiscal authorities.

Just as inflation risk increases in importance during periods of stimulated economic growth, so interest-rate risk increases as well. This means that the portion of portfolio devoted to fixed-payment instruments suffers not only a decline in real value but also a loss in dollar value. The more extended the period of economic growth, the more the interest rate tends to rise. The higher the interest rate goes, the greater the dollar loss realized in the fixed-payment portion of the portfolio. Under such circumstances, the investor is faced with the problem of deciding whether to reduce the portion of his assets allocated to fixed-payment instruments and accept the dollar loss resulting from the discounts, or to hold the instruments to maturity knowing that the higher inflationary rate is reducing the real value of the dollars regardless of the face value at maturity.

Between the first of 1961 and early 1967, yields on one-year maturities more than doubled. From this extreme change on one-year maturities, the interest-rate changes increased progressively less as maturities lengthened. That is, the yield curve slopes upward progressively less steeply. Accordingly, the severest price impact fell on the ten and twenty-year maturities because on these issues both interest-rate change and number of years to maturity were significant. In about five years, investors lost approximately 10 per cent of the dollar value of their holdings of bonds with ten to twenty-year maturities.

In order to protect against interest-rate risk, the portfolio manager may either shift his fixed-payment instruments into shorter maturities, or shift a portion of his fixed-payment instruments into equities. By shifting into short-term maturities, and continually replacing maturing securities with new ones, loss of dollars through discounts can be avoided and advantage can be taken of rising coupons on newly issued notes. By shifting into equities, discount losses can be avoided and advantage can be taken of rising stock prices.

This is a conservative portfolio policy, not an aggressive one. An aggressive policy would require that the portfolio manager attempt to anticipate periods of declining interest rates by purchasing larger proportions of fixed-payment instruments with longer maturities at discounts, assuming that subsequently declining interest rates would cause capitalizations to rise with the effect of increasing the value of the fixed-payment instruments held in the portfolio.

Fixed-income yields can be deflated or inflated by an estimated interest-rate change factor for comparative purposes. This factor will vary with the economic and financial conditions prevailing at any given time. During a period of growth, the factor will deflate the fixed-income yields to account for the increased interest-rate risk and increasing discounts. After several years of rapid expansion and sizeable interest-rate hikes, the investor may estimate that interest rates are more likely to fall than rise. Therefore, the interest-rate change factor would inflate the fixed-income yields to account for reduced interest-rate risk, smaller discounts, and expected appreciation of the fixed-income portion of the portfolio. On the one side, the deflated yield will make common stocks more desirable, whereas on the other, the inflated yield will make common stocks even less desirable than immediate, comparable yields might indicate.

The data indicate that some mutual fund managers have tended to make portfolio changes in response to changing risk patterns in the 1960's. Although this tendency does not appear in all funds, there is some indication that it is becoming more common. Other studies might indicate that the same tendency has been displayed by other portifolio managers.

Security analysts must recognize and point out to portfolio managers that risk analysis in the 1960's has taken on new meaning. As a stimulated growth economy becomes accepted as a fact of life on the American scene, analysts, mutual fund managers, and portfolio managers in general must adjust their evaluations and their holdings in response to changing risk patterns.

PART II

INDIVIDUAL
INVESTMENT
PROGRAMS

INTRODUCTION TO PART II

In the following six essays some of the more basic approaches to building an individual investment program are presented. In these selections, each author attempts to suggest an appropriate approach to the individual investor who is attempting to construct his own portfolio. After considering the problems facing the investor, the individual may decide that a conservative investment program is more appropriate in his case. On the other hand, the investor may see in the problems facing him a challenge to perform as an aggressive investor with the expectation of a greater than average return. Both viewpoints are represented in the following selections. Regardless of which approach each author takes, however, he is implicitly saying that some specific investment philosophy, or some specific portfolio policy, is essential to the accomplishment of a successful individual investment program.

In the first essay in this section Nathan Belfer suggests that investment management is part of the total problem of money management. He states that the total financial needs of a client must be considered and that security holdings of the individual will have to be constructed in relation to his total position. He formulates six guide lines—individual needs, concentration and diversification, supervision, balance, timing, and taxation—that should improve the structure and performance of individual portfolios. He concludes with extended comments on portfolio construction and the observation that the investment manager has a challenging assignment.

In the second and third selections Douglas Bellemore discusses the main requirements for the conservative and aggressive investors to follow in order to achieve their goals. Regarding the conservative investor, he illustrates how and why common stocks are more successful than savings accounts, he emphasizes that the investor must follow basic principles, and he gives gour primary reasons why investors fail to achieve their goals. Regarding the aggressive investor, he outlines his basic concept of how and why beginning investors can accumulate from $165,000 to $400,000, depending on the amount saved and their success, he evaluates and applies growth rates of specific programs for specific individuals in table form, and he notes three groups of stocks from which portfolio selection may be made to achieve aggressive investment success. Throughout his work, Bellemore emphasizes the concept of compounding and the significance that a systematic investment program may acquire.

In the fourth selection Thomas and David Babson discuss the problem of selecting from the vast number of stocks that may be properly classified as growth stocks. The authors suggest five characteristics that can assist the investor in reducing this problem to manageable proportions. The divident payout factor is evaluated in comparison with the deferred income advantage to the tax-conscious individual, since deferred income is one of the main advantages of growth stocks. Other features of growth stocks are mentioned in general, and the need for sound management is emphasized as a factor of paramount importance.

In the fifth essay Norman Miller reports on research completed at Indiana University on the subject of a growth industry approach to selecting growth companies. Contrary to popular opinion, this research indicates that industry growth is a poor basis for selection of growth stocks. Miller goes on to suggest reasons for the failure of this approach and indicates that there are other reasons, outside of economic growth, that influence the price appreciation of a specific stock.

In the last selection Arthur Weisenberger presents a short history of investment companies, tracing them from obscurity to prominence. The two major types of investment companies are presented in the light of the needs of the investing public for their services. Weisenberger relates many of the facts that have made investment companies, especially mutual funds, the multi-billion dollar business they are today and the "modern way to invest."

7

DETERMINING THE CONSTRUCTION AND COMPOSITION OF AN INDIVIDUAL SECURITIES PORTFOLIO*

NATHAN BELFER is a portfolio investment manager at Wood, Struthers & Winthrop. He lectures on Investment Management at the New York Institute of Finance.

Investment management is a part of the total problem of money management. The investment manager's function is to consider the client's total financial needs, his resources and the means by which the desired end can be most effectively achieved. In addition to direct investments in stocks and bonds, this will generally also involve such other financial areas as life insurance, real estate, estate planning and participation in business ventures. The security holdings of the individual will have to be constructed in relation to his total position. The subject matter of this article will be confined to the problems involved in the securities investment portion of the individual's financial structure.

In the management of individual portfolios the investment manager is to some extent like an architect. The building blocks consist of bonds, preferred stocks and common stocks. He must make a selection from the large array of items available to him in order to construct an edifice most suitable for the client. Unfortunately, investment management is not an exact science in the sense that the physical sciences are. As is well known, the physical sciences have such laws as those of gravity, thermodynamics, mass action, etcetera. Given the appropriate circumstances a definite reaction will always take place. A very simple example will suffice to highlight the difference between an exact science and investment management. Chemists know how to combine two parts of

---

*From *Financial Analysts Journal,* Vol. 21, No. 3 (May-June 1965), pp. 101-4. Reprinted by permission.

hydrogen and one part of oxygen to always produce water. Unfortunately, as every investor, security analyst and investment manager knows, the same predictability does not prevail in the investment world. A given set of circumstances will not necessarily lead to an exact predictable end. If it did, the investment management problem would be quite different from what it actually is in the real world. (In fact one might ask whether organized markets could exist if investment management were an exact science in the sense that the physical sciences are. Theoretically, analysts all over the country would be putting data into a computer. If the answer came out "buy," and every investment manager were simultaneously trying to buy the stock in question, there could be no organized market. For every buyer there must be a seller, which requires a difference of opinion concerning the future value of a particular security. If prediction were as exact and precise as in the physical sciences, it is obvious that the auction market as we know it today would be impossible.)

If investment management is not an exact science, what is it then? In the author's view it is at best a limited art. The investment manager must consider and evaluate all the information available to him. He must then try to utilize it in a manner which will produce the most rewarding results. Economics too is not an exact science, and one does not expect perfection from it. The environment of the economic, political and business world is constantly changing. This makes predictability and exactitude extremely difficult. In addition, all of the needed data may not be available.

What is the investment manager to do when confronted with a changing environment and possibly incomplete information? He cannot hope for mathematical certainty. However, he can apply his judgment, experience and knowledge to the available data. Over a period of time he should be able to do reasonably well for his clients.

While there are no firm rules in the investment management area, the author has developed for himself a number of guidelines for the construction of individual securities portfolios. The remainder of this article will be devoted to a consideration of them.

1. INDIVIDUAL NEEDS

There are various types of investors—the traditional widow and orphan, the aggressive young business man trying to build up capital, the individual preparing for his retirement, the pension fund with income needs, etc. They all have varying requirements which require different techniques of management. It is obvious that the same security is not suited for every portfolio. Fortunately, this need not be a problem for the investment manager. There are literally tens of thousands of individual securities available to the portfolio manager. He should be able to select securities which meet the needs of the individual involved. The investment manager must thus be a capable security analyst in order to be able to evaluate security recommendations and make appropriate selections for each portfolio.

While this guide line of individual need would appear to be an obvious one, in the author's experience it is too frequently violated. If a security has been found which has the promise of substantial price appreciation, life would be simplified for the manager if it could be purchased for every account under his supervision. Unfortunately, things are not that easy. A particular security may have great promise; however, its inclusion in portfolios must be considered in terms of the individual need of each client.

A corollary of this is the fact that the investment manager in addition to being a good security analyst must also have psychological insight. It is part of his task to determine what the individual client's real needs are and to try to fulfill them. It is essential that the client be happy with his investments.[1]

2. CONCENTRATION AND DIVERSIFICATION

These two guidelines can be discussed together. Diversification has, of course, always been stressed. In this author's view it has possibly been overemphasized. Many portfolios have far too many individual securities. It is impossible to supervise adequately too large a portfolio list. In addition, over-diversification can result in mediocrity in investment results. Even if a particular security shows substantial appreciation, the benefits to the entire portfolio will be negligible if this security holding represents only a small percentage of the total dollar value of the portfolio.

While diversification is essential, it can be achieved by investment in a limited number of items which the investment manager and his analytical staff know thoroughly. Concentration can be extremely rewarding if the proper security is chosen. Thus, at varying times in the past, concentration in such groups as the airlines, retail trade, drugs, sulfur, electronics, etc., would have resulted in very satisfactory investment results. To achieve the maximum benefits, however, a more than token investment in the selected group would be required. If one had a firm conviction on, say, the oils at a particular time, the investment manager could consider combined investment of as much as 20-25 per cent in several different issues in that industry group. To benefit from concentration it is necessary to have a thorough knowledge of the security or industry in which one intends to invest heavily. This also requires constant supervision, another guideline which will be discussed separately.

Some diversification is of course necessary. However, it is easy to slip into

---

[1]This theme concerning the need for the individual investor to be happy with his investments is interestingly developed by Linhart Stearns in his book *How to Live With Your Investments*, New York, Simon & Schuster, 1955.

the trap of over-diversification. Concentration will result in more substantial investment results. In summary, one should try to put many of the eggs into one basket and watch that basket constantly.

3. SUPERVISION

It is obvious that the individual securities in the portfolio must be carefully and constantly supervised. While this is a truism, it bears repetition. During the great postwar business and stock market boom from 1946 to 1960, it was possible to be successful by buying a security and putting it away. If the initial selection were reasonably sound, too much supervision might not have been necessary. In the period up to 1960, time and the general growth of the economy might have bailed one out of one's mistakes.

The period immediately ahead is unlikely to witness as dramatic an increase in stock prices as we enjoyed in the postwar period. Time by itself will not achieve satisfactory investment results. Markets in the future are likely to be brutally selective and price increments more modest than previously. There is, thus, an urgent need for increased effective supervision to achieve maximum investment results.

4. BALANCE

Balance in the portfolio refers first to the proportionate disposition of funds between stocks and bonds. Within the bond portfolio there should be some balance as to maturities. In the stock portfolio there should be some balance among growth stocks, cyclical stocks and defensive issues.

It is not possible to state precisely what the balance should be as between bonds and stocks. The individual needs of the particular client must be considered. The more venturesome portfolio might at times be 100 per cent in common stocks, should the market outlook justify it.[2] There are other portfolios, of course, in which the manager would wish to maintain a constant bond ratio of at least 40 per cent. The relationship between fixed income securities and common equities will be determined by the investment manager for each particular portfolio on the basis of individual needs and his conception of the stock market and business outlook at the time.

---

[2]The author must indicate at this point that he has a bias in favor of common stocks as long-term holdings. The increased efforts by the government to pursue an antirecession policy and to maintain the economy's growth rate, combined with the emergence of a semi-welfare state in the United States, has long-term implications pointing toward "creeping" inflation. With such an outlook fixed dollar investments will be less rewarding in the long run than common equities. A managed economy, however, will not completely eliminate short-term business fluctuations, and bond reserves are therefore necessary.

One must be flexible in approach and technique. The investment manager cannot be rigid and should not set fixed stock-bond ratios which are invariable at all times.

5. TIMING

Timing is essential in all areas of life. Many readers, no doubt, have had the frustrating experience of buying stocks which appeared to be cheap on fundamentals and which performed indifferently in the market. The technical position of a security in addition to the intrinsic value must be considered. This is not an argument for tape reading or the mystical use of chart techniques. However, the technical position of a security is important in the achievement of maximum long-term investment results. There is no point in buying a security which appears underpriced if it will lag the market on a short-term basis. The funds could be more advantageously employed elsewhere in the interim period. Timing will also be a factor in selling decisions.

This is not the place for a discussion of the technical approach to stock market investment. The portfolio manager should have a knowledge of the subject. Intrinsic value considerations should be predominant in the investment decision. However, an awareness of the technical market indicators will be of assistance in achieving optimum timing.

6. TAXATION

The investment manager must concern himself with the tax problem of his clients. Unfortunately, tax considerations intrude upon investment judgment. It is obvious that under our present tax laws a dollar of capital gains is worth more than a dollar of ordinary income. This, however, while important, should not be the basic factor in investment decisions. Too often individuals are loath to sell low cost stocks because of the tax which will have to be paid. Yet a growth company's outlook can change, making the stock relatively over-priced. In such a case the sale of a low cost holding is justified even when there is a large tax to pay. The stock sold could go down by more than the tax to be paid, or hopefully the proceeds could be reinvested in another security which will go up by more than the tax. This writer doubts that the capital gains tax will be repealed in the foreseeable future. In most cases it will have to be paid. The only way to avoid it is by death. (The Treasury even considered eliminating this possibility in the 1964 tax revision.) While tax payments are onerous they should not be allowed to interfere with sell recommendations that are justified for investment reasons.

Municipals bonds have a place in portfolios provided the tax bracket of the individual concerned is high enough. While there is no hard and fast rule on this, the use of municipal bonds may not be suitable in tax brackets below the 40 per cent level.

One other factor should be mentioned. It is not truly a guideline, but may be applicable in legal trusts. In the selection of securities for trusts and legal funds there may be various restrictions which the portfolio manager will have to observe. In general, it is wise for the settlers of trusts, and governing boards of pension and profit-sharing plans, to give the investment manager sufficient discretion to enable him to adjust to unforeseen changes in economic and stock market conditions.

The above guidelines will not assure investment success. However, they should improve the structure and performance of individual portfolios.

Two other items relevant to portfolio construction are perhaps worthy of mention. First, the reserve or fixed income portion of portfolios has generally consisted of bonds or preferreds. While these are perfectly suitable, it is possible to be more imaginative in the reserve portion of the portfolio. There are some securities with fixed income characteristics which may also hold out the possibility of capital appreciation.

Electric utilities have shown steady persistent growth in earnings, dividends and prices. They could have been very successfully employed as a form of semi-reserve. While electric utility prices will fluctuate more than bonds, they do have a defensive characteristic. Further, unlike bonds, they could show appreciation potential. A common stock such as Federal National Mortgage Association is another interesting reserve possibility. It too has shown appreciation and dividend increases over the last several years. First mortgage railroad bonds of many railroads could have been purchased at sharp discounts some years ago. Yields were well above those available on governments and grade A corporate bonds. With greater understanding of the bonds and an improving railroad picture, these bonds (e.g., Missouri-Pacific) have shown satisfactory price appreciation. Convertible bonds and convertible preferreds also offer the opportunity of price enhancement. These are examples of items which, while they function as reserves, also enable the portfolio to enjoy appreciation.

Second, for the foreseeable future the rate of growth in both the economy and the stock market may be somewhat less than during the postwar period. In such a market special situations may have a place in portfolios. Normally, liquidations, mergers and reorganizations offer only limited profit potential. However, when dynamic possibilities are difficult to find, special situations can be interesting. A profit, even though a small one, is still a profit. A sufficient number of them will improve results for the portfolio. Some recent examples of special situations which could have been profitably included in portfolios are Texas Gulf Producing, Franco Wyoming Oil, American Viscose, Champlin Oil, Garrett Corporation, Bethlehem Steel preferred and International Harvester preferred.

The investment manager has a challenging assignment. In the construction of an individual portfolio he must be both a first rate security analyst and an architect of ideas. While it is not an exact science, investment management can be a highly rewarding art.

8

REALISTIC GOALS FOR THE CONSERVATIVE INVESTOR*

DOUGLAS H. BELLEMORE is professor of finance at New York University

Successful investing for the conservative investor is neither difficult nor time-consuming; furthermore, it does not demand an unusual degree of judgment or skill. The main requirements are that this type of investor (1) have a systematic program of investing, (2) not try for spectacular results, (3) remain immune to changing moods and emotions of the market place, and (4) purchase only securities representing reasonable values based on established standards of value.

Conservative investors are defined here as investors who wish to minimize not only investment risks, but also the time and effort necessary to manage a common stock portfolio. Above all, they want peace of mind regarding their investment, and they expect their portfolio to do as well, but not better than, the indexes of common stocks over the long term. The base for all computations is an assumed compounded annual capital price appreciation rate of 3 per cent, a rate based on the long historical trend of common stock prices during the twentieth century, and one which we consider as a long-term minimum expectation. If the individual invests $500 annually, ages thirty to thirty-nine, and $1,000 per year between forty and sixty-five, the amount invested should appreciate to $51,000 at sixty-five if all dividends are spent as received and not reinvested.

*From *The Strategic Investor* (New York: Simmons-Boardman Publishing Corporation, 1963), pp. 9-15, copyright ©A 671203. Reprinted by permission.

But why invest in common stocks at a 3 per cent rate of capital appreciation when money accumulating in savings accounts can earn a compounded rate of 4 per cent (noticeably higher in California savings and loan associations)? It is, of course, true that at the 4 per cent savings bank rate, instead of 3 per cent, the total of savings *plus* all accumulated compounded interest at age sixty-five would exceed $51,000. However, the 3 per cent rate for appreciation of stocks is conservative—a minimum—and actual experience indicates that over the next 20 or 30 years a higher rate is very likely to be produced—probably at least the 3.66 per cent long-term record of the Dow Jones Industrial Average.

But far more important, the $51,000 accumulated in common stocks does not assume the reinvestment of income dividends, but merely allows for capital appreciation. Dividend income, which could either be spent as received or reinvested annually, has not been included in the $51,000 calculation. To make a fair comparison with savings accounts, therefore, an equal amount invested in savings and common stocks should be compared, excluding interest income on savings accounts. On this basis, total savings of $31,000 to age sixty-five would be accumulated, having had, of course, no capital appreciation. The individual having spent all interest income, would have deposited $31,000 over the years and would have amassed the same amount at sixty-five. Conversely, savings invested in common stocks (excluding dividends) would reach an estimated $51,000 allowing for capital appreciation on a compounding basis. Consequently, the investor would have invested $31,000, spent all dividend income, and still have realized $51,000.

Conservative investors accumulating capital funds over working years should not only invest annually as described above, but, *in addition, should reinvest all dividends,* and pay income taxes on the dividends from regular income. When annual dividends are added to regular periodic investments, it is logical to assume an over-all compounding rate of 6 per cent (3 per cent growth plus 3 per cent dividend income reinvested). Specifically, if dividends are reinvested annually, in addition to the $31,000 invested at age thirty to sixty-five inclusive, a compounded annual rate of 6 instead of 3 per cent is used. As a result, the estimated value of the common stock portfolio at sixty-five is $89,000, rounded to $90,000, instead of the $51,000 estimated if dividends are not reinvested. The 6 per cent rate is believed to be realistic and conservative. Some authorities use a 7½ per cent rate.[1]

In order to have accumulated a round figure of $100,000 of portfolio's value at age sixty-five, we suggest additional sporadic investments over the years totaling $6,000. Thus, an investment of $31,000 plus $6,000, or $37,000, plus

[1]Nicholas Moldovsky, "Stock Values and Stock Prices," *The Financial Analysts Journal,* Vol. 16, No. 3, May-June 1960, p. 81.

reinvestment of all dividends, should bring the portfolio's value up to an estimated value of approximately $100,000 at age sixty-five.

Specific monetary goals for the conservative investor depend, of course, on amounts invested regularly. Regularity of investment purchases is important in order to build capital consistently and to "dollar average" purchases over the years. A suggested minimum investment program follows for age thirty to retirement at sixty-five:

1. $500 annually—age thirty to thirty-nine inclusive—
total invested $ 5,000.00
2. $1,000 annually-age forty to sixty-five inclusive-
total invested $26,000.00
Total Invested $31,000.00

This program assumes that amounts invested will appreciate at an annual rate of 3 per cent compounded. Table 4 depicts the expected value of this portfolio at five-year age intervals from age thirty to sixty-five inclusive. The figures in the brief table below have been extracted from the complete Table 6. All estimates are minimum expectations.

Table 4.   *Estimated Value of Portfolio At Ages Indicated*
(Assumes No Reinvestment of Dividends) Investment Compounded At 3%
Annual Rate (Investment $500 Year Ages 30-39, $1,000 Year Ages 40-65)*

On Reaching Age	Total Amount Invested (Not Including Dividends Which Are Reinvested)	Total Estimated Value of Portfolio
35	$ 3,000	$ 3,234
40	6,000	5,904
45	11,000	13,312
50	16,000	19,742
55	21,000	29,354
60	26,000	39,345
65	31,000	50,921

*Table 9 (p. 76) shows estimated portfolio values for every age, 30-65 inclusive.

Table 6 indicates the following for accumulation by capital appreciation of portfolio to age sixty-five:

1. Five hundred dollars invested annually ages thirty to thirty-nine (total investment $5,000) with no further investment would appreciate to $12,369 at age sixty-five at a 3 per cent compounding rate and to $29,982 at a 6 per cent compounding rate.

Table 5.   Estimated Value of Portfolio
At Ages Indicated (Assumes Reinvestment
of Dividends Annually) Investment Compounded At 6%
Annual Rate (Investment $500 Year Ages 30-39, $1,000 Year Ages 40-65)*

On Reaching Age	Total Amount Invested	Total Estimated Value of Portfolio
35	$ 3,000	$ 3,488
40	6,000	6,986
45	11,000	16,324
50	16,000	26,482
55	21,000	42,414
60	26,000	61,397
65	31,000	89,137

*Table 9 (p. 76) shows estimated portfolio values for every age, 30-65 inclusive.

2. One thousand dollars invested annually ages thirty to thirty-nine (total investment $10,000) with no further investment would appreciate to $24,723 at a 3 per cent rate and $59,964 at a 6 per cent rate.

3. One thousand dollars invested annually ages forty to forty-nine inclusive (total investment $10,000) with no further investment would appreciate to $18,396 at a 3 per cent compounding rate and $33,483 at a 6 per cent compounding rate.

4. One thousand dollars invested annually ages fifty to fifty-nine inclusive (total investment $10,000) would appreciate to $13,688 at a 3 per cent compounding rate and $18,697 at a 6 per cent compounding rate.

5. One thousand dollars invested annually ages sixty to sixty-five inclusive (total investment $6,000) would appreciate to $6,468 at a 3 per cent compounding rate or $6,975 at a 6 per cent compounding rate.

6. Five hundred dollars invested annually ages thirty to thirty-nine inclusive and $1,000 annually ages forty to sixty-five inclusive would appreciate to $50,921 at a 3 per cent compounding rate and to $89,137 at a 6 per cent compounding rate.

7. One thousand dollars invested annually ages thirty to sixty-five inclusive would appreciate to $63,276 at a 3 per cent compounding rate and to $119,121 at a 6 per cent compounding rate.

8 The advantage of higher rates of compounding are illustrated as an investment of $31,000 rises to $50,921 at a 3 per cent rate but to $89,137 at a 6 per cent rate.

9. The advantage of investing at a relatively early working age is illustrated by the fact that $500 invested annually for ten years, ages thirty to

Table 6. Estimates of Capital Appreciation of Individual's Portfolio
Assuming Regular Investments Annually of Amounts as Indicated and Compounded at Rates Indicated

Age for Which Capital Values are Calculated	Accumulation of Annual Investments of $500 Ages 30-39 Inclusive		Accumulation of Annual Investments of $1,000 (Instead of $500) Ages 30-39 Inc.		Accumulation of Annual Investments of $1,000 Ages 40-49 Inclusive		Accumulation of Annual Investments of $1,000 Ages 50-59 Inclusive		Accumulation of Annual Investments of $1,000 Ages 60-65 Inclusive		Total Accumulated Value of Portfolio at Ages Indicated			
											At 3%		At 6%	
	At 3%	At 6%	At 3%	At 6%	At 3%	At 6%	At 3%	At 6%	At 3%	At 6%	Total of Columns 1,5,7,9	Total of Columns 3,5,7,9	Total of Columns 2,6,8,10	Total of Columns 4,6,8,10
	(1)	(2)	(3)	(4)	(5)	(6)	(7)	(8)	(9)	(10)				
Age 30	500	500	1,000	1,000							500	1,000	500	1,000
Age 35	3,234	3,488	6,468	6,975							3,234	6,468	3,488	6,975
Age 40	5,904	6,986	11,808	13,972							5,904	11,808	6,986	13,972
Age 45	6,844	9,349	13,688	18,697	6,468	6,975					13,312	20,156	16,324	25,672
Age 50	7,934	12,510	15,869	25,021	11,808	13,972					19,742	27,677	26,482	38,993
Age 55	9,198	16,742	18,396	33,688	13,688	18,697	6,468	6,975			29,354	38,552	42,414	59,360
Age 60	10,668	22,404	21,326	44,809	15,869	25,021	11,808	13,972			38,345	49,003	61,397	83,802
Age 65	12,369	29,982	24,723	59,964	18,396	33,483	13,688	18,697	6,468	6,975	50,921	63,275	89,137	119,119
Rounded for ease of reference											51,000	63,000	90,000	120,000
Total Amount of All Periodic Investments											31,000	36,000	31,000	36,000

Total Portfolio Values at Age 65

Recapitulation:

	3% (1,5,7,9)	3% (3,5,7,9)	6% (2,6,8,10)	6% (4,6,8,10)
	12,369	24,823	29,982	59,964
	18,396	18,396	33,483	33,483
	13,688	13,688	18,697	18,697
	6,468	6,468	6,975	6,975
	50,921	63,275	89,137	119,121

Note: (1) 3% rate of capital appreciation assumes no reinvestment of dividends.
       (2) 6% rate of capital appreciation assumes all dividends reinvested annually.

thirty-nine inclusive, rises to $12,369 at a 3 per cent compounding rate and $29,982 at a 6 per cent compounding rate at age sixty-five. On the other hand, $500 invested annually for ten years, ages fifty-five to sixty-four inclusive rises to only $5,904 at a 3 per cent rate and $6,986 at a 6 per cent rate by age sixty-five.

10. Table 6 assumes that an investment program starts at age thirty.

a. However, if the reader is forty and wishes to start investing $1,000 annually, he can calculate his estimated portfolio value at age sixty-five by simply ignoring investments made at earlier ages (thirty to thirty-nine) shown in columns 1 to 4 inclusive. He will simply take the totals of columns 5, 7, and 9 if assuming a 3 per cent rate of compounding, or columns 6, 8, and 10 if assuming a 6 per cent rate of compounding.

b. If the reader is fifty, he will simply use columns 7 and 9 if assuming a 3 per cent rate of compounding and 8 and 10 if using a 6 per cent rate.

In other words, an investment of $37,000 ($31,000 regularly invested plus $6,000 sporadic investments) would have approximately tripled in value by age sixty-five. Of course, if a conservative investor doubles the periodic investments outlined above, investing a total of $74,000 instead of $37,000 over the years thirty to sixty-five inclusive and would reinvest all dividends, he should accumulate approximately $200,000 by the time he reaches sixty-five, instead of $100,000.

Accumulation of $100,000 assumes that investors follow basic principles. While the accumulation of $100,000, as indicated above, is by no means difficult for the conservative investor, success on this level will still depend on:

1. Avoiding the pitfalls of investment.
2. Following meticulously the principles of portfolio management.
3. Buy and hold and rarely sell.

Actually, many investors who invest a total of $31,000 to $37,000 over their working years do not accumulate $100,000 for retirement, but, in fact, far less. Failures occur because (1) some investors become trapped by mistakes, (2) they are traders instead of investors, (3) they are not broadly diversified, and (4) they do not follow policies developed for success as conservative investors.

Tables 4, 5, 6, and the calculations above ignore taxes that must be paid on dividends received. The assumption is that the investor can pay this tax from regular income, so that all annual dividends will be reinvested. In effect, the tax paid on dividend income is a small but further contribution from regular income to the investment program.

Specifically, at forty if the individual has invested $500 per year beginning at thirty and has reinvested all dividends received, the estimated value of his portfolio would be $6,986 and the estimated dividend income would be 3 to 5 per cent of this amount or approximately $315. The income tax on this dividend income at a 30 per cent effective tax rate would be $95 and at a 40 per cent effective tax rate would be $126. At fifty the tax on dividends ($1,200) would amount to $360 at a 30 per cent rate and $480 at a 40 per cent rate.

ADVANTAGES OF COMPOUND INTEREST AND DOLLAR COST AVERAGING

The above calculations and estimates dramatically indicate the advantages of compound interest and dollar cost averaging. The value of compounding cannot be underestimated.

An illustration is the historic story of the advisor to the king who was promised any reward he desired. He asked the king for what appeared a nominal one—that is, that the first year he be granted one bushel of rice and that each year thereafter the grant be double that of the previous year's. The king agreed to this seemingly modest request. But before many years the annual contribution, because of compounding, was equal to the total product of all the land in the kingdom.

9
REALISTIC GOALS FOR THE AGGRESSIVE INVESTOR*

DOUGLAS H. BELLEMORE is professor of finance at New York University.

ACCUMULATING $165,000 TO $400,000

After examining the heavy odds against accumulating $1 million dollars, no reasonable investor would set it as his goal. Investors who press to amass a million dollars assume far greater risks and have poorer records than

*From *The Strategic Investor* (New York: Simmons-Boardman Publishing Corporation, 1963), pp. 16-22, copyright ©A 671203. Reprinted by permission.

investors with more modest goals. Like the horse races, the possibilities seem intriguing if the odds are not considered.

On the other hand, aggressive investors who (1) understand and avoid mistakes, (2) follow the guidelines, and (3) devote the time and effort necessary to manage successfully an aggressive-type portfolio can set goals of $165,000 to $400,000 depending upon the amount saved and invested: $1,000, $1,500, $2,000, or $2,500 per year.

Just how logical is such a bold statement? First, it is based on the author's professional review of hundreds of personal portfolios in post-World War II years. Second, this statement can be supported by the same type of statistical approach utilized in developing reasonable goals for the conservative investor.

The conservative investor, by investing $37,000, can expect a basic 3 per cent annual growth rate of price appreciation compounded, which together with the reinvestment of all dividends annually, will result in the accumulation of a portfolio at sixty-five of $100,000, resulting from the combined growth rate of 6 per cent compounded annually. In other words, his $37,000 investment would have nearly tripled over the years.

ANTICIPATING A GROWTH RATE OF CAPITAL INVESTED OF 6 PER CENT COMPOUNDED—OVER-ALL RATE 9 PER CENT

If the aggressive investor follows guidelines referred to above, he should certainly expect a base growth rate of 6 to 7½ per cent, at the very least, or twice the starting base rate used for the conservative investors not reinvesting all dividends received.

Furthermore, not only should the aggressive investor expect that invested capital should grow at a compounded base rate of 6 to 7½ per cent annually, but that he would receive some dividends despite his lack of interest in such income. If dividends are reinvested he should expect a minimum growth rate of 8 to 9 per cent. A 3 per cent growth rate compounded will double invested funds in 24 years; a 6 per cent growth rate in 12 years, a 7½ per cent rate in 10 years, and a 9 per cent rate in 8 years. Based on actual experience of investors following certain suggested principles, the aggressive investor can reasonably work on the assumption of a composite compounded growth rate of 9 per cent annually, or a doubling every 8 years.

Actually, approaching the 9 per cent rate from another viewpoint, all investors should work with projections of earnings five to six years ahead and the aggressive investor, whose goal is primarily capital gains, should assume that a commitment of the type in which he is interested should yield a 100 per cent capital gain within five years. In some cases it will take somewhat longer, but if his judgment has been at all correct, certainly rarely more than eight years. In some cases he will be pleasantly surprised by realizing 100 per cent capital gains in less than five years. Therefore, based on all the above premises, an expected doubling at a minimum of every eight years (a 9 per cent rate compounded) is not at all unreasonable.

Concerning growth rates, during the past 50 years stock prices, earnings, and dividends (Standard and Poor's "500" Index) have *all* grown at a compounded annual rate of 3¼ per cent, and for the longer period, 1871-1959, at 2½ per cent. For the Dow Jones Industrial Average since 1897 the rate has been 3.66 per cent. The record for all common stock portfolios as a class, *assuming the reinvestment of all dividends*, will probably yield a compounded rate of 6 to 7½ per cent in the future.

Only 20 per cent higher than the 7½ per cent rate, our 9 per cent rate for aggressive investors is realistic since it is based on reasonable premises.[1] If the conservative investor, by reinvesting all dividends, can expect a growth rate of 6 to 7½ per cent compounded annually, the aggressive investor should certainly do at least 20 to 50 per cent better—or a 9 per cent rate. To achieve this, he has to make portfolio selections from any one or from all of these three groups:

1. Growth stocks. Before investors in general recognize a specific growth stock, the aggressive investor should recognize and purchase securities of companies whose earnings are expected to grow at rates of at least 8 to 9 per cent compounded annually, or more than twice that of the economy as a whole. It is important in purchasing growth stocks to purchase shares before the market (investors in general) prices them so high as to discount earnings for many years in advance. However, investors will frequently have opportunities in bear markets, like 1962, to purchase growth stocks a second or third time at logical price/earnings ratios; for example, IBM in 1962.

2. Temporarily unpopular stocks or "comeback stocks." After lengthy and critical investigation the aggressive investor may decide that a particular stock or a specific group of them are heavily undervalued in the market because of temporary unpopularity. Before purchasing, however, he must estimate that they will regain at least some of their lost earning power and popularity and provide 100 per cent capital gain opportunities over the next five years. Full recovery in earnings is not necessary in order to provide 100 per cent capital gains. Frequently, such stocks will not take five years to recover, but

---

[1]Nicholas Molodovsky, a practicing Customers' Broker for a large New York Stock Exchange Member Firm, Associate Editor of the *Financial Analysts Journal* and author of many articles, stated in "Stock Values and Stock Prices, Part I," *Financial Analysts Journal,* May-June 1960, "By lifting the growth rate of the trend line of earnings and dividends of 2½ per cent while maintaining the 5 per cent current return, we have also increased in round figures the effective total return from dividends to 7½ per cent." Mr. Molodovsky does not assume any reinvestment of dividends in establishing any growth rate projections, and these are projections for the average for all stocks.

considerable patience is often required in such situations. One of the best examples of such temporary undervaluations was the international oils—Standard Oil of New Jersey and Royal Dutch in 1960 and January 1961—selling at about half their 1956-57 highs. Within two years they were up over 50 per cent. A second example was Chrysler, which almost quadrupled in 12 months, June 1962-June 1963, after falling to its lowest price since World War II. A third was Ford which in 1958 sold at $35 versus $65 in 1956, but by 1959 Ford rose to over $80 and by 1961 to $117 (all prices before the two-for-one split). The steels, papers, and tobaccos at the 1962 low were further examples. Standard Oil of New Jersey rose to $70 in 1963.

        3. "Special Situations." Occasionally, the aggressive investor will confront special situations, which provide opportunities for substantial capital gains.

Capital Appreciation at Various Growth Rates

        The following are examples of annual growth rates compounded which are required for a portfolio to double in market value. The aggressive investor can work with a 9 per cent rate for the previously cited reasons.

Table 7.   Results from Various Assumed
Growth Rates and Years Required to Double Investment

(%)	Years	(%)	Years	(%)	Years	(%)	Years
3	23½	7	10½	11	6½	15	5
4	18	8	9	12	6	16	4¾
5	15	9	8	13	5½	17	4½
6	12	10	7½	15	5½	19	4

The Results of 9 Per Cent Growth Rate

        We have seen that the conservative investor investing $500 annually between thirty and thirty-nine and $1000 per year thereafter until sixty-five can expect to accumulate a minimum capital of $51,000 if he does not reinvest dividends, and $89,000 to $100,000 if he reinvests all dividends annually.

        The aggressive investor, by investing the same amounts, $500 per year age thirty to thirty-nine and $1,000 per year thereafter, a total of $31,000, can expect to accumulate at a 9 per cent rate around $165,000. If, in addition to the amounts invested periodically, there are some sporadic investments of an additional $10,000 throughout the earning years, he can accumulate a minimum of $200,000. The total investment would be $31,000 in periodic investments and $10,000 in sporadic investments, or a total of $41,000. If $1,000 were invested annually instead of $500 in the thirty to thirty-nine age period, this would be a substitute for the $10,000 invested sporadically and could produce $237,000 without any additional investments above the $41,000.

The aggressive investor should reinvest whatever dividends he receives; however, unlike the conservative investor, dividend income may not be as significant for him, especially if he concentrates largely on growth stocks or "special situations." Nevertheless, investment in "come-back" stocks usually produce significant dividend yields even though the commitment is made solely for capital appreciation.

A combination of higher income and a desire to save and invest larger amounts than these should reap parallel rewards.

Table 8 depicts results which can be expected with larger periodic investments, assuming a composite over-all growth rate of 9 per cent compounded annually.

Table 8.   Results of Larger Periodic Investments
Assuming Composite Over-All Growth Rate of 9%

Case I	Annual Amounts Invested	Total Amounts Invested Cost of Investments	Total Estimated Value of Portfolio Age 65
Age 30-39	$ 500	$ 5,000	
Age 40-65	1,000	26,000	
Total Portfolio		31,000	Approx. $165,000
Case II			
Age 30-39	500	5,000	
Age 40-65	1,000	26,000	
Sporadic Investments - Total		10,000	
Total Portfolio		41,000	Approx. $200,000
Case III			
Age 30-65	1,000	36,000	
Total Portfolio		36,000	Approx. $236,000

Table 9 indicates the following for accumulation by capital appreciation of portfolio to age sixty-five:

1. Five hundred dollars invested annually ages thirty to thirty-nine inclusive (total investment $5,000) with no further investments would appreciate to $46,371 at age sixty-five at a 7½ per cent rate of compounding and to $71,400 at a 9 per cent rate of compounding.

Table 9. Estimated Capital Appreciation of Portfolio for Aggressive Investor
Regular Investments Annually Ages 30-65 Inclusive — Compounded at Rates Indicated

Age for Which Capital Values are Calculated	Accumulation to Age 65, $500 Invested Yearly Ages 30-39 Inclusive		Accumulation to Age 65, $1000 Invested Yearly (Instead of $500) Ages 30-39 Inclusive		Accumulation to Age 65, $1000 Invested Yearly Ages 40-49 Inclusive		Accumulation to Age 65, $1000 Invested Yearly Ages 50-59 Inclusive		Accumulation to Age 65, $1000 Invested Yearly Ages 60-65 Inclusive		Total Estimated Capital Accumulated			
	At 7½%	At 9%	At 7½%	At 9%	At 7½%	At 9%	At 7½%	At 9%	At 7½%	At 9%	7½% Columns 1,5,7,9	7½% Columns 3,5,7,9	9% Columns 2,6,8,10	9% Columns 4,6,8,10
	(1)	(2)	(3)	(4)	(5)	(6)	(7)	(8)	(9)	(10)	(11)	(12)	(13)	(14)
Age 30	500	500	1,000	1,000							500	1,000	500	1,000
Age 35	3,622	3,762	7,244	7,523							3,622	7,243	3,762	7,523
Age 40	7,604	8,289	15,208	16,560							7,604	15,208	8,289	16,560
Age 45	10,917	12,740	21,833	25,480	7,244	7,523					18,161	29,077	20,263	33,003
Age 50	15,172	19,597	31,344	39,204	15,208	16,560					30,380	46,552	36,157	55,764
Age 55	21,999	30,155	44,999	60,320	21,833	25,480	7,244	7,523			51,076	74,076	63,158	93,324
Age 60	32,301	46,405	63,602	92,810	31,344	39,204	15,208	16,560			78,853	110,154	102,170	148,574
Age 65	46,371	71,400	92,743	142,800	44,999	60,320	21,833	25,480	7,244	7,523	120,447	166,819	164,724	236,123

Total Portfolio Values at Age 65:   120,000   167,000   165,000   236,000

Total Amount of all Periodic Investments: 31,000   36,000   31,000   36,000

Recapitulations:

	Col (11)	Col (12)	Col (13)	Col (14)
	46,371	92,743	71,400	142,800
	44,999	44,999	60,320	60,320
	21,833	21,833	25,480	25,480
	7,244	7,244	7,523	7,523
	120,447	166,819	164,724	236,123

2. One thousand dollars invested annually ages thirty to thirty-nine inclusive, (total investment of $10,000) with no further investment would amount to $92,743 at a 7½ per cent rate of compounding and $142,800 at a 9 per cent rate of compounding.

3. One thousand dollars invested annually ages forty to forty-nine inclusive, (total investment of $10,000) with no further investment would appreciate to $44,999 at a 7½ per cent rate of compounding and $60,320 at a 9 per cent rate of compounding.

4. One thousand dollars invested annually ages fifty to fifty-nine inclusive with no further investment (total investment $10,000) would appreciate to $21,833 at a 7½ per cent compounding rate and to $25,480 at a 9 per cent compounding rate.

5. One thousand dollars invested annually ages sixty to sixty-five inclusive, with no further investments (total investment of $6,000) would appreciate to $7,244 at a 7½ per cent rate of compounding and $7,523 at a 9 per cent rate of compounding.

6. Five hundred dollars invested annually ages thirty to thirty-nine inclusive and $1,000 invested annually ages forty to sixty-five inclusive would appreciate to $120,447 at a 7½ per cent rate of compounding (columns 1, 5, 7, 9 at a 7½ per cent rate of compounding and $164,724 at a 9 per cent rate of compounding.

7. One thousand dollars invested annually ages thirty to sixty-five inclusive would appreciate to $166,819 at a compounding rate of 7½ per cent and to $236,123 at a compounding rate of 9 per cent.

8. The advantage of higher rates of compounding are illustrated as an investment of $31,000 rises to $120,447 at a 7½ per cent rate of compounding, but to $164,724 at a 9 per cent rate of compounding.

9. The advantage of investing at a relatively early working age is illustrated by the fact that $500 invested annually for ten years, ages thirty to thirty-nine inclusive, rises to $46,371 at a 7½ per cent rate of compounding and $71,400 at a 9 per cent rate of compounding. On the other hand $1,000 invested annually ages fifty-five to sixty inclusive would only rise by age sixty-five to $15,208 at a compounding rate of 7½ per cent and $16,560 at a compounding rate of 9 per cent.

10. The table assumes that an investment program starts at thirty. However, if the reader is forty and wishes to start investing $1,000 a year, he can calculate his estimated portfolio value at sixty-five simply by ignoring investments made at earlier ages (thirty to thirty-nine) shown in columns 1 to 4 inclusive and will simply take the totals of columns 5, 7, and 9 if assuming a 7½ per cent rate of compounding or columns 6, 8, and 10 if assuming a 9 per cent rate of compounding. Moreover, if the reader is fifty he will simply use columns 7 and 9 if assuming a 7½ per cent rate of compounding and columns 8 and 10 if assuming a 9 per cent rate of compounding.

10
WHY GROWTH STOCKS BEST MEET MODERN INVESTMENT NEEDS*

THOMAS E. BABSON and DAVID L. BABSON are associated with David L. Babson & Company.

There are some 4,000 corporations whose securities are listed on the nations's six major stock exchanges and many times that number whose shares are traded "over the counter." How can the individual select from this staggering quantity those whose shares may be properly classified as growth stocks?

RECOGNIZING GROWTH STOCKS

To simplify the task of selection, certain characteristics should be looked for, of which five are especially significant:

1. The company should be engaged in an industry whose rate of sales growth is faster than that of the national economy in periods of expansion and whose volume does not decline as much in periods of recession.

2. The company should be able to translate its increase in sales into a reasonably comparable rise in net profits per share. Although the dollar sales of some industries are expanding faster than the Gross National Product, their net income per share remains relatively stationary because of government regulation or other factors.

---

*Reprinted with permission of The Macmillan Company from *Investing for a Successful Future* by Thomas E. and David L. Babson, pp. 145-50. Copyright © 1959 by The Macmillan Company.

3. The company's management should be research-minded. This is an age of science, and the companies that have been making the greatest progress and are most likely to continue moving strongly ahead are those in the forefront of research. Exceptionally strong financial resources are required to sustain an adequate scientific effort today.

4. The company's outlay for direct labor should be in low ratio to its total production costs. This makes it less vulnerable to the continued advance in wage rates and fringe benefits. Moreover, wage scales in such companies are apt to be higher than average and the number of workers fewer, so that labor relations are likely to be better.

5. The company should have a record of consistently high profit margins. A generous margin allows management to finance the growth of its business to a greater degree by *in*ternal than by *ex*ternal means.

Expanding Companies in Expanding Industries

In what industries are these five growth qualifications most likely to be found? Let us begin by identifying some of the leading areas of activity where output

*Table 34. Average Annual Rates of Growth in
Physical Volume of Major Industries, 1947-1956 and 1951-1956*

Industry	1947-56 (per cent)	1951-56 (per cent)	Industry	1947-56 (per cent)	1951-56 (per cent)
Air transport	16	15	Indus. machinery	6	5
Life insurance	14	13	Automobile	6	2
Plywood	14	13	Instruments	5	6
Aluminum	13	15	Paper	5	4
Plastics	13	10	ALL INDUSTRIES	5	4
Electric power	9	10	Petroleum	4	3
Natural gas	9	7	Steel	4	2
Ethical drug*	8	6	Rubber	3	4
Chemical	8	6	Copper	2	2
Gypsum	8	5	Cigarettes	2	0
Electric apparatus	7	9	Lumber	1	0
Wood pulp	7	6	All fibers	1	−1
Flat glass	6	5	Railroad freight	0	0
Cement	6	5	Coal, bituminous	−2	−1

*Based on dollar sales—physical production data not available.
Sources: Francis L. Hirt, Department of Commerce: David L. Babson & Company, Inc.

has been expanding faster than the Federal Reserve Board Index of Industrial Production (the universally accepted measure of the nation's volume of production of goods and services expressed in tons, man-hours etc., rather than in dollars).

Table 34 shows the average annual rate of growth in the *physical* volume of most important industries from 1947 to 1956 and 1951 to 1956. In the nine-year period total industrial production advanced at an average annual rate of 5 per cent, and in the five-year span at 4 per cent. Hence the industries with above-average rates of growth can be readily noted.

A table of the rates of growth for a wide list of products, many of which are components of the above industrial groups, is given as an Appendix to this volume. It is interesting to compare the yearly rates of increase for individual products with those of the broad industrial group of which they are components—for example detergents averaging a gain of 26 per cent annually and sulphur 4 per cent, compared with 8 per cent for the entire chemical industry.

The widely differing rates of growth reflect the powerful forces that have been discussed in previous chapters. For instance, the rapid increase in such items as electronics and polyethylene, the contrasting trends in synthetic fibers and antibiotics on the one hand and wool and sulfa drugs on the other, stem from the greatly expanded research activities since prewar days.

Note in Table 34 the disparity between the growth rates of aluminum (13 per cent) and those of steel (4 per cent) and copper (2 per cent). The reasons for the remarkable rise in usage of the lighter metal are given in Chapter 15.

The sharp uptrend in demand for home labor-saving devices such as dishwashers and power-mowers, for convenience items such as coffee-makers and frozen foods, and for leisure-time products such as TV sets and outboard engines, is the result of high employment, the increase in discretionary income and the trend toward suburban living.

The ideal investment situation is one in which the long-range annual rate of growth in demand is not only rapid but is relatively resistant to periods of business decline. The largest drop in over-all industrial production from any one year to the next during the period 1947-1956 was 7 per cent. Hence those industries listed in Table 35 that have not shown a decline of as much as 7 per cent in output in any year during that decade have exhibited above-average stability.

Increased Sales, Increased Profits

The second essential characteristic of a growth-type investment is the ability to convert increased sales volume into a corresponding rise in profits per share. In the case of some companies that are growing physically at an above-average rate, expansion of net profits may be held down by factors beyond the control of their managements.

Table 35.　Relative Stability in Rates
of Production for Various Products, 1947-1956

No Decline in Any Year		Decline of Less Than 7 Per Cent in Any Year	
Electronics	Cement	Chemicals	Paper & board
Petroleum	Plywood	Aluminum	Life insurance
Natural gas	Air transport	Plastics	Wood pulp
Electric power		Cigarettes	

Decline Between 7 and 15 Per Cent in Any Year		Decline Exceeding 15 Per Cent in Any Year	
Rubber	Synthetic fibers	Automobile	Soft coal
Copper	Industrial	Steel	All fibers
Instruments	machinery	Railroad freight	Lumber
Gypsum	Electric apparatus		
	Flat glass		

For example, some industries are subject to governmental control as to rates or prices they are permitted to charge. This tends to temper, in various degrees, the *earnings* progress of publicly regulated companies such as those providing electric power, natural gas distribution, telephone service and air, rail and bus transportation. Public commission awards of competing airline routes or natural gas pipeline licenses or broadcasting channels may affect future growth prospects of established companies.

Importance of Research

The third qualification is that the industry or company must have a strong position in research. It is impossible to overstress the importance of this factor as a key to progress. As outlined in Chapter 5, the increasing attention being directed by both corporations and government to the development of new products and processes is one of the most important reasons for faith in the continued dynamic progress of the American economy. Research is a self-regenerative force that can prevent a company's position from deteriorating to the point where it must compete with similar products of others purely on a price basis.

People are more anxious to buy new, improved items than to replace the old or worn with others of the same type—particularly so when the new offer the advantages of greater labor saving, convenience, pleasure or health. Industry is eager for new materials and processes that will cut costs and enhance the appeal of products or services.

Research activities are most effective and most broadly pursued in industries where the known technological factors are numerous and new ones are most rapidly yielding to investigation, making for an infinite number of possible end results, such as the chemical, drug, electronics, labor-saving machinery and metallurgical fields. This is an important investment consideration.

The Payroll Factor

The fourth factor to look for in selecting a growth stock is a low proportion of direct labor costs. High ratios of labor to total costs are a characteristic of industries whose production methods do not lend themselves readily to mechanization or in which the cost of automatizing is prohibitive. Although progress has been made in reducing direct labor by the automobile, steel, machinery and railroad industries, the wage component is still relatively high in these fields. These industries are strongly unionized, and demands for shorter hours, higher pay and fringe benefits, as well as "featherbedding" tactics, are problems constantly harassing management.

Certain kinds of labor are almost immune to replacement by machinery, such as skilled repairing, delivery, credit-processing and functions involving human relations, as in selling. Companies engaged in service industries such as merchandising have been and will continue to be faced with a tendency of labor rates to creep upward faster than their efficiency can be raised. The more successful, financially strong retailing organizations have attacked this obstacle by establishing shopping centers and supermarkets and introducing self-service, thus cutting general overhead and increasing the ratio of sales to clerical man-hours. But the problem of maintaining adequate margins in the personal-service industries promises to continue a pressing one.

One the other hand the unit labor cost for the manufacture of petroleum products and chemicals, the processing and packaging of most drugs and foods, and the transportation of natural gas and generation of electricity varies from less-than-average down almost to zero, except for supervision and service. For instance one petrochemical plant in the South turns out over $5 million of products annually with total operating personnel of eight.

The Profit Margin

The fifth measurement that helps to identify a true growth company is its profit margins, which must be broad. The fact that a company can sell its goods or services at prices that exceed its costs by substantial amounts indicates the existence of at least one and usually several of the following conditions:

1. That most of its products are continually in good demand.

2. That they or the methods of making them are protected by strong patents or know-how.

3. That the amount of investment in plant required to produce like products is so great as to discourage competition.

4. That the management is exceptionally successful in controlling costs.

Wide profit margins betoken sound business health. Furthermore they are of particular significance to the investor building a lifetime portfolio, because they make it possible for a company's stock to pass the first of the three qualifying tests outlined in the preceding chapter—that of deferment of income.

Since this matter of deferred income is one often overlooked and not clearly understood by investors, it should be explained in some detail. Under today's high tax rates one must find a way of investing what savings he is able to set aside in such a manner that as much as possible of the income, at least, escapes personal taxes. It is therefore to his advantage to invest in companies that pay out little of their current earnings and plow back the remainder into additional plant and research projects. These reinvested earnings generate future earning power, and the more generous the profit margins, the more money thus is reinvested free of the investor's personal taxes.

Table 36 compares the average pre-tax margins and the average percentage of earnings retained of a group of typical growth companies with those of a group of stable-industry, income-type companies over the five-year period 1952–1956.

It is not the purpose of these figures to imply that margins of stable-industry companies are unduly low or that too large a percentage of earnings is paid out, but rather to emphasize, by contrast, the characteristically higher return enjoyed by growth companies and the large proportion of their earnings plowed back into the business.

Money to meet costs of plant expansion must come either from outside sources or from a company's own reserves. External financing is the method generally followed by firms that pay out most of their earnings in dividends. When such companies need funds for new plants, they raise the money either by borrowing, which lowers the company's credit position, or by selling additional stock, which dilutes the equity of those already owning shares.

The internal-financing method consists of paying out a low proportion of earnings and using the remainder to pay for expansion of the business. It adds to

assets and keeps the capital structure strong; it is the course followed by growth
companies under normal conditions, and is one of the several reasons for the
above-average rise in the value of their shares over the years.

Just how does this internal-financing policy contribute to the "deferred
income" requirement of the estate-building investor? As an example, if a
company pays out in dividends only 30 cents of each dollar of earnings and
plows back the balance in research and expanded plant capacity, the 70 cents
reinvested, although it belongs to the stockholder, is not taxable to him. It
increases the value of his equity.

*Table 36.   Five-Year (1952–1956) Average Profit
Margins and Percentage of Earnings Retained of Typical
Growth-Industry Companies vs. Typical Income-Industry Companies*

Industry	Company	Pre-Tax Profit Margin (per cent)	Percentage of Profits Plowed Back in Business
GROWTH-INDUSTRY COMPANIES			
Chemical	Dow Chemical	20	46
Glass research	Corning Glass	23	50
Labor-saving machinery	Int'l Business Machines	21	66
Research & development	Minnesota Mining	22	56
Photo supplies	Eastman Kodak	23	46
Ethical drug	Charles Pfizer	20	50
STABLE-INDUSTRY COMPANIES			
Tobacco	American Tobacco	9	28
Food	General Foods	8	43
Shoe manufacture	International Shoe	8	19
Variety chain	Woolworth	8	22
Transportation	General Amer. Transport.	12	45
Food	Corn Products	13	32

The new products developed by research and the new plant capacity
financed by these withheld earnings make possible broader earning power,
increased dividend-paying ability and greater capital growth over the years. The
investor secures his portion of these earnings—his "deferred income"—in later
dividend increases and long-term growth in the value of his shares.

The advantages to the high-bracket taxpayer of owning shares in companies that grow through internal rather than external methods of financing cannot be overemphasized. The fact that one is building a fund for retirement or some other future purpose presupposes that the income from his business or profession is in excess of his current living expenses so that he is able to reinvest all of the income he receives from his investments.

Should an individual subject to high personal taxes own the stock of a company that finances externally, such as American Telephone? Over the years, it has been paying out 80 to 85 per cent of its earnings in dividends. Thus only the 15 to 20 per cent it retains and reinvests is free of this man's high personal income taxes. Or should he own the stock of a company that expands primarily by internal financing methods, such as Gulf Oil, which has made a practice of paying out about one-third of its earnings in dividends and reinvesting the balance in expansion?

Table 37 summarizes the far greater *after-tax* benefits derived by an investor in a 50 per cent personal income tax bracket from Gulf Oil than from American Telephone. The figures are based on March, 1955, prices of one share of Telephone at $180 and 3 shares of Gulf Oil at $60 each, 1954 earnings and dividends.

Table 37.   Effect on Taxpayer in 50 Per Cent Tax Bracket of Reinvestment of Earnings, American Telephone vs. Gulf Oil

Allocation of Earnings	American Telephone	Gulf Oil
1. Earnings per $180 invested	$11.92	$21.48
2. Subtract earnings paid out in dividends	9.00	6.00
3. Leaves earnings kept by company to reinvest in business free of investor's personal tax	2.92	15.48
4. Amount of dividend left for reinvestment after investor's personal tax (50 per cent of item 2)	4.50	3.00
5. Total available for reinvestment (sum of items 3 and 4)	7.42	18.48
6. Per cent reinvestment to assumed market value (Line 5 as percentage of $180)	4.1%	10.3%
7. Item 6 in terms of dollars per $1,000 invested	$41.00	$103.00

Source: *How to Invest for Retirement,* David L. Babson & Company, Inc., Boston, 1955.

As this table shows, for every $1,000 this investor placed in Telephone he had an effective after-tax reinvestment of $41. But for every $1,000 invested in Gulf, he had an after-tax reinvestment of $103, almost three times as much.

Now note the effect of this greater reinvestment of profits on the earning power and dividend-paying ability, *per share*, of the respective corporations. The net income of American Telephone in 1954 was 200% more than in 1937—the peak prewar business year. But, because the company had created 29 million additional shares since 1937 in order to finance its growth, the 1954 net income per share was only 22 per cent higher than in 1937 ($11.92 versus $9.76).

In 1954 Gulf Oil earned 473 per cent more net income than it did in 1937. But this increased net income was divided among only 25 per cent more shares than were outstanding in the earlier year (adjusting for stock dividends and splits). Hence, net earnings per share in 1954 were $7.16, or four times the $1.76 earned in 1937.

It is not surprising, therefore, that Gulf Oil shares sold in 1955 at three times their 1937 average price, while Telephone's shares were quoted at about the same as in the earlier year; or that Gulf's annual dividend was four times as great as in 1937 (representing twice its purchasing power of that year) while Telephone's annual payment was no more than it was 17 years earlier (or, in terms of purchasing power, only half as much as in 1937).

It is obvious from the above illustration that the reinvestment method of utilizing profits is greatly to the advantage of the life-time investor, who should be accepting a lower *current* return to secure greater *future* income. The retained earnings belong to him, but he pays no income tax on them. The company invests and manages these withheld earnings for him at its above-average profit margins. His rate of return is clearly better than would be the case if he received in dividends most of the earnings of high-pay-out companies and reinvested in their stocks what remained after his taxes. The latter process, repeated time and again, drains off capital values that he would retain under the former.

To sum up this discussion of "deferred income", two powerful factors work for the benefit of the investor who buys growth stocks to implement his long-range program. These are:

1. The large percentage of retained and plowed-back earnings, on which he does not pay a tax and which create more earning power, higher dividend-paying ability and greater growth of his capital over the years.

2. A relatively large pre-tax profit margin, which, with its compounding effect, builds up his capital at an above-average rate.

Other Features of Growth Stocks

There are two other tests that investments must pass if they are to be suitable for the portfolios of those who are building for the future: they must possess capacity to continue increasing in value, and they must be of the requisite strength to protect the principal invested in them.

The basic forces promoting continued expansion in sales, earning power and dividend-paying ability—population growth, technological progress, higher consumption standards—have been described in detail in Chapters 5, 6 and 7. When doubts arise as to the further growth of firms such as Dow Chemical, Texas Company or International Business Machines, it should be remembered that since the early 1930's, when it was the generally accepted view that the American economy had "matured," these and numerous similar concerns have increased their sales and earnings many times over. The individual characteristics of these enterprises, and the factors that have brought about their impressive growth, have not changed.

As for the third test that a suitable commitment for long-range investing purposes must pass—i.e., protection against loss of principal—a cautionary note should be sounded. The term "growth stock" is frequently misapplied by enthusiastic promoters to equities of new, unseasoned companies currently registering impressive expansion but without the assurance of size, stability or long records of success; or even to speculative stocks that are expected to register an immediate rise in market price.

Here the term "growth stocks" is intended to apply only to the shares of those companies having the five characteristics outlined earlier in this chapter: they must be engaged in growing industries, must have achieved a long-term

*Table 38.   Age and Dividend-Paying
Records of Typical Growth Companies*

Typical Growth Companies	*Years in Business (as of 1956)*	*Number of Years of Uninterrupted Dividend Payments*
Corning Glass Works	105	76
Dow Chemical	59	46
E. I. du Pont	154	53
Eastman Kodak	55	55
International Business Machines	45	41
Minneapolis—Honeywell Regulator	30	29
Minnesota Mining & Manufacturing	54	41
National Lead	65	51
Owens-Illinois Glass	54	50
Parke, Davis	92	79
Pfizer, Charles	107	56
Scott Paper	77	42
Standard Oil, New Jersey	75	75
Texas Company	54	54

uptrend in earnings per share, and must have research-minded managements, low direct-labor costs and wide profit margins. In addition, they must be solidly established and well seasoned. Companies that so qualify are among the strongest, best-managed corporations in America today. Listed in Table 38 are a few outstanding growth companies, with the length of their business lives and the number of years in which they have paid dividends without interruption.

The Importance of Sound Management

While opportunities for profitable operations vary from industry to industry, depending upon the relative weight of factors within as against those beyond the control of management, the quality of a company's leadership is of very great importance in making stock selections. This attribute does not lend itself to exact measurement. But if, between two companies in the same industry and operating under a uniform set of general conditions, one makes markedly greater sales and earnings progress than the other, this result may safely be attributed to superior management ability.

It is management that fixes the amount and emphasis of a company's research program, appraises the potential markets for new products so developed, selects those that may be profitable, sets the location and capacity of plants to make them and decides how such facilities are to be financed. An imaginative new management team may sometimes be able to change the character of a company whose affairs have been deteriorating under handicaps, such as a limited line of products in a highly competitive field. Conversely, a company operating in an industry of great potentiality can stagnate under leaders who are complacent or unprogressive.

The most reliable measure of management quality, however, is to be found in a company's past record and current trends. In appraising the ability of corporate leadership, it is better to rely upon demonstrated performance than upon what a new managing team might be able to do with a company whose performance has been poor or is worsening.

INVESTMENT, NOT SPECULATION

It will be noted that this whole approach to investing is far removed from that of speculative trading or market guessing, which are so broadly believed to be the only courses open to equity investors. Instead of dealing with the hopes and fears of the moment or the narrow superficialities of *current* market prices, earnings or dividends, it reaches back into the fundamentals of what makes a company really successful.

11
ARE GROWTH STOCKS
REALLY PROFITABLE?*

*NORMAN O. MILLER is an assistant professor
of finance at the University of Texas.*

For some years now the fashion in Wall Street has been to invest in "growth stocks." Amateur investors with relatively small sums to commit in securities have been seeking industriously to pick those particular common stocks that will experience unusual growth in market value and in size of dividend payments over a period of years. Professional security analysts have struggled valiantly with the problem of identifying and selecting stocks with unusual appreciation prospects.

One of the most popular rules for selection of growth stocks is that they are usually to be found in growth industries. Concepts of growth industries vary somewhat, but they are commonly defined as those increasing their sales at a greater rate than the rate of growth of the total economy. The theory is that a company in a growth industry is likely to experience a greater-than-average increase in sales, which is likely to result in a pronounced improvement in profitability, an increase in earnings and dividends per share, and appreciation in market price for common stock.

Research recently completed at Indiana University shows there is very little basis in the experience of the past twenty years for the growth-industry idea and that, in fact, industry growth is a poor basis for selection of growth stocks. A survey of nine leading industries revealed that the greatest improvement in profitability in the period 1935-54 occurred in an industry that has expanded at about the same rate as the national economy, namely, the steel industry. The third greatest improvement in profitability was found in copper metals and mining, an industry that has been declining relative to the national

*From *Business Horizons,* Vol. 1, No. 5 (Winter 1958-59), pp. 45-50. Reprinted by permission.

economy. One of the industries with the strongest growth trends, the chemical industry, ranked seventh among the nine industries in rate of increase in profitability. This study shows that, even if one had been able to forecast accurately in the 1930's the future growth of our major industries, the forecast would not have provided a reliable basis for selection of common stocks.

GROWTH AND PROFITABILITY

One of the difficulties of the "growth industry" idea is the loose use of the term. Many people who use it do not define it, and many others seem to regard any industry that shows an increase in sales over a period of years as a growth industry. In the expanding economy of the United States, growth is a relative term. An industry is a growth industry only if it is growing relative to the total economy. An industry that is increasing its sales in absolute dollar amounts, but at a lesser rate than the expansion of the total economy, is actually a relatively declining industry.

In this statistical study we have measured the absolute growth in nine major manufacturing and mining industries by constructing for each industry an annual index of sales (average annual sales for 1935-39=100). To measure the growth of the economy in terms of sales of the manufacturing and mining companies we took the aggregate annual sales of 143 companies in 18 different industries and made an index for aggregate sales (1935-39=100). The sales index for each of the nine industries was then divided by the aggregate sales index for the 18 industries to obtain a *relative* sales index for each industry, which shows the growth of an industry in relation to the growth of industrial companies in general. An industry experiencing a more rapid expansion of sales than industrial companies generally has a sales index rising above 100, while one experiencing a less rapid expansion of sales than industrial companies generally declines below 100.

By this method three of the nine industries studied were identified as growth industries, four as neutral industries, and two as declining industries (Table 1).

Relative growth in sales for an industry, according to the growth industry thesis, is supposed to cause an increase in the profitability of companies engaged in that industry. The term "profitability" is often loosely used, but we have defined it for the purpose of this study as the relationship between amount of profit and amount of total capital. Profit is the annual amount remaining after all income and expenses except fixed charges, income taxes, and preferred dividends. Total capital is the sum of noncurrent debt, preferred stock, common stock, and surplus. Thus, profitability is measured as a rate of profit on total capital, and changes in profitability appear as changes in this rate.

We have measured changes in relative profitability of the nine industries over the twenty year period by the same statistical technique as was used to measure relative growth of sales. The annual rate of profit for each industry was converted to an index with the average of 1935-39=100. The same kind of index was computed for the aggregate of 18 industries. Thus, an industry that has had an improvement in profitability greater than that of industrial companies generally has a relative profitability index above 100, while an industry whose profitability has improved less shows a relative profitability index below 100.

Table 1.   *Classification of Industries by Relative Growth in Sales*

	Relative Sales Index, 1952-54*
Growth industries	
Paper and paper products	149
Chemical	130
Tire and rubber	127
Neutral industries	
Oil	104
Steel	103
Cotton textile	97
Food products	93
Declining industries	
Copper metals and mining	79
Cigarette tobacco	76

*Growth over the 20-year period is measured by averaging the annual relative indexes for the last three years of the period.

Source: All of the data used in this study are derived from an investment service published by Studley, Shupert & Company, Inc., of Boston, Mass. The industry classifications used are those established by this service. The companies included in each industry are the principal companies in which there is a public investment interest.

Comparison of the relative sales indexes for the several industries with the relative profitability indexes shows very little correlation (Table 2).

There is some support for the growth industry approach to common stock selection in the fact that two of the three growth industries experienced relative growth in profitability and, in a negative way, by the fact that the industry with the least growth in sales shows the lowest relative index of profitability. Other facts, however, are quite inconsistent with the growth industry idea. The steel industry, which has expanded only at about the same rate as the total economy, had a considerably greater improvement in relative profitability than any of the growth industries. The chemical industry, with the second greatest rate of growth, had the seventh greatest rate of improvement in relative profitability; and the copper industry, which has experienced a marked relative decline in sales, had a better improvement in relative profitability than two of the three growth industries.

Table 2.   Relative Indexes of Industry Growth and Profitability

	Sales Index	Profit-ability Index	Order of Sales Index	Order of Profit-ability Index
Growth Industries				
Paper and paper products	149	143	1	2
Chemical	130	82	2	7
Tire and rubber	127	118	3	4
Neutral Industries				
Oil	104	101	4	6
Steel	103	179	5	1
Cotton textile	97	104	6	5
Food products	93	67	7	8
Declining Industries				
Copper metals and mining	79	121	8	3
Cigarette tobacco	76	46	9	9

Source: Derived from data published by Studley, Shupert & Co., Boston, Mass.

THEORY AND EXPERIENCE

There are some good reasons for thinking that a particularly favorable growth trend in an industry should result in a better-than-average improvement in profitability. A marked improvement in sales ought to permit a spreading of fixed costs over a constantly increasing volume of production and thus exert a favorable influence upon profit margins. A relatively rapidly growing industry also has the best opportunity for rapid upgrading of fixed assets, that is, of adding new plant and equipment of the latest design and efficiency. Upgrading of assets should result in cost reduction and improvement of profit margins to the extent that economies can be retained. It might be expected, too, that in the more rapidly growing industries the competitive pressures would be somewhat less because of the favorable development of markets.

Probably all of these influences upon profitability tend to operate to some extent in growth industries, but in any particular period of time their effect often tends to be diluted or offset by other influences. Thus, the effect of spreading fixed costs over greater volume may be offset over a period of time by an increase in fixed costs due to price inflation. The greater efficiency of new plant and equipment may be counterbalanced by increases in labor costs per unit of product. Even in the more rapidly growing industries, price competition may press very severely upon profit margins.

In any such statistical study as this, an important influence upon the results is the general prosperity of the economy at the beginning and the end of the period of observation. Some industries are much more sensitive profitwise to the business cycle than others, and any historical record of changes in profitability is bound to be distorted to some extent by cyclical fluctuations. We have endeavored to measure trends over a relatively long period of time—a score of years—and we have tried to minimize cyclical fluctuations by averaging annual data for the five years 1935-39 as the base period and for the three years 1952-54 as the terminal period. The fact remains that the economy was more prosperous in 1952-54 than it was in 1935-39.

The difference in prosperity of the country during the two periods certainly had an influence upon the relative trend of profitability for the several industries in this study. In general, the more stable industries through the business cycle experienced less benefit profitwise from the higher level of business activity in 1952-54, and the more unstable industries experienced the greater profit. The steel industry led all the rest in increase in relative profitability because it was experiencing a very low rate of profit on total capital during the relatively depressed period of the late 1930's. Its profitability was greatly improved by the much more favorable business conditions of the early 1950's. The paper and paper products industry, too, was relatively depressed in the latter 1930's and booming in the early 1950's. In both industries the difference in general business conditions in the two periods probably had more to do with change in their relative profitability than did influences attributable particularly to long-term growth.

On the other hand, the cigarette tobacco industry, which makes the poorest showing of the nine industries in terms of relative profitability, is a notably stable industry. It was earning an excellent rate of profit on capital in the 1935-39 period and about the same rate in the 1952-54 period. Because the already high rate of profit did not increase, as did the rates for other industries that were depressed in the latter 1930's, the relative profitability of the tobacco industry declined. The showing of the chemical industry was also affected by its comparatively favorable profit experience in 1935-39. In spite of its distinct growth trend, the industry was not able to increase its good rate of profit as much as some other industries with less favorable profit experience in the earlier period.

It may be that differences in the general prosperity of the economy from one period to another, combined with differences in the sensitivity of profits in different industries to the condition of the economy, largely invalidate any conclusions that may be drawn from a statistical study of the growth and profit experience of industries over two decades of time. If this is so, it supports the conclusion that the long-term growth trends of industries are by no means a controlling influence upon changes in the relative profitability of industries. It suggests, instead, that even over comparatively long time periods, changes in the relative prosperity of the total economy are a major influence.

EQUITY CAPITAL PROFITABILITY

The rate of profit on total capital measures most accurately the profitability of an industry or a company. It does not, however, measure exactly changes in the profitability of common equity capital, and common stock investors are particularly interested in the returns on common stock and surplus. Between profit on total capital and profit on equity capital lie income taxes and, for many companies, interest on noncurrent debt or preferred dividends, or both. Changes in these expenses may cause changes in the profitability of equity capital different from changes in the profitability of total capital. Table 3 shows that, in fact, there have been considerable differences between the relative indexes of rate of profit on total capital and rate of profit on equity capital for the industries in this study.

The correlation between industry growth and rate of profit on equity capital is even less than that of industry growth and profitability of total capital. Of the three growth industries in this study, only the paper and paper products industry experienced a greater than average increase in rate of profit on equity capital. Its improvement ranked third among the nine industries in size of relative increase. The first and second industries in order of size of improvement were neutral industries—the oil and the steel industries. A declining industry, copper metals and mining, was the fourth industry that showed a relative increase in rate of profit on equity capital. It is worth noting that two of the growth industries ranked sixth and seventh among the nine industries in relative improvement in profitability of use of equity capital.

One cause of difference between rate of profit on total capital and rate of profit on equity capital is income taxes. During the period of this study, the rates of the federal income tax increased markedly with corresponding increases in the proportion of sales absorbed by federal income tax payments. However, the increase in tax rates had no general effect on our relative indexes of rate of profit on equity capital, since the indexes for each industry were computed on an after-tax basis, as was the index for 18 industries.

The relative indexes of profit on equity capital for the different industries varied from their relative indexes of profit on total capital because of change in

Table 3.   Profitability of Total Capital and of Equity Capital

		Relative Index Numbers*		Order of Magnitude	
	Sales	Total Profit	Equity Profit †	Total Profit Index	Equity Profit Index
Growth Industries					
Paper and paper products	149	143	124	2	3
Chemical	130	82	70	7	6
Tire and rubber	127	118	66	4	7
Neutral Industries					
Oil	104	101	125	6	2
Steel	103	179	261	1	1
Cotton textile	97	104	94	5	5
Food products	93	67	55	8	8
Declining Industries					
Copper metals and mining	79	121	106	3	4
Cigarette tobacco	76	46	39	9	9

*For 1952-54 based on 1935-39 as 100.
†The relative indexes of rate of profit on equity capital have been computed by the same method as the relative indexes of rate of profit on total capital.
Source: Derived from data published by Studley, Shupert & Company, Inc.

"leverage." (The term "leverage" is generally used to mean the proportion of the total capital structure of a company represented by senior securities, that is, bonds and preferred stock.) A successful company with senior securities in its capitalization normally "makes money" for its common stockholders by the use of this senior capital because the rate of interest on bonds, or of dividends on preferred stock, is less than the rate of profit earned by such a company on its senior capital. The excess of earnings on senior capital over its cost reverts to the equity owners of a business. Thus, for a successful company, an increase in the proportion of senior securities over a period of time causes the rate of earnings on equity capital to improve more than the improvement in rate of earnings on total capital.

Only three of the nine industries in our study increased the proportional use of senior capital from 1935-39 to 1952-54. One was a growth industry, one a neutral industry, and one a declining industry. Apparently the increase in leverage in these industries—chemical, food products, and cigarette tobacco—was influenced more by the relative cyclical stability of their earnings than by long-term growth.

Two of the three growth industries, paper and paper products and tire and rubber, greatly reduced the proportion of senior securities in their capital structures, and this development in financial policy caused a decline in their relative indexes of rate of profit on equity capital.

Among the growth industries, the chemical industry was the only one that increased the proportion of senior securities in its capitalization. This change tended to benefit the rate of earnings on equity capital even though the rate declined relative to that for the 143-company aggregate. The benefit is evidenced by the fact that the chemical industry's relative index of equity profit in 1952-54 was sixth in size among the nine industries, while its relative index of profit on total capital was seventh.

Both the paper and paper products industry and the tire and rubber industry had a very large proportion of senior capital in the base period 1935-39, and both industries substantially reduced the percentage of bonds and preferred stock in the period to 1952-54. The reduction in leverage had an adverse influence upon the rate of profit on equity capital. During this period, the tire and rubber industry, which ranked fourth in rate of profit on total capital, ranked seventh in rate of profit on equity capital.

EVALUATION

This survey shows little relationship between the rate of growth of industries (as measured by their annual sales and improvement) and the rate of profit earned on common equity capital. There may be a basic tendency for the more rapidly growing industries to improve their earnings on total capital to a greater extent than industries growing less rapidly, but the tendency is only one of a number of variables affecting earnings and dividends per share of common stock and the value of stock in the market.

We have observed that the business cycle is an influence, even upon experience over a considerable period of years. In our study the more cyclical industries tended to show better experience profitwise because the initial period of observation was one of relative economic depression and the terminal period was one of relative economic prosperity. Price inflation, the rate of technological development of products, the rate of improvement in production processes, and change in the intensity of competition also tend to affect the profitability of different industries.

The policies of industries and companies in the use of senior capital is a second major variable. Change in degree of senior capital leverage may cause the rate of profit on equity capital to change in a considerably different manner than change in the rate of profit on total capital.

Common stock investors also have to take into account the fact that the profit experience of different companies in the same industry often varies widely, with some succeeding amazingly while others fail. They must remember that the growth of earnings per share of common stock is affected not only by the rate of profit on equity capital but also by the increase from year to year in amount of equity capital per share caused by retention of earnings. And, finally, there is the well-known emotionalism of investors that causes them at one time to pay one price for a dollar of earnings and at another time to pay twice as much for the same dollar of earnings.

Andrew Carnegie is said to have paraphrased a patriarchal maxim to read, "Put all your eggs in one basket and watch the basket." This remark has been seized upon by some observers and applied, in a rather indiscriminate way, to the investment of money . . . . Mr. Carnegie's epigram may be intelligently applied to any line of enterprise in which a man's talents, knowledge, and capital are involved, but not to the investment of his surplus wealth.

—Thomas Gibson

Simple Principles of Investment

12
THE MODERN WAY TO INVEST*

ARTHUR WEISENBERGER is associated with Arthur Weisenberger & Company.

Of the more than twenty million Americans who own stocks, at least one in every six now uses the services of investment companies—often referred to as mutual funds. Investment companies have brought about a new concept of investing, which has spread rapidly since the end of World War II.

---

*Reprinted from *Investment Companies 1967* by permission of Arthur Weisenberger & Company, copyright ©1967.

What is this new concept? It is simply the new application of a very old method of solving financial problems. The technique of combining forces to obtain benefits not possible otherwise is as ancient as civilization itself; it is the basis of government, of trade, of industry, of banking, and of life insurance. The investment company is a way of extending the advantages of pooling resources to everyone who wants to invest in corporate stocks and bonds.

It has naturally followed that many people have now become investors who never before considered stock ownership appropriate to their circumstances. Investment companies have made it practical as well as possible for all to share in the rewards (and, necessarily, in the concomitant risks) of owning a stake in our country's economic future. At the same time, investment companies have also shown many substantial, experienced investors that their financial problems can be simplified and their results improved.

FROM OBSCURITY TO PROMINENCE

Although still relatively small in comparison with such older institutions as life insurance companies, banks and trust companies, and savings and loan associations, investment companies have grown in a little over twenty-five years from obscurity to prominence in the financial field. They unquestionably qualify as one of the fastest-growing investment mediums in the United States—and very likely in the entire world.

Most of this growth has derived from the popularity of mutual funds, the better known and more predominant form of investment company. The other type, which has no short, colloquial name, is the closed-end investment company. Although the two differ in certain mechanical features and to some extent in usefulness, they are sufficiently alike in purpose and in operation for one definition, one description, to apply to both.

WHAT IS AN INVESTMENT COMPANY?

Nothing could be simpler than the basic idea of an investment company. It is a corporation or trust whose only business is the proper investment of its shareholders' money, generally in common stocks or a combination of stocks and bonds, in the hope of achieving a specific investment goal. It brings together the investable funds of many people with similar needs and purposes, and it undertakes to do a better job of investing those funds and managing the investments than the people, individually, could do for themselves.

The investment company's likelihood of accomplishing its purpose is based upon its ability to spread its large amount of money over a wide variety of different securities, thus reducing risk—and to provide continuous professional supervision in the selection and administration of its investments. In effect, an investment company is a single large investment account, owned by many separate people who share its income and its expenses, its profits and its losses, in proportion to their individual shares in the account. It is a way of providing for anyone, of whatever means, the same advantages and safeguards that wealthy people and large institutions have relied upon for many years.

Like any other corporation, an investment company issues shares of its own stock. Each share represents the same fractional interest as any other share in the investment account or portfolio of securities. Income from the account, after deduction of necessary expenses, is received in the form of periodic dividends. Investment profits and losses are reflected in the price of the shares and in distributions to shareholders of profits, when realized on balance. It is only through purchase of the company's shares that an investor may receive the benefits of the company's investment advisory and management services.

EARLY BEGINNINGS

The idea of the investment company is by no means a new one. Its origins can be traced back to the early nineteenth century in Europe and, in much its present form, to England and Scotland during the 1860's. There, during the succeeding two decades, the investment company became a very popular medium, especially for overseas investment, in which both the risks and the returns were high and the benefits of diversification and management were obvious.

No comparable development occurred in the United States until the mid-1920's. Although Boston Personal Property Trust had its beginning in 1894 and The Colonial Fund in 1904, and a few other companies were formed between 1920 and 1923, the year 1924 may be considered the true birth-date of investment companies as they are now known in this country.

In 1924, three large companies were organized—Massachusetts Investors Trust, State Street Investment Corporation (a private company until two years later), and U.S. & Foreign Securities Corporation. Present among this small group were many of the major characteristics of the modern investment company as it is known today.

A CLOSED-END PIONEER

The first large, diversified investment company in this country to be organized and sold as such, U.S. & Foreign Securities, was formed in 1924 by a well-known New York investment banking firm, Dillon, Read & Company; it began its existence with $10 million to invest. At the time of its founding, U.S.

& Foreign won considerably more immediate recognition than did either Massachusetts Investors Trust or State Street.

Like that of other corporations, U.S. & Foreign's capitalization at the time of organization was "fixed." The number of shares of its stock (including two classes of preferred as well as common stock) remained unchanged for a long time after it was first issued. Investors who, after the initial offering, wanted to become shareholders had to obtain stock from other investors willing to sell. For this reason, supply and demand determined the price at which shares were bought or sold. The market price of the common stock could be far above the actual underlying value of the investments it represented (selling at a premium) or far below (selling at a discount).

The existence of U.S. & Foreign's preferred stocks caused the common shares to be highly speculative, because their effect was much like that of borrowed money in a margin account. As long as the company's investments increased in value, the common stockholders were in an enviable position. But when the trend was reversed, their "equity" dropped rapidly; it could even disappear completely. The use of senior capital by an investment company is referred to as "leverage."

Investment companies like U.S. & Foreign became very popular during the five years following 1924. They are known as closed-end companies, because of their relatively fixed capitalizations. Nearly fifty companies of this type are still in active existence, most of them formed during the late 1920's. Twenty-one are listed on The New York Stock Exchange; others are traded on smaller exchanges or over-the-counter. Their mechanical features are still similar to those of U.S. & Foreign at its beginning, except that few now provide leverage to their common shares through borrowing money or having preferred stock outstanding.

BIRTH OF THE MUTUAL FUND

The organizational history of Massachusetts Investors Trust differs from that of U.S. & Foreign in nearly every respect. Its initial capital was only $50,000; but provision was made from the very beginning to issue new shares whenever there was demand for them—and to work toward the creation of such demand. Shortly after the company's founding, all shares were made redeemable upon request, at a price based on the current value of the Trust's assets, minus a small fee.

Only common shares were issued. Because of this, and because of the redemption feature, the investor in Massachusetts Investors Trust was affected neither by the margin-like consequences of using senior capital nor by the effects of supply and demand, with regard to the Trust's shares. In contrast to the practice of many closed-end investment companies in their early days, M.I.T.

adopted a policy of issuing to its shareholders regular reports of all details of its operations and portfolio holdings.

Massachusetts Investors Trust was the prototype of the open-end investment company, or—as it has been popularly known since the late 1930's—the mutual fund. While many valuable services have been added more recently, and while there are now over three hundred mutual funds with combined assets of more than $36 billion, the basic operation of a mutual fund today is little changed from the pattern originated in Boston by M.I.T. forty-two years ago.

1929–AND AFTER

Unfortunately for many investors, the closed-end type of investment company—especially that making heavy use of borrowed money to magnify the effects of stock market swings—was far more popular than the open-end, or mutual fund type, during the speculative frenzy of the late 1920's. By the time of the historic stock market crash, there were many hundreds of closed-end companies, with assets of about $7 billion, whereas the nineteen mutual funds had total assets of less than $200 million.

A few closed-end companies, with more conservative objectives and policies, survived the crash with distinction. The majority did not. The effects of high leverage in a long bear market proved disastrous for most. Many of the early closed-end companies reflected the enthusiasms and hopes of their natal times; under laws which now exist, their experience can never be repeated.

Of course, the early mutual funds also suffered from the decline. Asset values shrank drastically, as did all security prices. But no mutual fund shares became completely worthless, and in every known case at least some dividends were paid throughout the depression.

INVESTMENT COMPANIES COME OF AGE

The 1929 debacle and the difficult years following clearly demonstrated the pressing need for competent investment management. During the early 1930's, a sizable number of mutual funds were organized and achieved moderate success in distributing their shares to the public. But between 1936 and 1940 the entire investment company business underwent a searching investigation by the Securities and Exchange Commission. This study was conducted to the accompaniment of widespread publicity, largely confined to the abuses which were uncovered. The Investment Company Act of 1940 was passed as an outgrowth of this investigation.

Passage of the 1940 Act, many of whose provisions codified practices followed by most mutual funds from the start, marked the beginning of the real growth of investment companies in the United States. Federal regulation, even though it is not concerned with actual management practices, policies, or investment decisions, has done much to promote public confidence in investment companies. Their total combined assets are now nearly forty times what they were when the Act was passed.

THE MODERN PERIOD

During the war years, investment companies could do little more than mark time. Immediately after the war's end, growing public confidence (spurred by the passage of the 1940 Act) ushered in the most recent period of investment company history—a period which has produced the industry's greatest growth and innovation. A part of this growth can be attributed to the general post-war climate of progress, prosperity and optimism. The long rise in common stock prices, the increasingly widespread availability of investment capital, and the demonstrated results of inflation added to the attractiveness of investment company shares. But a most significant contributor was the creativity, the enthusiasm, and the accomplishments of the people who manage funds and bring them to the public.

For example, it was only twenty years ago that a mutual fund first developed a program by which an investor might conveniently accumulate shares on an informal basis, for as little as $25 a month. After a slow start, the idea caught fire. An earlier, comparable arrangement, now known as the contractual plan, began to show rapid growth. The New York Stock Exchange developed its Monthly Investment Program, applying the concept to listed stocks, including shares of closed-end companies. Over a third of all mutual fund accounts in existence today are of an accumulating nature. Periodic small investment has become, for millions of people who had never before thought of themselves as investors, a practical way of building capital.

Most mutual funds and a few closed-end companies have enabled investors to reinvest their dividends and other distributions automatically. Thus, accelerated progress toward long-term goals has been facilitated and encouraged. Many funds have also developed arrangements for the orderly withdrawal of accumulated capital and income, through equal monthly payments. As the funds have added such features, not easily obtainable elsewhere, their identity as a special kind of investment medium, rather than simply as a different type of security, has become more widely understood.

MANAGEMENT'S ACCOMPLISHMENTS

The major promise of investment companies is that they can do a

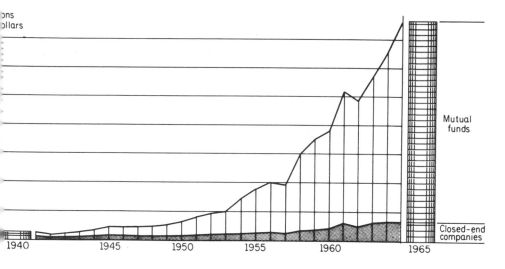

Table 1. Growth of Investment Company Assets Since 1940

Year	Mutual Funds*	Closed-End Companies†	Total
1965	$35,220,243,000	$3,514,577,000	$38,734,820,000
1964	29,116,254,000	3,523,413,000	32,639,667,000
1963	25,214,436,000	3,217,936,000	28,432,372,000
1962	21,270,735,000	2,783,219,000	24,053,954,000
1960	17,025,684,000	2,083,898,000	19,109,582,000
1958	13,242,388,000	1,931,402,000	15,173,790,000
1956	9,046,431,000	1,525,748,000	10,572,179,000
1954	6,109,390,000	1,246,351,000	7,355,741,000
1952	3,931,407,000	1,011,089,000	4,942,496,000
1950	2,530,563,000	871,962,000	3,402,525,000
1948	1,505,762,000	767,028,000	2,272,790,000
1946	1,311,108,000	851,409,000	2,162,517,000
1944	882,191,000	739,021,000	1,621,212,000
1942	486,850,000	557,264,000	1,044,114,000
1940	447,959,000	613,589,000	1,061,548,000

*A tabulation showing growth in number of shareholders, gross sales, redemptions and net sales appears in Chapter II.

†Including funded debt and bank loans. Decline from 1964 to 1965 reflects liquidation in 1965 of The M. A. Hanna Company.

Sources: Open-End–Investment Company Institute. Data include member companies only. Closed-End-Arthur Weisenberger & Company, 1947-65. Investment Company Institute, 1940-46.

better job for the investor than he can do for himself. The record of investment company management during the past decade is set forth in a later chapter. Whether the record demonstrates that the promise has been fulfilled can neither be proved nor disproved. What investors, individually and collectively, actually did for themselves during the same period cannot be measured. However, the growth of investment companies and their increasing use by substantial investors are strong indications that many people believe the accomplishments of professional management have at least approached the promise.

To the informed observer, the results produced by many investment companies in the post-war years, as well as earlier—and the fact that these results are a matter of public record, easily available to all—appear to have been among the most important elements in bringing about the industry's present size and position.

Mutual funds have, of course, become highly competitive with each other, as more and more new funds have been formed. If pride alone had not forced the funds to seek constant improvement in their methods of research and securities analysis, rivalry for investor favor would certainly have done so. A mutual fund cannot for long afford to produce results notably inferior to those of other, equally available managements.

WHO USES INVESTMENT COMPANIES?

The growing ranks of investment company shareholders represent a cross-section of investing America. All economic levels are represented as well as all levels of experience. Significantly, the majority of shareholders are in modest income brackets.

A recent survey of mutual fund shareholders showed that 60 per cent had annual incomes of less than $10,000. The median fund shareholding was not quite $5,600 for those who had made lump-sum investments, and less than $2,400 for those accumulating shares under a periodic payment plan.

There are also many investors holding large blocks of shares, and their number is increasing. Most funds show many individual holdings in amounts well over $100,000. Many other large holdings represent the investments of pension and profit-sharing funds, schools, colleges, and similar institutions.

ADAPTABILITY THROUGH VARIETY

If investment companies were all very much alike in their purposes and policies, their usefulness would be limited, for individual investors have widely differing needs and preferences. The degree of risk that should be assumed; the relative importance of current income and future income; the emphasis that should be placed on the pursuit of capital growth; the best route to be taken toward any of these objectives—all these factors vary with each investor. The investment company business recognizes these important differences of investor need. Rare is the individual whose needs cannot be met either by one investment company or by a combination of several.

The initial decision to be made by the investor and his adviser is to determine his investment needs and preferences. The next step is to select the fund or funds that appear to best satisfy those requirements. This determination is facilitated by the publication of a wealth of data by the investment companies themselves as well as the ready availability of comparative performance records. Having at hand a company's objectives as well as a record measuring its results toward accomplishing those objectives, the investor can intelligently choose the appropriate vehicle.

POLICY CLASSIFICATIONS

Since the portfolio composition of any investment company reflects the aims and policies of its management, a natural classification may be based on the structure of that portfolio.

There are companies, primarily mutual funds, which are managed as if they represented an individual's entire long-term investment program. These are called Balanced Funds. A diversified portfolio is maintained at all times, consisting of bonds, preferred stocks, and common stocks. The proportions usually vary with the level of the market, or with the management's view of market trends. Balanced Funds are found only among open-end investment companies.

Next in order are investment companies whose purpose is to provide a cross-section of common stocks or other equity-type issues. The majority of both open-end and closed-end companies are of this diversified Common Stock Fund type. They are suitable for that part of an individual's or an institution's total capital that is to be invested in equities.

Common Stock Funds as a group, however, include a broad range of companies with significantly different portfolio policies and objectives. Opportunity for growth in rising markets, the extent of risk in declining ones, and emphasis on producing current income are factors which vary from fund to fund.

There are also investment company securities intended for those portions of an investor's assets to be held in bonds and preferred stocks. A few mutual funds provide this service by limiting their portfolio holdings to bonds, preferred stocks, or a combination of the two. Preferred stocks of a few closed-end investment companies are also available.

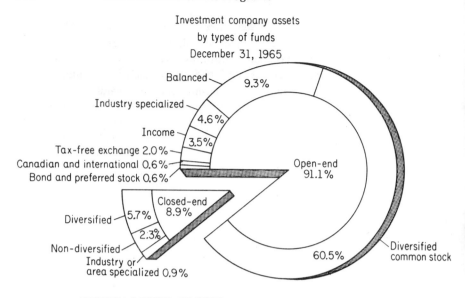

Investment company assets
by types of funds
December 31, 1965

Balanced — 9.3%
Industry specialized — 4.6%
Income — 3.5%
Tax-free exchange 2.0%
Canadian and international 0.6%
Bond and preferred stock 0.6%
Open-end 91.1%
Closed-end 8.9%
Diversified — 5.7%
2.3%
Non-diversified
Industry or area specialized 0.9%
60.5%
Diversified common stock

SPECIALIZED TYPES

Finally, there are a number of investment companies intended only for a limited portion of the equity component of an investor's portfolio. These companies, which exist in both mutual fund and closed-end forms, tend to concentrate their investments within a single industry or group of related industries, such as aviation, life insurance, or petroleum. Less specialized, though sometimes included in this category, are those investment companies which invest only in securities native to a particular country, section of the United States, or part of the world.

Recent trends have been to broaden the restrictive and specialized policies of such companies, in order to minimize the risks inherent in specialization. Thus an atomic energy fund may widen its horizons to include a variety of the natural sciences. A portfolio heretofore limited to oil and gas may be expanded to include other forms of energy. Companies formed to invest predominantly in Canada have become international.

A few closed-end companies follow a policy of investing in special situations in which they take an active management interest. They are included in this broad group of specialized companies.

SOURCES OF ASSISTANCE

The growth of investment companies in recent years has been accompanied by the development of a large group of men and women whose business it is to help investors use these funds to their best advantage. The group comprises the independent brokers and investment dealers, and the representatives of mutual fund sponsors. They provide the vital links between investment companies and the public. Many are specialists who are well qualified by training and experience to advise investors about the purposes, policies and uses of specific investment companies.

The individual who wishes to decide for himself should carefully examine individual fund prospectuses in conjunction with the other available literature.

A GROWING NEED OF THE TIMES

The growth of the investment company movement has coincided with an era of rapid industrial progress. More people today earn more money, with a resultant higher standard of living and increased savings available for investment. Ownership of the nation's great productive enterprises by people in all walks of life is no longer a dream—it is a reality. To the man or woman receiving an investment company dividend check, the term "people's capitalism" is a particularly meaningful phrase.

The United States and its millions of citizens are fortunate in having a ready-made and democratic way of participating in the progress that lies ahead. It is a way through which present and prospective investors may avoid some of the headaches and heartaches of a venture into an unfamiliar field. It is the modern way to invest—the investment company.

PART **III**

INSTITUTIONAL
INVESTMENT
PROBLEMS

INTRODUCTION TO PART III

Although institutional investment problems have been around for a long time, the growth of institutional investing and influence has focused much more attention on the problems of institutional investors. With the rapid growth of mutual funds, pension funds, and trust funds, their significance in the markets and in the economy has increased markedly. Furthermore, accompanying the growth of the fund assets, an increased awareness of institutional performance has placed increasing pressures on the institutional portfolio managers. In our stimulated growth economy, the institutional manager is in the difficult position of a fiduciary charged with the responsibility of conserving the capital in his fund in the face of greater inflation risk and considerable pressure for capital appreciation performance. In the following essays, six authors discuss some of the pressing problems facing the institutional investor, his reactions, and the impact of his reactions upon the economic and financial environment in which he must function.

In the first essay John Heimann examines the question of prudent investment policy. He emphasizes that protection of dollar capital is paramount, but that the preservation of purchasing power with a minimum of financial risk is similarly of prime importance. He examines equity and fixed-income securities in the light of these objectives, along with the evaluation of specific securities in a discussion focused on the role of the pension fund trustee, his obligations and duties in both the short run and long run.

In the second essay Harold Elsom develops the theme that the manner of achieving legally acceptable discretion is better defined than is commonly supposed. He examines the common law on the subject and specifically treats the key areas of "reasonable care," "reasonable skill," "safety of capital," "risk," and "diversification", among others. He concludes his essay by posing the question of why corporate trustees are so preoccupied with the law of trust investment and suggests possible answers.

In the third essay Jack Treynor presents a method of rating quantitatively the management performance of mutual, trust, and pension funds, a subject that has long been open to much speculation. Working with the rate of return and risk for the individual, Treynor develops a method that goes a long way toward overcoming the inherent limitations involved in rating investment fund performance and answering the needs of fund managers and investment analysts.

In the fourth selection Jack Treynor and Kay Mazuy evaluate the widely held idea that mutual fund managers can successfully anticipate major market turns, basing their analysis on the technique developed by Treynor in the preceding essay. It is their conclusion that mutual fund managers cannot outguess the market. The implications of this study are directly applicable to the responsibilities of portfolio managers and to stockholders' expectations of management performance.

In the fifth selection Albert Bingham voices concern over the current attitudes and practices of his fellow financial analysts, specifically with regard to their involvement with the "performance kick" and percentage-based appreciation comparisons. He suggests that the factor of risk is not being adequately recognized, and that many investors want income, not short-term appreciation.

In the last essay in Part III David Eiteman examines some of the changes that have been made since the publication of "The Report of Special Study of Securities Markets of the Securities and Exchange Commission" and reports on their effectiveness and shortcomings. Special attention is given to the areas of floor trading, specialist activities, and odd-lot operations. Other areas are examined also; and emphasis is placed upon the impact of these developments in the investment markets.

13
WHAT IS THE PRUDENT POLICY TODAY IN INVESTING PENSION FUND ASSETS?*

JOHN G. HEIMANN is with the Pension Fund Investment Department of Smith, Barner & Co., New York City.

Long- and short-run advice on what constitutes prudent pension fund investment policy defines prudency as the preservation of dollar capital as well as that capital's purchasing power with a minimum of risk in flexibly seizing attractive investment opportunities. Current market conditions are said to warrant deviation from long-run emphasis on stocks to bonds and mortgages and adoption of more conservative ratio of fund's bonds to stocks. Stock selection, however, at any time is judged best when gauged in terms of average or better long-term performance.

During the past 15 years, a multitude of theories have been argued regarding the investment of pension fund assets. These discussions have ranged far and wide across the investment horizon and have included the extremes of the total fixed fund (insured) to the completely variable fund (100% in common stocks). No two investment theories could conceivably be any more opposite, yet both have been realistically and well defended. The result has been something of a compromise. The trustees of a great majority of pension funds have adopted some of the thinking of both sides, resulting in the practices of the "balanced fund" which includes both fixed and variable types of investment in differing proportions. Let us explore this question of prudence in logical fashion (1) What is prudence? (2) What is prudent for the trustees of a pension fund? (3) Did the popularly accepted investment policies of the past answer this concept? and (4) What investment policies should be followed at the present time?

*From *The Commercial & Financial Chronicle*, Vol. 194, No. 6098 (Thursday, October 12, 1961), pp. 1, 24-25. Reprinted by permission of the *Chronicle*, 25 Park Place, New York City 10007.

The answer begins with *Harvard College v. Amory*[1] where the court stated: "He (the trustee) is to observe how men of prudence, discretion and intelligence manage their own affairs, not in regard to speculation, but in regard to the permanent disposition of their funds, considering the probable income as well as the safety of the capital to be invested." This was modified in *Marshall v. Frazier*[2] in which the court recognized some of the realities of human nature by concluding that even prudent men take risks for themselves which should not be assumed for another.

From these earliest decisions, the body of law regarding the actions of a prudent man has been slowly built by court interpretation. An interesting recent study on the prudent man theory and what it means to a trustee can be found in an article by Harold B. Elsom in the *Financial Analyst's Journal*[3] in which he concludes that " . . . the concern for safety of capital dollars is . . . logically, chronologically and technically correct. The sequence . . . shows the idea of safety to be associated with *wealth* (italics added), not funds . . . We have then a reasonable interpretation of court opinion suggesting that wealth-protective measures are in order . . . If safety of wealth rather than a sum certain were ever in question, doubt has been removed." Or, in non-legal language, the courts have strongly suggested that they consider it prudent for a trustee to invest in securities which protect *wealth* (purchasing power) in addition to or in replacement of those securites which only protect dollar capital.

These factors not withstanding, it is important to realize that the courts have consistently concerned themselves with the problem of "preservation" but nowhere have the courts stated or even intimated that it is the duty of a prudent man to *create* dollar capital other than that necessary to preserve the purchasing power of those dollars.

However, as far as I know, there has been no court ruling on factors pertaining to what would be considered prudent for the trustee of a pension fund. Therefore, our next step is to examine the requirements of a special type of trust fund—the pension fund—in order to apply our knowledge of prudence to this specific problem.

WHAT IS A PENSION FUND?

The typical pension fund is a trust which has been established to provide a certain schedule of retirement benefits. These benefits are obtainable by those individuals who are covered by the particular trust and who meet a detailed schedule of requirements. If the covered individual satisfies the requirement, then he is entitled to the benefit which most often is expressed in dollar amounts.

We are all aware of the facts of life in a collectively-bargained industrial

---

[1]9 Pick 446, 461 (Mass. 1830).
[2]80 P. 2nd 42, 55 (Oregon 1938); see also in re Cook's Estate, 171 Atl. 730 (Delaware 1934).
[3]Volume XVI, No. 4, July-August, 1960, p. 27.

society in which the dollar benefit is subject to periodic renegotiation and change. But the trustee's task, at any given moment, is to make certain that the fund is sufficiently sound to meet the existing dollar payment when it comes due. All other considerations are less important.

There are many types of plans available to the trustee and variety of investment theories from which he can choose. Be this as it may, his primary responsibility does not change regardless of the route finally chosen. His first thought and responsibility is still the preservation of that dollar capital and, if possible, the preservation of the purchasing power of that capital. This is the basic task with which he has been charged.

For many years the theory of dollar capital preservation was paramount with the trustees of pension funds. For this reason, most funds turned to insurance companies, who, for a scheduled premium payment, guaranteed the fixed-dollar benefit. In the 1930's, the insurance companies held the bulk of pension fund reserves. This, however, has changed dramatically during the past 15 years. During the late 1940's, the trustees of many funds became aware that the self-insured method of funding was considerably more attractive than that of purchasing annuities in one form or another. The reasons for this shift were manifold. For one thing, the acceptance by the courts of the theory of preservation of wealth (purchasing power) opened the doors to new types of investment. This factor, combined with the continuation of inflation and the rise in the market values of common stocks, gave impetus to the acceptance of equity investment. Other reasons that contributed to the change included the fact that life insurance companies were taxed on their earnings; whereas the pension fund was a tax-free institution; non-insured funds had greater flexibility concerning contributions and the like; and, in many cases it could be proved that the self-insured fund was less expensive than the insured fund.

The end result of these trends has been an explosive growth in the assets of the self-insured funds. By the end of 1960, 62.0% of total pension fund assets was self-insured compared to 38.0% administered by the insurance companies.

There is little question in my mind that this change in philosophy was "prudent" when it was undertaken in the late 1940's and 1950's. We shall discuss this at greater length later. However, it is worth repeating that this change was a direct result of the acceptance of the theory that "prudence" consisted not only of the preservation of dollar capital but also the preservation of the purchasing power of that capital. The switch to investment in common stocks was a partial recognition of this theory and has, for the most part, proven successful to date.

THE INVESTMENT PROBLEM FOR THE PRUDENT TRUSTEE

Few investment professionals would question the theory that an investment policy must be flexible. A specific approach is valid until (1) either the outlook for the economy or the condition of the securities markets change in such a way as to modify the original investment policy or (2) the specific needs of the fund change sufficiently to require a different policy.

The primary task for the trustee of a pension fund is to undertake an investment program which will preserve both capital and purchasing power. The trustee or his professional advisor is charged with the problem of choosing the investment route which will satisfy these needs most satisfactorily. The solution must be based upon current considerations, in light of historical patterns.

All investors should recognize any investment entails the acceptance of some degree of risk. There is no such thing as a riskless investment, including the retention of cash (the ownership of cash during the past 20 years certainly did not preserve purchasing power even though it preserved capital). For this reason, all investment programs entail the measurement and balance of risk exposure. The more capital is exposed to risk, the greater should be the rewards to the investor. There is nothing new in this theory. It only makes financial sense to expect a higher rate of return from an investment which exposes the investor to a greater degree of risk than from some other type of investment, available at the same time, but whose exposure to risk is less. For this reason, common stocks historically yielded more than corporate bonds and corporate bonds have yielded more than government bonds.

Therefore, in order to answer our question, "What is a prudent investment for a pension fund?" and simultaneously, give recognition to the ever-changing climate of investment markets, I think that it would be fair to divide our question as follows:

(1) What can be considered a prudent investment for a pension fund on a long-term basis?

(2) What can be considered a prudent investment for a pension fund *at the present time?*

Since we are now concerned with investment in light of that which we have discovered can be considered prudent, there are additional characteristics of a pension fund that bear importantly upon investment matters. Specifically, a pension fund is tax-exempt; it has a long period of accumulation and distribution of funds; inflow of money may exceed outflow for many years to come; it is not subject to substantial hazard; and, there are no legislative investment restrictions governing the selection of securities other than those that might have been voluntarily included in the trust instrument.

THE EARNINGS FACTOR

In addition, all pension funds have calculated into their basic structure an earnings factor, typically called the actuarial assumption on interest earnings. This figure is arrived at by the fund's actuary when he calculates the cost of the fund. It usually represents a conservative estimate of long-term return and is a minimum earnings objective for the fund. However, if the earnings experience exceeds the actuarial assumption, the benefit to the fund can be considerable. Suppose that the actuarial assumption required for a particular fund is 3%. If, over a period of time, the overall yield on that fund is 4%, 1% in excess of the actuarial assumption, then in 25 years the fund will have earned sufficient excess funds to provide either a 25% increase in benefits or a 20% savings in costs or some combination of the two.

Before attempting to answer the questions posed previously, we should recognize that any discussion such as this must be essentially general regarding the peculiar requirements of an individual fund. No two funds are exactly alike. Each fund deserves individual attention to its problems so that a suitable investment policy can be formed. Our task today is to discuss the general investment problems of this type of fund and to attempt to arrive at an investment philosophy which most closely satisfies the question of prudence. What we discover can be applied to a specific fund and its particular investment portfolio.

THE LONG-TERM SOLUTION

The self-insured fund has available two types of investment; fixed-income securities such as bonds and mortgages and variable-income securities such as common stocks and real estate. Studies based upon statistics collected and collated from 1879 through the present show that the average yield on representative fixed-income securites has been 4.32% per year. For the same period of time, a broad cross-section of common stocks has shown an annual return of 8.12%, including both dividend earnings and appreciation in the price of the stock. Of this, 4.91% came from dividend income and 3.21% from appreciation.

In recognition of these long-term trends, the investment solution has been the substantial increase in the ownership of common stocks by pension funds. In addition, to the long-term advantage in return over other types of investment which were mentioned previously, the process of investing in common stock was supported by studies which led to the conclusion that, over a long period of time, this type of investment tended to compensate for the steady depreciation in the purchasing power of the dollar. Inflation has accounted for an approximate 2% per year depreciation in the purchasing power of the dollar since the turn of the century, whereas, common stocks have appreciated 3.21% per annum for the same period of time. It is important to recognize that neither inflation nor the rise in the prices of common stocks proceed at the same rate in any given period of time. These patterns are only valuable if viewed as an extremely long-term measurement. There have been periods in our history when there was no inflation and the prices of stocks rose and vice versa.

EQUITY HOLDINGS INCREASED

Because of all these various factors, the percentage of common stocks owned by the funds increased rapidly. This was due not only to a greater allotment of the annual contributions invested in stocks but also due to the rise in common stock prices. During the late 1940's and early 1950's when the common stock philosophy first came to the fore, Moody's Corporate bonds were yielding approximately 3%-3½%, whereas, at the same time Moody's 125 Industrial common stocks were yielding between 4% and 7%. Obviously, the attraction of high-grade commons plus the potential capital appreciation possibilities made this type of investment a logical vehicle for the trustees of a self-insured fund.

The end result has been that by 1960 all corporate pension funds showed 43.6% invested in common stocks at market value, compared with 33.1% at book or cost, the 10.2 point differential resulting from the appreciation in prices. Numerous examples of the acceptance of this long-term philosophy can be mentioned. In general, though, it should be sufficient to note that in 1951 only 21.6% of pension fund receipts was invested in common stocks. This rose to approximately 50% by the end of 1960.

This increased reliance upon common stock investment has proven quite successful to date. Even now, any truly long-term extrapolation of historical statistics would continue to favor stock investment for a pension fund. Therefore, in answer to our first question, "What can be considered prudent pension investment for the long-term?" the answer remains in favor of a substantial commitment in common stocks.

However, we must not allow ourselves to be so blinded by history that we stumble over the immediate future. No investment policy can be pursued successfully if it does not consider tomorrow even if its eye is upon the future. A man looking through a pair of binoculars may be able to view a distant object clearly, but if he should take a step while looking at that object and not look down, he could break his neck. A pension fund has much the same problem. Money must be invested continuously, each investment another immediate step. So, perhaps, the time has come for us to look at the ground directly beneath us.

PRESENT INVESTMENT CONDITIONS

Most investment professionals will agree, I believe, that the long-term future for our economy is bright barring the incidence of a major catastrophe. It is upon this forecast that a long-term investment in common stock is predicated. Personally, I do not take issue with these predictions though I must confess that I am not as optimistic as many others. What I would like to investigate, however, is the current relative value of the different types of securities usually purchased by pension funds. This investigation would be pursued in light of past performance, future potentials, and securities which conform most closely to the dictates of prudence within this framework.

This is not to be an essay in market timing nor will I attempt to guess the future short-term course of market prices. Rather, this is an evaluation of the present opportunities in investment with some judgment as to which type or types of securities are now most attractive for a pension fund.

The stock market reached an all-time high a few weeks ago. Likewise, the evaluation of earnings in relationship to the price of the stock (price times earnings ratio) has approached historical highs. Conversely, as prices have gone up, current yields have dropped so that at the present time they average less than 3% on a broad cross-section of common stocks.

Only four times in the last 80 years have common stock yields been so low (in 1899, in 1933, in 1936, and in July and August 1959). More significant, perhaps, is the fact that since 1880 common stock yields have averaged 3.2% only 13 times. In each instance, stock prices have turned downward not more than 13 months later. The decrease in prices ranged from 16% to 90%; there were 25% to 50% declines in nine of the 13 instances. This relationship between stock price peaks and unusually low dividend yields has appeared regardless of the business cycle or of circumstances such as war, peace, speculative enthusiasm, monetary stringency or ease, etc., and regardless of the trend of dividend payments.

3% VERSUS 4.91%

This current yield of less than 3% must be considered in light of the long-term yield on common stocks of 4.91%. Our acceptance of this yield indicates that we are willing to pay a premium for our common stocks of 38.9% above the historical values.

Representative bonds, on the other hand, are currently priced to provide a yield somewhat in excess of the 4.32% average on a long-term basis. Presently, Moody's AAA Industrials yield to maturity 4.30% and newly issued corporate bonds provide yields of 4.55% to 5.00% depending upon maturity, quality, and the like. Furthermore, it should be recognized that even though the long-term average yield for bonds is 4.32%, there have been periods in our history for as long as 20 years when bond yields never climbed above 4.00%.

MORTGAGES ATTRACTIVE

Up to this point, we have not discussed mortgages as a form of investment for pension funds since at the present time they only account for a very small percentage of total pension fund assets. However, interest in mortgage investment is growing rapidly and, in my opinion, rightly so. An investment in mortgages makes a great deal of financial sense for the typical pension fund if they are purchased in proper relationship to the other securities in the fund's portfolio. Skipping the factors of social usefulness and other non-investment considerations, mortgages currently provide an attractive rate of return. For example, a government insured mortgage, net after servicing charges, is priced to provide a yield to maturity of approximately 5% or better depending upon location of the underlying property and the like.

This review of current conditions certainly indicates that, on a basis of history, bonds now provide a rate of return somewhat better than the long-term averages, whereas common stocks are so priced as to provide a current rate of return substantially below the long-term average. Plain common sense dictates that we look a lot closer at our common stock investments since this warning cannot be ignored. Furthermore, any trustee charged with prudence must consider the factor of relative risk. Since his investment choices include securities of varying degrees of risk, he should view with a cold eye those whose purchase involves more risk than those in which his dollar capital is relatively safe.

As pointed out previously the long-term rate of return for common stocks has averaged 8.12% per year. This is the result of both dividends and price appreciation to which a pension fund draws no distinction because of its tax-exemption. Since our current yield on stocks is approximately 3%, this would indicate that we are looking for an additional 5.12% per annum, either from increased dividends or price appreciation, to remain abreast of the long-term average. Where will this come from, if it is at all available?

EARNINGS CRUCIAL FACTOR

Equity investment is based upon the theory that as a company prospers, so will its stockholders. This will be the result of both increased dividends paid to the stockholder plus appreciation in the price of the stock. For this reason, one of the most important methods of evaluating a particular company's past record is a study of growth or lack of growth in earnings per share. Furthermore, earnings per share are of utmost importance to the stockholder since it is out of earnings that dividends are paid and it is partially out of earnings that a company will finance its future expansion.

We all realize that there are other factors which affect the price of a stock such as public psychology. But, in the long run, either a company prospers and earns more money for its stockholders or it does not. Since the typical pension fund is a long-term investor and should be concerned with long-term value, this investigation of earnings is of great importance.

If we buy a stock today which yields but 3%, and our reason for the purchase of any common stock is predicated upon the long-term efficacy of this form of investment, then we would need an additional 5.12% to keep us even with the average. Since this 5% plus will be a direct result, over the years, of earnings per share, does the specific investment being considered show this type of annual increase for a representative period of time? If it does not and there are no extenuating circumstances, why should it be purchased at all? Let's look at some typical pension fund stock investments and see how they compare with this yardstick.

LOOKING BACKWARD

In 1954 the New York State Banking Department compiled a study of pension funds managed by the major New York City banks on a discretionary basis. At that time, a list was provided of the 10 stocks which were then the favorites of the pension trust departments. I realize, of course, that some of these companies may no longer be in favor with the pension trust departments of those banks and that others may have been added. However, of these 10 stocks seven appeared in the Fall, 1961 edition of "The Favorite 50" indicating that these stocks are still very much in favor with certain segments of the investment community. Each one of these 10 companies has been measured in a way to provide:

(1) The compound annual rate of increase or decrease in earnings per share.

(2) The compound annual rate of increase or decrease in market price per share.

Since the end of World War II, no period of time has been what we could fairly title as "typical." Certainly, our present semi-peace, semi-war economy is not typical. Therefore, I have selected two post-war periods of time for this study. 1951-1960 and 1957-1961 inclusive (earnings for 1961 are estimated). This dual view should present a fair or at least representative picture of the earnings trends of these companies.

RECORD IS ILLUMINATING

The accompanying table provides some illuminating facts. For example during the 10-year period, 1951-1960, The Standard & Poor's Composite Index showed an annual rate of increase in earnings per share of 1.5% and an annual rate of increase in the market value of the index of 11.8%. During the latter five-year period, 1957-1961, earnings remained unchanged, whereas market prices went up 6.3%. The figures speak for themselves and are hardly conducive to comfort regarding current market values. Another way of looking at what has happened to the prices of stocks is that they have risen 45% since 1955 when their profits reached an all-time high, a point to which we have not as yet returned. Will corporate earnings justify the faith of the investing public? Perhaps, they will. The point is that the current market is discounting a good portion of the immediate future. They do not represent outstanding values in anyone's book.

Compound Annual Rate
of Increase or Decrease in Earnings Per Share and Mean Market Price

	1951–1960 Comp. Ann. Rate of Inc. or (Dec.), %		1957–1961* Comp. Ann. Rate of Inc. or (Dec.), %			Annual Inc. in EPS Required
	Earnings Per Sh.	Mean Mkt. Price	Earnings Per Sh.	Mean Mkt. Price	Curr. Yield,	to Equal First Ave., %
American Tel. & Tel. ‡	3.0	6.3	6.5	14.7	3.0	5.12
General Electric ‡	1.0	18.7	0.3	2.8	2.9	5.22
General Motors ‡	0.7	12.5	(1.5)	0.1	4.4	3.72
IBM ‡	15.9	27.2	20.2	39.9	0.5	7.62
International Paper ‡	(3.4)	10.8	(6.3)	(3.8)	2.9	5.22
J.C. Penney	0.0	7.0	1.1	7.9	3.1	5.02
Socony Mobil	1.6	8.7	(5.7)	(5.4)	4.5	3.62
Standard Oil, N.J. ‡	3.5	12.9	(4.3)	(4.2)	5.1	3.02
Texaco ‡	8.9	15.8	4.6	10.7	2.9	5.22
Westinghouse	(1.9)	13.0	(†)	9.0	2.8	5.32
Dow Jones Industrials	0.5	11.2	(1.1)	6.3	2.8	5.32
Standard & Poor's Comp. 500	1.5	11.8	0.0	6.3	2.9	5.22

*Estimated 1961 earnings.

†Earnings for 1956 (base year) distorted due to strike; reported $0.05 per share.

‡One of the Vicker's Favorite 50 for Investment Companies, Fall 1931.

The table also lists the current return on these 10 companies plus an indication of the rate of growth necessary in earnings per share to justify investment on a historical basis. What we have calculated is the direct result of subtracting current yield from our long-term objective and arriving at a figure which represents the necessary minimum growth in earnings per share in order for that investment to come up to par with the average. Suppose we purchase General Electric with a current yield of 2.9%. This means that we would need an additional 5.22% per annum to achieve the historical standard. Does GE make it on the basis of earnings experience for the past 10 years. Earnings per share grew at a compounded rate of 1.0% and for the latter five-year period at a rate of 0.3%. This does not mean that GE cannot improve its earnings in the future but past facts indicate the necessity for closely scrutinizing the future prospects of the company.

On the five year basis, only two of these 10 companies would satisfy this requirement—IBM and American Telephone. On the basis of 10 years, three companies make the mark: IBM, Standard Oil of New Jersey and Texaco. Note, however, that two of the three are international oil companies whose future prospects have dimmed somewhat in recent years. Since the results of this study speak for themselves I do not wish to belabor that which can be reviewed at leisure. Certainly, it is reasonable to conclude that the prospects of most of these 10 companies are something less than inspiring.

SELECTIVITY VS. AVERAGES

Of necessity, our discussions have concerned themselves thus far with averages. This makes no allowance for better-than-average selectivity of individual investment commitments. There is no substitute for selection since it should be apparent that all individual investments either are better or worse than the arithmetic average. Investment is not now nor ever has been an absolute science based upon some mathematic formula. Many intangibles come to play in the selection of a security such as an evaluation of the capabilities of management. Therefore, this factor of selectivity is of major importance. Whether a fund's investment performance will better the averages will depend directly upon the sagacity of the investment policies and investment selection of that fund. This is not predictable. Therefore, we must concern ourselves with the guideposts of the averages. For this reason, the recommendations which follow must be viewed as a flexible framework within which specific judgments are to be made. There is no one answer which will satisfactorily answer the needs and problems of all pension funds. If there were, it would have been discovered long ago.

AN INVESTMENT POLICY FOR TODAY

If an investment policy is to be successful over a long period of time, it must dodge the rigidity of a fixed formula which is applied regardless of current conditions. That which was applicable in the past, may no longer be valid or justified. That which is applicable today, may be discarded in the future not because of a lack of success but because of a fundamental change in those conditions governing the investment policies of a fund. What we must do is evaluate the present in terms of the fund and weigh the alternative investment routes in order to ascertain that which is justifiable for a prudent trustee. The past is a guide, the future is unpredictable. But we are able to evaluate the present.

As mentioned at some length previously, it is the responsibility of a trustee to select his investments in order to protect the dollar capital of the fund and, hopefully, preserve its purchasing power with a minimum of risk. His choice of investments is as broad today as it was in years past. Only the relative positions and values of these securities have changed with the years. Under present conditions, bonds provide a higher yield. Simultaneously we are all in accord with the idea that, as far as safety of principal is concerned, bonds are a better protection than common stocks. What is prudent today? I think that it is clear that greater emphasis should be given to bond and mortgage investment than in the recent past. If the yield relationships should return to their normal pattern, then the prices of bonds will go up or stock prices will fall or some combination of the two. If on the other hand, history does not repeat itself and the future portends a continuance of higher than common stock yields for bonds, the typical pension fund with its cash flow can easily return to the purchase of common stocks.

THE CASE FOR BONDS

Since I do not believe that it is the province of a trustee to take unwarranted risk, then increasing the emphasis on bond investment in light of all the historical data available would appear to me to be exercising prudent judgment. Obviously, if there is a substantial justification of relative yields between bonds and stocks and we return to a more normal relationship, then another change in policy should be seriously considered.

A further refinement of this thinking would be that applied to the selection of individual stock investments. The best way to approach this problem is to consider for a moment something about the type of stock a fund should not purchase. Since the rationalization of stock ownership for a pension fund is based upon long-term performance, it only makes sense that no commitment should be made in any security which does not equal the average. Certainly, there will be exceptions to the rule. In general, however, this long-term performance is as good a guide as any available and can be applied without too much difficulty.

I do not wish to lay down any hard and fast rule regarding what percentage should be invested in bonds and mortgages versus the percentage in common stocks, at the present time. This can only be judged on a fund by fund basis and depends directly upon its specific requirements. What is the current percentage diversification of assets between these types of securities? How long has it been investing its money? Whatever the specific answers happen to be and assuming they had been well conceived prior to this time, then I think that a more conservative attitude is warranted in light of present market conditions.

How prudent are your pension investments? The answer is two-fold and predicated upon the recognition that prudence is primarily concerned with preservation—the preservation of dollar capital and the preservation of the purchasing power of that dollar capital. Furthermore, this preservation must be accomplished with a minimum acceptance of risk by the prudent trustee.

On a long-term basis, a substantial reliance upon common stocks apparently satisfies the definition of prudence as well as taking advantage of undeniable long-term trends. As far as current policies are concerned, I believe that prudence would dictate some deviation from the long-term solution, namely, more reliance upon bonds and mortgages.

I have attempted to place the investment problem within the framework of current conditions. Surely changes can and will take place in the future and when they happen our investment programs will change in order to take full advantage of the new conditions. The point to remember is that security markets are hardly static and it is both prudent and sage to sieze attractive opportunities when they exist. Any unquestioning reliance upon a fixed formula can lead to disaster.

Prudent investment can be achieved if the trustees are willing to consider objectively the investment alternatives, selecting that medium which will provide the necessary preservation with the least amount of risk under current market conditions. This measurement is not necessarily difficult. It only needs to be done.

14
THE LAW OF TRUST INVESTMENT

. . . In Which the

"Prudent Man" Theory

Is Evaluated*

HAROLD B. ELSOM, vice president and trust officer, Texas National Bank of Houston, is completing his 27th year with that organization. He has also served in all executive capacities for the Houston Corporate Fiduciary Association.

The corporate trustee is a growing factor in the American economy—a buyer and seller of securities, a provider of capital, an income

*From *Financial Analysts Journal,* Vol. 16, No. 4 (July-August 1960), pp. 27-33. Reprinted by permission of the publisher and the author.

producer for dependent individuals and institutions, and finally as a prospective employer of many wage earners, including Financial Security Analysts.

That this fact is not always well attended is apparent from the occasional failures of the financial community to understand this market which it seeks to cultivate. It is also apparent in some instances where Financial Analysts desire to establish associations with corporate trustees. And of importance in this failure of understanding is the law of trust investment.

Many persons (some trustees themselves) conceive of this subject as an ambiguity whose edges blend imperceptibly into areas of surcharge—a word of anathema signifying the trustee must foot the bill for his mistakes. Our theme begins, therefore, with the simple assertion that the manner of achieving legally acceptable discretion is better defined than is commonly supposed, owing to the convergence of several simple rules on any given problem. In a word, the overlapping of these rules lends clarity which no single one of them exhibits within itself.

We shall deal with the "Prudent Man Statute" of the State of Texas (Sec. 46 of the Texas Trust Act) and the related law of Texas and other states. The statute varies little from similar statutes of other states. We shall also observe the general body of the law of trust investment because the Texas Trust Act recognizes the common law. Our remarks have no point in states which do not follow the "Prudent Man" rule. The Texas statute reads in part:

> .... the trustee shall exercise the judgement and care under the circumstances then prevailing, which men of ordinary prudence, discretion and intelligence exercise in the management of their own affairs, not in regard to speculation, but in regard to the permanent disposition of their funds, considering the probable income therefrom as well as the probable safety of their capital. Within the limitations of the foregoing standard, the trustee is authorized to acquire and retain every kind of property, real, personal or mixed, and every kind of investment . . . which men of ordinary prudence, discretion and intelligence acquire or retain for their own account . . .

The Legislature could not have used more comforting language, providing it meant literally what it said (an unlikely occurrence). Every kind of investment is authorized. Nothing is said about analytical standards; and most prudent men are not Financial Security Analysts.

Looking to the statute alone, it would not be difficult for a trustee, having expended all of the funds of a trust in real estate, and finding himself beset by litigants, to produce as expert witnesses men of conceded probity, intelligence and discretion, who invest their funds solely in the good earth; and who do so, not from speculative motives but with pure investment objectives, due regard for permanent disposition of their funds, probable income and probable safety of their capital. Having been actuated by identical consideration, the trustee would be shielded from liability. Similarly, prudent men can be found who invest only in single stocks, only in oil properties, only in government bonds, etc.

Thus, to the average reader, the fairly implied spirit of the statute is generous. This implication is deceptive. The phrases used do not have the inferences attributed to them by ordinary gentry. Much of the language was extracted from a case decided in 1930, since modified. Again, trust investment is affected by custom, official rules, and case law not alluded to in the enactment, except for the reference to the common law. Hence, trust men and attorneys do not rely on the conclusions which our examples suggest.

Resorting to the cases, we find few that are helpful—i.e, few that were decided after the effective dates of such legislation. We have examined several legal opinions which culminate in stating that prudence is a question of fact to be determined by a jury or by a court, in the light of all the circumstances bearing on the case at issue.

This is not very helpful. We hasten to add, however, that it would be unfair to expect our lawyer friends to produce law which isn't there. It is also oversimplification; there is some law which attorneys bring to our attention with competence. The current of our thought is nonetheless true: there are few case guides on the statutes.

We are not sure, for instance, what is meant by "permanent disposition of their funds." We are not sure the legislature means it when it says, "which men of ordinary prudence, discretion and intelligence exercise in the management of *their own affairs.*" If so, it upset an established common law precedent. Or, what did the lawmakers intend when they utilized the phrase, "probable safety of their capital?" "Funds" is used in connection with permanence of investment, "capital" in connection with safety. Are they contradistinct?; or are they used interchangeably?

STATUTE CREATES A PUZZLE

An important point lurks here. "Funds" could be taken to mean money set aside for a purpose, the emphasis being on dollars or their equivalent, available either constantly or at a future time, or on the happening of an event. "Capital" in an ordinary sense might signify wealth or anything of economic value usable for the production of more wealth. If "capital" were used to denote safety of funds, a dollar conservative approach would be enjoined, based on the trustee's ability to deliver the money originally entrusted to him, or its equivalent. If "safety of capital" were used to describe economic good or value, then the trustee would be required to conserve the economic value or relative wealth quantity of the trust.

These observations establish the difficulty of obtaining a sound concept from inspection of the act itself. We believe the older cases are helpful; that some of them are still good law; and that it is probable that where such decisions led to phraseology within the act, the judicially determined meanings inhere in the statute.

Broadly, what rules did these cases enunciate?

The first great question deals with: What sort of prudence? The answer begins with *Harvard* vs. *Amory* (9 Pick. 446; 461 Mass. 1930) where the court stated: "He (meaning the trustee) is to observe how men of prudence, discretion and intelligence manage their own affairs, not in regard to speculation, but in regard to permanent disposition of their funds, considering the probable income, as well as the probable safety of the capital to be invested." This sounds familiar, after examination of several "prudent man" statutes. Please note the phrases, "permanent disposition"; "manage their own affairs"; and "probable safety of capital." Note also the use of the words "funds" and "capital." Obviously, here is the origin of the statutes. Let us see what weight the courts have given it, bearing in mind the while that statutes are subject to judicial interpretation, and not losing sight of our question: What sort of prudence?

Speaking four years later we have a court modifying *Harvard* vs. *Amory:* " . . . the external standard of 'such care and skill as a man of ordinary prudence would exercise in dealing with his own property' is not the standard he would use . . . if he had only himself to consider . . . he must take no risks which would not be taken by an ordinarily prudent man who is trustee of another person's property." (Cooks Estate 171 Atl. 730; *Marshal* vs. *Frazier,* 80 P. 2d 42). The realities of human nature were recognized quickly; it was concluded that even prudent men take risks for themselves which should not be assumed for another.

We begin our answer to the question. What sort of prudence? by concluding that legal prudence differs from everyday prudence; and that it is a measuring device external to any particular case, as a ruler is external to the object it measures. Our prudent man is a synthetic individual of the law engaged in the management, not of his own affairs as stated in *Harvard* vs. *Amory* and in the statutes which lifted their phrasing from that case, but those of a dependent.

If the law is to hold us to a standard apart from ordinary horse sense, we must determine its other parts as well. The cases tell us that another basic element is the duty to use "reasonable care," seemingly innocent thought, but not so in fact. For instance, many intelligent individuals have done well in their investments utilizing the advice of brokers, financial services, knowledgeable friends or similar sources, relying wholly on the opinions obtained. Our fictional counterpart, the "ordinary prudent man" may not follow so comfortable a course. He must, himself, bring reasonable care to the task. He must, himself, investigate the safety and expectable income. He must weigh the background of the security. The effective opinion and the decisive conclusion must be his own.

It is no defense to show that he acted on the advice of others, however highly qualified, if later events disclose that diligent personal investigation would have revealed a deficiency in the investment under the test of legal standards. It has been held that reliance on opinions from these sources was not defensible. Brokers, attorneys, friends (on whom the trustee was long accustomed to rely), bankers, financiers, business men, financial publications, and the general reputation or "blue chip" standing of a security or company, is held invalid. This is not to say that factual material from reputable sources may not be accepted, or that opinions may not be given consideration. It is to say that fact and opinion must be distinguished and that the trustee have sufficient data to produce his own opinion based on investigation of all material data. It is also to say that a working knowledge of the law of trust investment should be an elementary qualification of any Financial Analyst toiling for a corporate trustee.

Case law also demands "reasonable skill" of the fiduciary. Once more the law has its own vantage point. Once more the standard is external to the fact. A trustee, having suffered losses for his beneficiaries through failure to apply sound principles and techniques of analysis, would find no defense in this circumstance. If he does not have the required degree of skill, he must acquire it; for we have seen that he may not resort to outside sources, or refuse to act as a fiduciary.

The other side of the coin is different. If he has greater facilities and skill, he must apply them earnestly or be held derelict. Judges are prone to reason that corporate trustees should be held accountable for greater skill and knowledge than individual trustees, despite an old common law rule to the contrary. A Wisconsin cause (Estate of Ellis, 191 Wisconsin 23; 209 N. W. 945) ruled that, "when the trustee is a company organized for the purpose of caring for trust estates, which holds itself out as possessing a special skill in the performance of the duties of a trustee, and which makes a charge for its services" a unique importance attaches to the skill requirement. A later case emphasized the point by saying that corporate trustees are professionals having a large volume of business and expensive facilities.

CERTAIN ADVANTAGES OF A BANK

A New York court put it this way: "a bank has certain advantages . . . . It not only has its trust officer who is supposed to be more or less familiar with market prices of securities and whose business it is to be posted concerning market conditions, but over the trust officer are officials of the bank, men of affairs assumed to be chosen because of their business judgment." (*Matter of Baker,* 292 N. Y. Supp. 122).

One judge at least (*Matter of Balfe,* 280 N. Y. Supp. 128) observed that failure to sell securities could not be overlooked merely because they had fallen in value generally. By implication, corporate trustees would be expected to anticipate substantial market declines. He mitigated his remarks by adding that the trustee could not be deemed a guarantor of value. If the failure to sell was not accompanied by negligence, no surcharge could ensue. He should be able to show, however, that careful consideration was given to sale or retention and that the record shows that he acted with prudence (minutes of investment committee). That the judicial tendency is toward a stricter view toward corporate trustees is witnessed by further decisions in New Jersey (*Liberty Title & Trust Company* vs. *Plews,* 142 N. J. Eq. 493; 60 Atl. 2d 630, 1948) and Oklahoma (*Finley* vs. *Exchange Trust Company,* 183 Oklahoma 167).

Although logic would lead one to conclude that reasonable skill is the same animal at all times and places, we find it is not one thing at all. One ruler measures a foot for an individual trustee, another and longer one a foot for a bank trust department. Mayhap this is proper. We do hold ourselves out to the public in a reassuring, confident way.

The prudent man of the jurists must also exhibit caution. In the eyes of the Bench, this virtue cannot be equated with care as perhaps would be done by the man in the street. Cases on caution go more to the question of motivation. Trustees may not seek speculative gain or place exceptional emphasis on prospective principal gain or growth in income. A flesh-and-blood prudent man may bring care and skill of the highest order to the selection of investments, yet be assuming risks which the law witholds from his legal twin. In *King* vs. *Talbot* (40 N. Y. 76) the court said: ". . . it does not follow . . . that trustees may do the same." The law of the husbandman applies again. Trustees' purposes shall be those appropriate to the prudent man morally and legally bound to provide for dependents. He must satisfy himself with results obtainable by reliance on probabilities developed from a preponderance of financial evidence. In the nature of things, this must be constituted of tangibles growing out of the company's record, position in its industry, etc., determined by procedures of measurement. Otherwise, how can he demonstrate his prudence, if challenged? There are overtones of interest to Financial Analysts here.

Thus far, we have treated only basic elements. We see them cropping out like geologic substrata in existing statutory and regulatory law. We assume that the newer law does not set aside the older case law, but crystallizes the major portion. Legal prudence still consists of care (knowledge, intelligence and diligence); skill (experience and facilities); and caution (proper motivation). Additionally, the law moves toward holding corporate trustees to distinctly higher standards in the consideration of these elements.

Yet withal, whether we have met the law's injunctions is one of fact as well as law, of particulars, not generalities. Since the courts seem to regard a fact finding in an adjudicated case as having converted that fact situation virtually into law, we may look to the facts of earlier cases with reason.

SPREADING OF RISK NECESSARY

We find great diversity but certain ideas seem generally accepted. For example, the spreading of risk among several investments is recognized as necessary. Professor Austin Wakeman Scott, a frequently cited authority expresses it thus: "The trustee . . . should not therefore invest more than a reasonable proportion of the trust estate in a single security or, it would seem, in a single type of security. This is a commonplace among experts in the art of making investments."

The extent of liability is not well defined, however, since many jurisdictions have not adjudicated the question. In others, its presentation to appellate courts has been obscured by collateral issues such as the measure of damages and whether failure of diversification was the proximate cause of loss. Recognition of the principle is present, despite the confusing factors.

General agreement also exists that trustees may not acquire investments on credit, carry on a business, buy securities of new or unproven enterprises, purchase realty or personalty for resale, invest in junior liens, or make unsecured loans.

Most of the cases mentioned were decided in the 1930's. The defendants were usually banks or business men who acted without intent to commit wrong. According to their experience they were doing workmanlike jobs for their clients. It was the extraordinary sequence of the years 1926-1930 which probed their weakness and brought them to the bar for judgment by principles and tests of which they had been ignorant, some of which, indeed, were wrought out of their own experiences.

We opine, therefore, that a normal investment environment produces little investment case law. It will be our adjustments to the unusual, unforeseeable events of the future which will call our prudence into question. How shall we fare under our "prudent man" statutes?

Oddly enough, we begin with another look at the past. Two cases will serve: the first, *Chemical Bank & Trust Company* vs. *Reynaud* (270 N. Y. Supp. 301, 1933) contained this language: "On the question whether an investment was a prudent one, the testimony of persons expert in financial affairs is admissible." The second, *Scoville* vs. *Brock* (81 Vermont 405) had this to say: "Evidence is admissible as to what insurance companies, trust companies and others purchase."

Seemingly, there is nothing new here. Such evidence was admissible then, and it is admissible now. What consequence? Simply this: This is the highway of development within the law. Here it may be altered without cases or statutes. It is also one of the places to look to estimate what the law may have come to be. Whatever we may do to protect against the onslaughts of the future has origins here.

For a beginning, the Great Depression led to a more orderly, more detailed approach to security analysis. The Securities Exchange Commission forced issuers of securities to divulge data not theretofore obtainable. The breakup of utility holding companies focused attention on evaluation and corporate structure. Earning power, book values, depreciation practices, inventory, and property accounting received thorough scrutiny for the first time. Railroad reorganizations, corporate bond defaults, and other corporate disasters had similar results. Federal Estate Tax litigation brought inquiry into factors of value. The work was done, the data recorded, the principles tested by expert disputation. Today it is probable that competent counsel would be more capable of convincing a court that a corporate trustee had failed in the matter of prudence—provided he had actually been mistaken, ignorant, or used poor procedures—than in the 1930's, since many of the results of these studies have been widely accepted. The effective step in insuring legal prudence is to utilize analytical methods in the hands of qualified personnel.

MINIMUM DIVERSIFICATION CITED

Official acceptance of this line of thought may be shown by reference to Regulation F of the Board of Governors of the Federal Reserve System having to do with trust departments operated by national banks. As an example, no common trust fund subject to Board regulation may invest more than 10% of its assets, at cost, in the securities of one company. Surely, there is no more clear cut statement of what constitutes minimum diversification.

The purchase of more than 5% of the outstanding shares of any corporation is also prohibited. Translation is easy: trust departments may not invest for purposes of control, nor to the extent that their holdings will carry any burden of participating in management—a crystallization of the case law rule against carrying on a business.

The Board was aware as well of the basic elements of diligence, skill, care and caution. Witness the imposition of these regulations concerning the exercise of investment discretion by trust departments: A committee of at least three *capable* and experienced officers is accorded this task. The Board thinks they should work at their job: "It is contemplated that there shall be a committee the members of which shall have a *continuity* of responsibility . . . ."

That thought, effort and application are expected, is underlined by provisions relating to alternates: "However, alternates appointed by the Board of Directors may serve in place of regular members . . . who are *unable to serve on account of vacations, illness, or other good and sufficient reasons if the minutes of the committee show the reason for the service of such alternate in place of the regular member.*" [Italics supplied] .

The Board seeks to forestall any evasion of decision through ignorance or lassitude. It demands a definite committee act as a condition precedent to every purchase, sale or retention. Its disposition in the matters acted upon must be recorded (note the case alluded to earlier, Matter of Balfe). Inaction is not permitted and retention is accorded equal weight with purchase or sale. Portfolios must be reviewed periodically, and one of the three possible decisions arrived at for each asset. Each of the three decisions involves all of the elements of legal prudence. Investment via default is abhorrent.

On the question, Are corporate trustees to be held to higher standards?, Regulation F states: "Every such national bank shall conform to sound principles in the operation of its trust department." This is followed by a footnote to the effect that the Statement of Principles of Trust Institutions of the American Bankers Association is commended. The Board then caused the statement to be appended to Regulation F, thus lending an aspect of official injunction. A pertinent part of the Statement: "A trust institution should devote to its trust investments all the care and skill that it has or *can reasonably acquire.*" (Italics supplied). Again case law protrudes.

The Board of Governors was likewise cognizant perhaps of the cases dealing with caution, as we put it, motivation, wherein we learned that the courts were not impressed with attempts to obtain competitive advantage through spectacular results. At any rate, Regulation F prohibits advertising of investment results of common trust funds.

KNOW THE "PRUDENT MAN" LAW

In sum, the lineaments of case law are visible in our statutes and regulations. The major change is in the body of evidence available and the crystallization of principles. It is well, therefore, for corporate trustees to arrange their policies and procedures with an eye to the law of trust investment. The routine of investment should remove the hazard of culpable oversight, or mistake, just as operating and accounting practices in the commercial bank are designed to remove misgiving as to examination or audit. Financial Analysts are equipped to cope with this problem so long as one of the weapons in their arsenal is a cursory knowledge of "prudent man" law.

Earlier, we raised questions as to the meaning of the statutory phrase "permanent disposition of their funds," and the seemingly interchangeable use of the words "funds" and "capital." We do not wish to straddle those questions.

Vagueness as to the meaning of "permanent disposition" arose because jurists were not required at that moment to render their thinking explicit. All that was needed was to distinguish between ideas and objectives. On one side they grouped these activities:

Business operations—the buying and selling of goods or services with attendant operations.

Trading—the taking of positions in commodities or securities for ensuing sale or purchase at a profit on the capital employed plus any borrowed funds.

Speculation—the purchase or sale of securities based on an opinion that extraordinary events or development, not supported by a proven record of probability and conventional investment techniques, will occur.

To the judges, these were impermanent. Sale was contemplated in the act of purchase. Income was a secondary or non-existent consideration. They realized that success in these operations was reserved for the few possessing unique faculties and temperament, whereas the trustee, if he were to serve a social need, would be most frequently an individual of usual proportions. He might conceive himself a wizard of finance. In rare instances, he might be such. But it was felt that disaster for the many outweighed possible benefits to the few.

On the other side were investment operations thought to be of lasting nature:

Bond purchases—where the issuer exhibited financial strength over good times and bad.

Mortgages—where secured by first liens on real estate of much greater value and demonstrated responsibility of the borrower.

Stocks—where determined to be sound income producing enterprises through the application of accepted investment criteria.

Other investments subject to similar standards.

These were called permanent, where not acquired for trading purposes, control or transitory reasons. As to securities, this thought was based on the habits and experience of mankind. The great basic industries persist from one generation to another. Large, successful corporations have positions of leadership which are fixed by the convergence of many forces—the interests of management and millions of stockholders; the myriad suppliers from whom they buy; their millions of customers; their relationships with the financial community; and with governments, our own and others. These entities were deemed economic phenomena engrained in the mind and habit of economic man. Selections from among them may be made by the use of diligence and intelligence with no special faculties required. Clearly, the jurists were speaking, not so much of chronology as of character and a state of mind. The trustee is free to sell; in fact, he is under a duty to do so under the stimuli of sensible reasons.

A CASE OF SEMANTICS

We come now to the terms "funds" and "capital." It is possible the judges were unaware of the fine differences in the meanings of these words. The character of their thought does not imply it. We believe these gentlemen pictured a trustee with cash or "funds" on hand for the making of investments, necessarily to be paid for with "funds." They then envisioned the trustee as having acquired the stock or bond. Instantly, the legal mind translated "funds" into "capital" which agrees nicely with the economic meaning of "wealth or anything of value used to produce more wealth." The concern for safety of capital in the cases and in the statutes is therefore logically, chronologically, and technically correct. The sequence of use of these words shows the idea of safety to be associated with wealth, not funds.

This outlook has been reinforced by events. At the end of World War II, trust literature was interlarded with concern as to whether trustees might buy common stocks, these being considered inflation hedges, but subject to fluctuations which could imperil safety of "funds." Some states had prohibitions against such investment, some limitations. This led many to fear the main body of the law might be influenced thereby, even though no case law or other prohibition existed—and, in some instances, even though "prudent man" statutes had been enacted.

Any such hazard seems to have been removed by corporate trustees themselves. A check of institutional policies in 1958 showed portfolio percentages devoted to common stocks to vary from 35% to 65%. Perhaps the average moved up in 1959.

We have then a reasonable interpretation of court opinion, suggesting that wealth-protective measures are in order. We have also the rule of evidence requiring admission of testimony as to the activities of trust institutions (such evidence would be overwhelming). If safety of wealth rather than a sum certain were ever in question, doubt has been removed. Courts will not require prudent men to lock their scales in the vault and stack their gold on the floor outside.

We have not treated analytical material here because that is a separate study. It is true, however, that analytical methods may be used to measure and clarify virtually every point of law mentioned. It is practicable for the corporate trustee, merely in the process of doing a good job, to evidence his prudence as he goes.

Our remarks end with a question and an observation:

The question: Why are corporate trustees so preoccupied with the law of trust investment? Are not security dealers, oil enterprises, and other businesses festooned with laws and regulations? Yet seldom do we find these other groups chronically concerned with things legal to the degree that is characteristic of trust officers. Perhaps the answer lies in the nature of their routine. Everything the trust officer does proceeds from some legal instrument: a will, a trust agreement, a divorce and property settlement, a court decree, a conveyance, an indenture.

VAST SUM OF KNOWLEDGE NEEDED

There is a deep compatibility between trust men, the law and the legal fraternity. This is weighted further by a most practical consideration—trustee's fees are low. We cannot know exactly what annual compensation the average corporate trustee receives. Our guess would be about one half of one percent of fair market value per annum, or roughly equal to the wage of investment counseling firms or mutual fund management companies.

But before he turns to the investment problem he must have provided for intricate and voluminous accounting procedures encompassing all sorts of transactions in all kinds of properties. He must have equipped himself to deal with Federal estate taxes, state inheritance taxes and income taxes. He must have arranged to take cognizance of births, deaths, marriages, birthdays, and the onslaught of all forms of legal imcompetence, and to follow intelligently the complexities of provisions in lengthy legal documents. He must have provided for personal understanding, sympathy and firmness in dealing with the lame, the halt, the blind, the unhappy, the alcoholic, the venal, the wise and the silly, the egocentric and the neurotic—along with the fine folk who comprise his main custom. Of a certainty, that portion of his fee, thereafter attributable to the investment chore, is not large. He would be something less than brilliant were he to risk the heavy hand of the law for so modest a prize.

The observation: Trust investment policy should not originate in apprehension. No court has ever held that the trustee must be right in all cases or in any particular instance. No court has ever held there is but one true answer to any investment problem and that the trustee must have it. The law demands only that the trustee be prudent within the rules of the game, so to speak. Within these rules he may be aggressive, defensive or neutral according to his nature, his judgment and, very importantly, the way he goes about it. He labors under no disability. The law would have him perform well, not timidly.

The trust business itself is founded on excellence. It would not exist without integrity and responsibility. Inefficiency would remove it from the banking scene. Trust investment demands the same standards. Indeed, the aim of excellent results in varied financial weather is the soundest, most efficient, least costly, and most defensible policy. We believe most trust institutions ascribe to it.

We have no real fear that anyone will accept what has been said here as gospel. Our intent has been one of exposition, to provide perspective, rather than minutial and exhaustiveness. One must resort to counsel for authoritative opinion on any set of particulars.

15

HOW TO RATE MANAGEMENT OF INVESTMENT FUNDS*

JACK L. TREYNOR is associated with Arthur D. Little, Inc.

Investment management has become an important industry in the United States. The responsibilities of investment managers are enormous, and their potential rewards are great. In order to reward management for good performance in this field, however, it is necessary to be able to recognize it. Unfortunately, pension funds, trust funds, and mutual funds all share one serious problem: to the extent that they are heavily invested in common stocks, the return achieved in any one period is subject to wide fluctuations which are beyond the control of investment management. The result has been that, although many believe the quality of investment management is important, no one has devised a satisfactory way to measure its impact on performance.

In this article we shall look at a new way to rate the performance of a fund's investment managers. The comprehensiveness of this rating is a question for the reader to decide for himself, depending on how he thinks about the "quality" of investment management. Most readers are likely to agree, however, that at least one dimension—and a critical one—of the quality of the investment management is analyzed by this new method.

ANALYZING RISK

It is almost ironic that the presence of market risk should pose such a serious problem. The assets controlled by investment managers are remarkably liquid. To a degree almost unmatched in other enterprises, the investment

*From Harvard Business Review, Vol. 43, No. 1 (January-February 1965), pp. 63-76. Reprinted by permission.

manager is free to act independently of the investment decisions of his predecessors. Furthermore, although there are varying institutional restrictions placed on the investment manager's decisions, by and large he competes directly with other investment managers, buying and selling securities in the same market. If it were not for the problems created by market risk, therefore, performance comparisons in the investment management industry would be more meaningful than in many other industries.

Actually, of course, there is more than one kind of risk in a diversified fund. There is a risk produced by general market fluctuations—the volatility of the stock market. There is also a risk resulting from fluctuations in the particular securities held by the fund. In any event, here are important practical consequences of either or both of these risks:

(1) The effect of management on the rate of return on investments made in any one period is usually swamped by fluctuations in the general market. Depending on whether, during the period in question, the general market is rising or falling, the more volatile funds (stock funds) will look better or worse than the less volatile funds (balanced funds). As the Wharton Report points out, the difficulty is not solved by averaging return over a number of periods.[1] For any sample interval of reasonable length, average return is still dominated by market trends.

(2) Measures of average return make no allowance for investors' aversions to risk. The importance of fluctuations in one or a few stocks from the investor's point of view is apparent when one considers that, after all, if this kind of risk were not important, investors would not diversify. It is sometimes argued that because the importance attached to risk varies from investor to investor, no absolute measure of fund performance is possible.

Overcoming Difficulties

In order to have any practical value, a measure of management performance in handling a trust fund invested in equities or in handling pension or mutual funds must deal effectively with both problems. It should tend to remain constant so long as management performance is constant—even in the face of severe market fluctuations. Also, it should take into account the aversion of individual shareholders or beneficiaries to investment risk. The method to be described here overcomes both difficulties.

---

[1]In discussing the cumulative performance of investment funds between January 1, 1953, and September 30, 1958, the report says ". . . the interpretation of the net result is to be made against the background of the movements in security market prices during this period . . . general fund performance and comparisons among funds of different types might be quite different in other time periods . . . ," *A Study of Mutual Funds* (Washington, Government Printing Office, 1962), p. 308.

This article has three parts. The first describes a simple graphical method for capturing the essence of what is permanent and distinctive about the performance of a fund, including the effects of fund management. The second develops a concept of fund performance which takes investment risk into account. The third develops a measure for rating fund-management performance which can be applied directly, using the graphical technique developed in the first part. For the statistician, an Appendix details certain of the relationships used.

THE CHARACTERISTIC LINE

The first main step to obtaining a satisfactory performance measure is to relate the expected rate of return of a trust, pension, or mutual fund to the rate of return of a suitable market average. The device for accomplishing this is the *characteristic line.* Let us examine its nature and significance.

Application to Funds

If the rate of return taking into account both market appreciation and dividends—is plotted for a fund invested substantially in common stocks, wide swings from period to period are often evident. It is not generally known, however, that most managed funds actually demonstrate a remarkably stable performance pattern over time when viewed in terms of the simple graphical device which I call the characteristic line.

Exhibit I summarizes the performance history of four actual managed funds:

• The horizontal and vertical axes in these figures are measured in terms of percent rate of return. (For both individual funds and market averages, rate of return is computed by dividing the sum of dividends, interest, and market appreciation on the funds available at the beginning of the year by the value of the funds available at the beginning of the year. Any increase in asset value during the year due to infusion of new funds is eliminated, as is any reduction due to distributions to beneficiaries or shareholders. Rates of return defined in this way are obviously approximations, because the value of funds available for investment typically fluctuates more or less continuously throughout the year.)

• The horizontal axis measures the corresponding rate of return recorded for a general *market* average (the Dow-Jones Industrial Average); the vertical axis shows the rate of return for the *fund.*

• Each point represents a year in the ten-year interval ending January 1,

1963. The small points represent the five years in the latter half of the ten-year interval; the large points, the years in the former half.

Exhibit I. Characteristic Lines

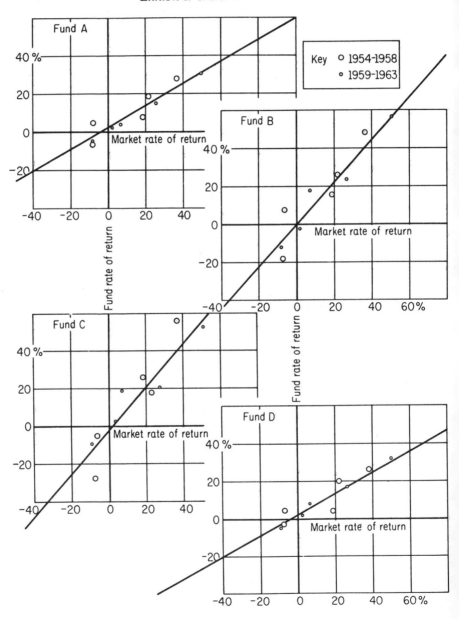

Although the funds exhibited wide swings in rate of return over the ten-year interval, the rate of return in each year fell into a straight-line pattern which remained virtually fixed throughout the ten-year interval. This line—the characteristic line—can be fitted by eye or by statistical methods. The significant thing about it is that it tends to be stationary over time, despite wide fluctuations in short-term rate of return.

Information Revealed

The characteristic line contains information about both expected rate of return and risk. The slope of the line measures volatility. Thus, a steep slope means that the actual rate of return for the fund in question is relatively sensitive to fluctuations in the general stock market; a gentle slope indicates that the fund in question is relatively insensitive to market fluctuations.

The slope angle of the characteristic line obviously provides a more refined measure of a fund's volatility than the usual categories of "balanced fund," "stock fund," or "growth fund." The range of volatilities observed in actual practice is enormous. Among mutual funds, for example, I have found that volatilities range from roughly one-third to about two. A volatility of two means that a 1% increase (or decrease) in the rate of return demonstrated by the Dow-Jones Average is accompanied, on the average, by a 2% increase (or decrease) in the rate of return demonstrated by the particular fund in question.

For any individual investor who is risk-averse, the observed differences in volatility are surely large enough to be worth measuring. The differences also disclose important contrasts in management policy.

What Deviations Mean

As users of the characteristic-line method will discover, the plotted points in a typical chart will not all lie on the characteristic line. What this means is that not all of the risk in the fund in question is explained by fluctuations in the general market level.

As pointed out earlier, one can consider that investment risk in a diversified fund is the sum of responses to (1) general market fluctuations and (2) fluctuations peculiar to the particular securities held by the fund. If a fund is properly diversified, the latter risk, which tends to be causally unrelated one security from another, tends to average out. The former risk, being common to all common stocks in greater or lesser degree, does not tend to average out.

If the management of a fund attempts to maintain a constant degree of volatility, then the slope of the characteristic line will tend to measure that volatility. If there are excessive deviations from the characteristic line, we have a strong indication that:

• Either the fund is not efficiently diversified to minimize risk unrelated to the general market (in which case the owner or beneficiary incurs additional risk without any compensating prospects of additional return).

• Or, perhaps inadvertently or perhaps as a matter of deliberate policy, management has altered the volatility of the fund. By increasing fund volatility when it is optimistic and decreasing volatility when it is pessimistic, management can speculate for the fund beneficiaries on fluctuations in the general market.

The appropriateness of such action is an interesting question but outside the scope of this article. It is worth noting, though, that in a sample I have taken of 54 American mutual funds, 4 out of 5 demonstrate fairly clear-cut characteristic-line patterns, with correlation coefficients equal to or exceeding 90%.

Possibly this pattern indicates wide agreement that causing fund volatility to vary greatly leaves the individual owner unable to rely on a stable estimate of the risk in the portion of his personal portfolio represented by the fund in question. His ability to strike what for him is the optimal over-all portfolio balance between expected return and risk is then impaired. But if, in retrospect, fund management has speculated successfully with the volatility of a fund, it is conceivable that beneficiaries may consider the disadvantage more than offset by the improved rate of return.

Suppose the characteristic line itself shifts? This may happen when fund volatility remains constant but fund performance varies widely from year to year. A sweeping change in the personnel constituting fund management, for example, might be accompanied by a sudden shift in fund performance.

Comparing Performance

The characteristic line also contains information about management's ability to obtain a consistently higher return than the competition's. If, for example, two trust or mutual funds demonstrate precisely the same volatility, their respective characteristic lines would have the same slope, but one line would be consistently higher than the other (unless they coincide). For instance, suppose a certain fund had exactly the same slope as Fund A in Exhibit I. If its characteristic line were plotted on the chart, it would run parallel to Fund A's but higher or lower. The fund with the higher line would demonstrate consistently higher performance—in good years and bad.

Although the problem of comparing performances of fund managements is obviously not so simple when the slopes differ, the characteristic line does contain, as we shall see presently, the information necessary to make such comparisons.

Implications for Control

The characteristic line has implications for management control, too. No matter how widely the rate of return for a fund may fluctuate, management performance is unchanged so long as the actual rate of return continues to lie on the characteristic line. One can establish control limits on either side of the line; points falling within these limits are assumed to represent a continuation of past management performance, while points falling outside the limits require special scrutiny. Without the characteristic line it is virtually impossible to tell whether the rate of return demonstrated in a given year represents a real change in the quality of fund management. With it, early detection of important changes becomes possible.

In summary, therefore, the graphical method provides a simple test of:

1. The extent to which a fund has adhered, purposely or not, to a single characteristic line.

2. The degree of volatility associated with the fund.

3. The success of fund management in maintaining a high rate of return under a variety of market conditions.

PERFORMANCE MEASURE

We turn now to a second line. This one deals not with an individual fund but with a *portfolio* containing a certain fund. The purpose of the line is to relate the expected return of a portfolio containing the fund to the portfolio owner's risk preferences. This line can be called the *portfolio-possibility* line. We shall see that the slope of this line is a measure of fund performance which transcends differences in investors' attitudes toward risk.

Risk Preference

Whether the performance pattern of a given fund rates high or low should depend on whether individual investors choose it in preference to the pattern demonstrated by other funds. During the last few years we have witnessed the rapid development of a theory of rational choice among portfolios.[2] The theory is too complex to be reviewed here in detail, but certain fragments of it provide the basis for a concept of fund-management performance.

---

[2]See, for example, H. M. Markowitz, *Portfolio Selection: Efficient Diversification of Investments* (New York, John Wiley & Sons, 1959); and D. E. Farrar, *The Investment Decision Under Uncertainty* (Englewood Cliffs, Prentice-Hall, Inc., 1962).

It is interesting to note that when one talks about the historical performance pattern of a fund, he is looking at the past; but when he considers the preferences of individual investors and their choices among funds, he is talking about their appraisal of the future. We shall continue to talk about the performance of funds in terms of historical performance patterns, even though actual investor choices among funds are necessarily based on expectations regarding future performance patterns. The implication is that a good historical performance pattern is one which, if continued into the future, would cause investors to prefer it to others.

Economists sometimes study the investor's choice among possible portfolios in terms of a risk-return diagram (like that in Exhibit II):

• The vertical axis in the exhibit measures the return which the investor would expect to get, on the average, from a given portfolio. The horizontal axis is some appropriate measure of risk.

(As a technical note for those interested in detail, let me add that it is traditional to measure the respective axes in terms of *expected rate of return,* where the rate is a weighted mean of possible future outcomes, and *standard error,* where standard error is a statistical measure of potential variability around the expected performance. Under certain assumptions regarding the nature of investment uncertainty, expected return and standard error completely characterize a given portfolio. These assumptions seem to fit actual stock-market experience fairly well. When the performance pattern of a mutual fund is clustered closely around the characteristic line, the slope of this line, which is our graphical measure of risk, is statistically an excellent measure of the standard error.)

• The rate of return is for a standard time period—perhaps a month, quarter, or year—per dollar of the individual investor's initial capital.
• The curved lines in the diagram are called indifference curves for the reason that the investor is indifferent to portfolio choices lying on a particular indifference curve; that is, he would just as soon have, say 5% more return at 4½% more risk as 8% more return at 6½% more risk, and so on (see the curve at right of chart).[3]
• There is a useful analogy between the investor's relative preference, as shown by indifference curves, and relative heights, as shown by contour lines on a topographical map—that is, lines along which elevation is constant. The arrows

---

[3]For elegant mathematical proof of the validity of indifference curves, see James Tobin, "Liquidity Performance as Behavior Towards Risk," *Review of Economic Studies,* February 1958, p. 65; a subsequently written, unpublished manuscript by the author carries the discussion further.

Exhibit II. Investor's Indifference Curves

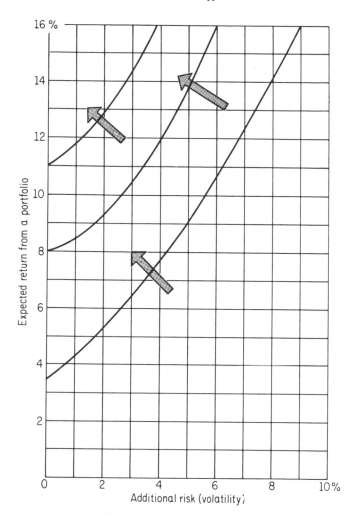

in the figure show the direction in which one moves to go from less to more desirable portfolios (or, to complete the topographical analogy, uphill).

Portfolio Choices

What kinds of portfolio choices are available to the investor? The assets he can include in his portfolio consist of two fundamentally different kinds:

• Money-fixed claims, such as checking deposits; savings deposits; government, municipal, and corporate bonds.

• Equity assets, including equity in personal business and partnerships and corporate common stocks.

The investor who holds money-fixed claims is subject to the risk of changes in both the interest rate and price level. Although both risks are real, in American financial history they have been small compared to the risk entailed in owning equities. The relative insignificance of market risk in money-fixed claims is reflected in the narrow range of net returns available in such claims. We shall simplify slightly and represent all assets of this type by a single point on the vertical axis of the risk-return diagram (Point B in Exhibit III).

If the investor wants to raise the expected rate of return of his over-all portfolio above the rate offered by money-fixed claims, he must undertake some equity risk. On the risk-return diagram in Exhibit III, the investor has available to him the opportunity to invest in shares in a particular balanced or growth fund, Fund A, as well as the opportunity to invest in money-fixed claims, B. If he is free to vary the investment in each outlet more or less continuously, then the locus of portfolio combinations available to him is the straight line—viz., the portfolio-possibility line—joining points A and B. The combination which is best for him will lie at point D along the line which is farthest "uphill" as indicated by the "contour lines" on his indifference map. The preferred combinations for other investors will differ, depending on the precise shape of their indifference curves.

Now consider a second investment, Fund C (top right of Exhibit III). The line BC is the locus of possible portfolios made available to our investor by the existence of this investment. As in the case of locus BA, there will, in general, be a single point, E, along BC, which is the farthest "uphill" for the investor.

The significant fact is that, although the location of the points of optimum balance along lines BC and BA will differ from one investor to another, the optimum point D along line BA will always be superior for a given investor to the optimum point E along line BC. For every possible level of risk an investor might choose, the return on a combined portfolio containing Fund A is greater than the return on a portfolio containing Fund C, which provides the same level of risk. This ensures that, whatever the optimum point along line BC may be for a particular investor, the point on BA directly above it (that is, with the same risk) will have a greater expected return. This will be true for every investor who is risk averse, quite independently of the precise shape of his indifference curve.

But if, for every risk-averse investor, line BA is superior to line BC, then, in terms of the portfolio possibilities this line makes available to investors, Fund A is absolutely superior to Fund C. Now it is apparent from Exhibit III that lines BA and BC differ only in slope. Line BA, which is superior to line BC, slopes upward more sharply, showing that the rate of gain from shifting the investor's portfolio in the direction of greater risk is greater for Fund A than for Fund C. *The steepness of the portfolio-possibility line associated with a given fund is thus a direct measure of the desirability of the fund to the risk-averse investor.* The

Exhibit III.   Risk-Return Diagram for an Investor

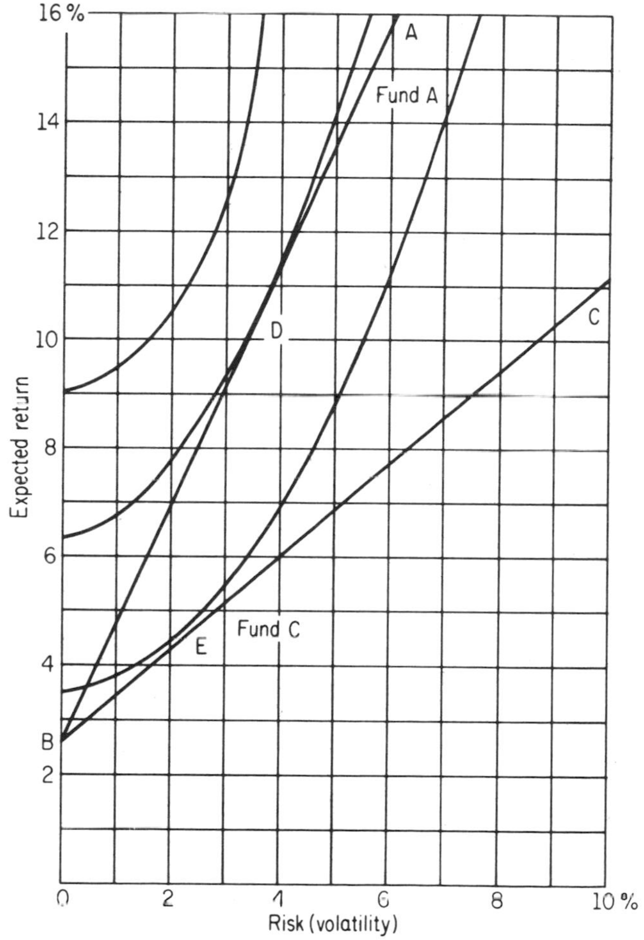

force of the preceding argument is not diminished by the fact that many investment funds contain money-fixed claims as well as equities.

Pension & Trust Funds

All very well for mutual funds, you may say. After all, the investor in mutual funds is free to adjust the fraction of his portfolio invested in each one pretty much as he pleases. But what about cases involving pension funds and trust funds, in which the individual beneficiary has no freedom whatever to alter the fraction of his total assets which are managed by the fund? To answer this question, let us take an illustration:

> Suppose a man has a certain fraction of his assets invested in a pension fund. Suppose further that the management performance of the pension fund (measured in terms of the slope of the portfolio-possibility line) ranks just equal to the performance of a certain mutual fund. A certain segment of the portfolio-possibility line for the mutual fund will be unavailable to the investor if part of his funds are irrevocably committed to the pension fund, since he is not free to convert all his assets to money-fixed claims. Within the range of the portfolio-possibility line available to him, however, he can achieve the same portfolio behavior with part of his capital committed to the pension fund as he could achieve if he were free to compose the risky portion of his portfolio entirely from the mutual fund in question. If his attitude toward portfolio risk leads him to choose a portfolio in this range, then he will be indifferent as to a choice of a pension fund or a mutual fund with an equal performance ranking. If, on the other hand, his choice lies outside this range, then the pension fund is less useful to him than a mutual fund with similarly sloped portfolio-possibility line.

Quantitative Measure

The performance demonstrated by a fund can be measured by the tangent of the slope angle, symbolized by the figure $\propto$. (For instance, the slope angle for Fund C in Exhibit III would be the difference between the slope of line BC and a horizontal line going through B; the slope angle for Fund A, which is larger, is the difference between BA and a horizontal.)

The formula for tangent $\propto$ follows directly from the geometry of Exhibit III. As detailed in the Appendix, it is:

$$\text{tangent } \propto = \frac{\mu - \mu^*}{\sigma}$$

where μ equals the expected fund rate of return at a particular market rate of return, μ^* is measured from a horizontal line through a point that would represent a fund consisting only of fixed-income securities, and σ is the symbol for volatility (which can serve as an approximate measure of investment risk as plotted on the horizontal axis of Exhibit III).

RATING MANAGEMENT

We are now ready to begin with the practical application of the concepts previously described. We will see how performance ratings can be read directly from the characteristic line.

Relative Ranking

In order to plot a fund, and the associated portfolio-possibility line, on a risk-return chart of the type discussed in the last section, one needs both an expected rate of return and an appropriate measure of risk. A measure of risk is provided by the slope of the characteristic line. The characteristic line also enables management to estimate the expected rate of return. In order to obtain a value for the expected rate of return for the fund, however, it is necessary to assume a rate-of-return value for the market. Depending on the choice of market rate of return, expected return for the fund—hence the slope of the opportunity locus—will vary. The effect of changing the assumed market rate is illustrated in Exhibits IV and V as follows:

• Exhibit IV portrays a sample of characteristic lines for 20 actual managed funds based on rate-of-return data for the years 1953 through 1962. By making specific assumptions about the market rate of return, the characteristic lines for these funds can be transformed into points on the risk-return charts shown in Parts A and B of Exhibit V. (The term "volatility" on the horizontal axes of these charts, as indicated before, refers to the amount of risk in the fund due to fluctuations in the general market.)

• Part A of Exhibit V was plotted by assuming a market return of 10%. (The characteristic line for each fund is inspected to determine its pattern of return when the market's return is 10%, and this pattern is converted to a point reflecting risk and return.) Given this assumption, the funds in question can easily be ranked visually; by drawing straight lines from Point Q to these points, one can obtain the portfolio-possibility lines for the funds in question. The problem is, of course, that the market-return assumption is arbitrary and other returns depend on it.

• Part B results when a market rate of return of 30% is assumed instead. Although the risk values for the individual funds are unchanged, the expected rates of return are affected, and a new set of portfolio-possibility lines results.

Inspection shows that the ranking of the funds is unchanged in Parts A and B of Exhibit V: For example, the highest- and lowest-ranking funds in Part A are, respectively, the highest- and lowest-ranking funds in Part B, despite the fact that the two diagrams are based on widely differing assumptions about the expected rate of return for the general market. This illustrates what is actually a quite general result: although the absolute position of funds on a risk-return

Exhibit IV. Comparison of 20 Managed Funds

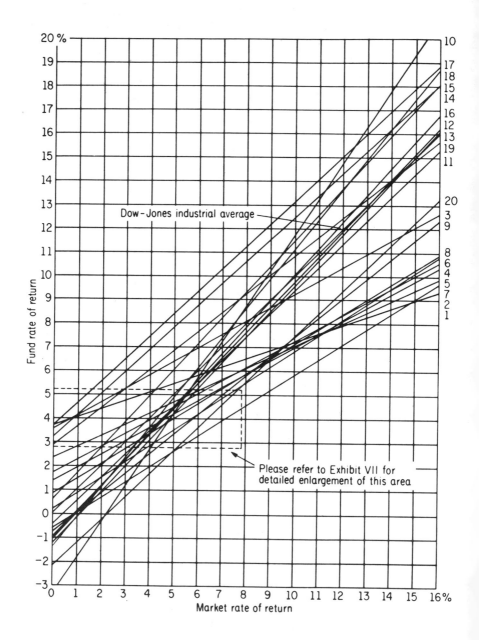

Exhibit V. Fund Rankings Under Different Market Conditions

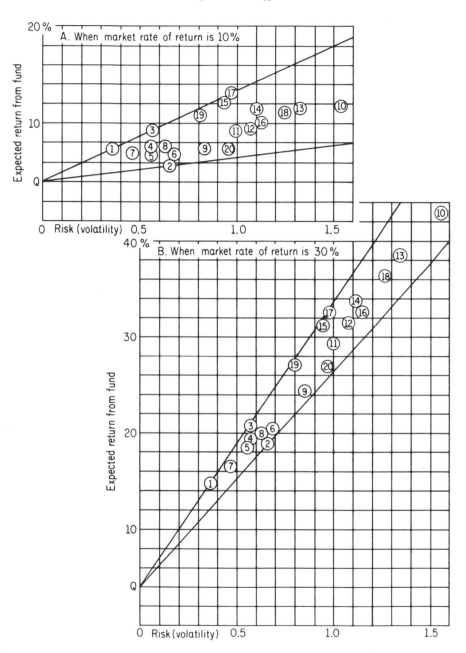

chart (and their corresponding portfolio-possibility lines) may vary with the level of market rate of return assumed, *the ranking of funds with respect to each other does not.*

Numerical Measure

What is desired, therefore, is a number which will measure the relative ranking of a fund—preferably without being affected by changes in the absolute level of rate of return of the kind illustrated by Parts A and B of Exhibit V. It happens that there is a number which has these properties: it is the level of rate of return for the general market at which the fund in question will produce the same return as that produced by a fund consisting solely of riskless investment. As Exhibit VI shows, its value can be read directly from the characteristic line:

Exhibit VI. Ranking Number of a Fund

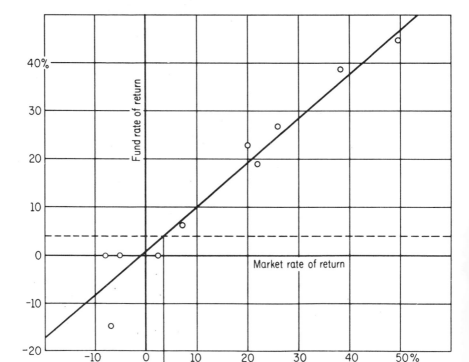

A horizontal line is drawn so as to intersect the vertical axis at a point representing the rate of return available on money-fixed claims. In Exhibit VI the horizontal line is drawn at 4%. (The choice of rate within the range of 3½% to 5% is somewhat arbitrary, but not especially critical as regards its effect on performance ratings.) The point at which the horizontal line intersects the characteristic line determines the rating of the fund, which is read off the horizontal axis as a percentage. The lower this percentage, the higher the rating of the pension, trust, or mutual fund. For those interested in a formal proof that the number just defined will have the special properties desired, the Appendix sets forth the steps in the reasoning.

In order to demonstrate the practical significance of the rating technique, let us refer back to Exhibit IV. Each of the performance ratings of the twenty funds whose characteristic lines are shown in this chart could be read directly from the figure if a horizontal line corresponding to the rate of return on a riskless portfolio (here 4%) were added. The performance rating for each fund could be determined by the value of market rate of return at which its characteristic line intersects the horizontal 4% line. Now see Exhibit VII. The characteristic lines are the same as the ones in Exhibit IV, but a 4% horizontal has been added, and the area of intersection with it has been expanded for ease in reading. Note that the performance ratings for the twenty funds (read off the horizontal axis) range from less than 1% to more than 7%.

Exhibit VII. Performance of Funds

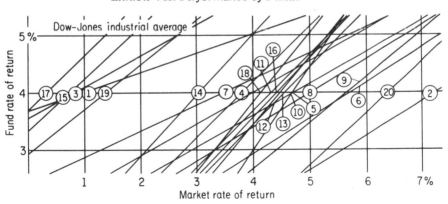

Differences Important?

Is the difference between the best and worst rated fund in Exhibit VII large enough to be significant to an investor? Let us take an illustration: Suppose that an investor specifies his portfolio volatility should be equal to one. The amount of "riskless" investment or borrowing which he undertakes will depend on the volatility of the fund. Let us say that Fund XYZ has a volatility of two. Since the desired portfolio volatility is one, then the portfolio must be blended of equal parts (in terms of dollars invested) of the fund and riskless investment. If, for example, the beneficiary's capital is initially worth $10,000, then. since a 1% reduction in the market rate of return will be accompanied on the average by a 2% reduction in the rate of return on $5,000 invested in the fund, the effective reduction in *portfolio* rate of return is 1% since:

$$\frac{0.02 \times \$5,000}{\$10,000} = 0.01$$

Now assume that the fund in question has a volatility of three-quarters. If the investor's desired portfolio volatility is one, he must invest an amount exceeding his own capital. If his capital is again $10,000, and he borrows $3,333 and invests that sum in Fund XYZ, then a 1% reduction in the market rate of return will be accompanied on the average by a 0.0075% reduction in the rate of return on $13,333 invested in the fund. The effective reduction in *portfolio* rate of return is then 1% because:

$$\frac{0.0075 \times \$13,333}{\$10,000} = 0.01$$

In both cases the portfolios have a volatility equal to one—the value specified—but the differing fund volatilities necessitate quite different investment strategies.

Is the significance of rating differences for a sample of funds influenced by market conditions? It is to a certain extent. We have already seen that one cannot employ characteristic-line data to obtain an expected rate of return for a fund without first assuming a value for the market rate of return. It is consequently not possible to make categorical statements about the spread in expected portfolio performance between the best and worst managed funds which results when an investor specifies a certain level of portfolio volatility. It is nevertheless possible to get a rough idea of the significance of the spread in performance ratings observed in a sample by making different assumptions about the market. If we take the extreme cases in the sample of twenty funds already described, for instance, we find these differences in investment return:

Expected market rate of return	10.0%	30.0%
Return of highest-ranked fund	13.6%	33.4%
Return of lowest-ranked fund	6.6%	26.6%

These figures suggest the following conclusions about differences in ratings:

(1) In the range of normal market rate of return, the difference in portfolio rate of return between funds ranked high and low is substantial.

(2) The difference seems relatively less important, the higher the performance of the general market is. Hence the consequences of rating differences for portfolio performance will be relatively more significant in a normal market than during the bull market of recent history.

CONCLUSION

In this article we have seen that there is a good way of cutting through the confusion of facts and figures in the marketplace to compare the performance of individual trust, pension, and mutual funds. The new method described is surely not a perfect answer to the needs of fund managers and investment analysts; for it requires the making of certain assumptions about fund performance with which not all men will completely agree (e.g., the desirability of a fund's holding to a consistent investment policy). But the method goes at least part of the way, I believe, to providing answers that have long eluded executives in the investment business.

We have seen that, consistent with any specified level of the market rate of return, there is associated with each fund a range of combinations of expected portfolio return and risk. The slope of the portfolio-possibility line measures the rate at which the individual investor increases the expected rate of return of his portfolio as his burden of portfolio risk increases. A comparison of slopes among funds provides a means of rating funds which transcends variations in individual investors' attitudes toward risk. Although the slopes vary just as the market rate of return varies, it can be proved that the ranking of the funds represented remains unchanged. The relative rankings can be read directly from the characteristic lines of funds to be compared.

Differences in ranking based on the characteristic lines can be quite significant for individual investors, even though they take varying attitudes toward risk. Also, the differences are independent of market fluctuations. Because the ranking measure has these properties, it provides a useful basis for reviewing the performance of fund management.

APPENDIX

Figure A shows the characteristic line for a typical fund. For each possible value of the market rate of return, the characteristic line predicts the corresponding rate of return for the fund pictures. The slope of the characteristic line is measured by tangent B; the vertical intercept is h. For the particular market rate of return D, the expected fund rate of return is μ. A horizontal line drawn a distance μ^* above the horizontal axis depicts the behavior of a fund consisting solely of fixed income securities. The ranking measure r is determined by the intersection of the characteristic line and the horizontal line at height μ^*.

The question is whether the ranking measure r has the properties specified; that is, whether it will —

... rank funds in the order of their respective values of tangent α (the slope of the opportunity locus as discussed earlier in the article);

... have the same value for a given fund, independently of fluctuations in the market rate of return.

Figure A. Characteristic Line and Value for a Typical Fund

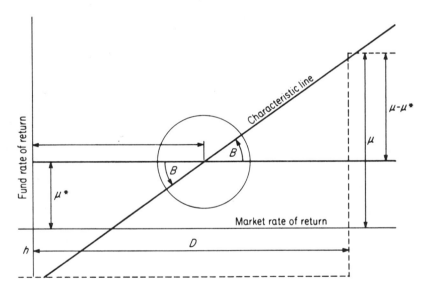

A moment's reflection shows that no number can have both properties simultaneously unless the general result alluded to in the main text holds true; that is, unless the *relative* ranking of funds—in terms of the slope of the portfolio-possibility line—is unaffected by fluctuations in the general market. Inasmuch as the proof demonstrates that the number in question does indeed have both properties, the general result follows.

From the geometry of the diagram, we have for the volatility:

$$\sigma = \frac{\mu - \mu^*}{D - r} = \text{tangent } B$$

Solving for r, we obtain:

$$r = D - \frac{\mu - \mu^*}{\sigma}$$

The expression in parentheses is the ranking measure discussed in the section on portfolio-possibility lines (see "Performance Measure," p. 143), with the volatility, σ, serving as the approximate measure of investment risk. We conclude that, for any given level of market rate of return D, r is uniquely related to the ranking fraction.

$$\frac{\mu - \mu^*}{\sigma} \quad \text{(which equals tangent } \alpha\text{)}$$

We note that a relatively large value of r signifies a relatively low level of performance for fund management. A second important property of r is obtained when the following relationship, based on the geometry of the diagram, is substituted in the previous expression for r:

$$\mu = D\alpha + h = D \text{ tangent } B + h$$

Substituting for μ, we find that:

$$r = \frac{\mu^* - h}{\sigma}$$

Now μ^* is the same for all funds and independent of market fluctuations; and h and σ are the intercept and slope, respectively, of the characteristic line. It is clear in this formulation that r is independent of D, the market rate of return. Hence r tends to have the same value independently of fluctuations in the general market.

You pays your money and you takes your choice.

–Punch, Vol. X, p. 16. 1846

16

CAN MUTUAL FUNDS OUTGUESS THE MARKET?*

JACK L. TREYNOR and KAY K. MAZUY are
associated with Arthur D. Little, Inc.

Are mutual fund managers successfully anticipating major turns in the stock market? There is a widely held belief that they are. Whether investment managers themselves actually share this belief is hard to say. At one time or another in promoting their services, however, a number of mutual funds have used the claim that they can anticipate major stock market movements.

We have devised a statistical test of mutual funds' historical success in anticipating major turns in the stock market. Applying this test to the performance record of 57 open-end mutual funds (as reported in this article), we find no evidence to support the belief that mutual fund managers can outguess the market.

DEBATED RESPONSIBILITIES

The question we have studied has an important bearing on the responsibilities which investment managers can properly be asked to assume. For instance, today almost everyone agrees that the market was dangerously high in early 1929 and that stocks were a bargain in the 1950's. On hindsight, laymen are tempted to think that these extremes should have been "obvious" to fund managers at the time, and that they should have sold or bought common stocks accordingly. In actuality, of course, fund managers did *not* always sell in 1929 and buy in the 1950's.

What position should the fund manager take to protect himself against

*From *Harvard Business Review,* Vol. 44, No. 4 (July-August 1966), pp. 131-36. Reprinted by permission.

accusations that he should have anticipated market movements in this way? More broadly, what does the shareholder have a right to expect from the fund manager? Is the fund manager speculating if he attempts to anticipate major market movements? Or is he negligent if he fails to try? It seems to us that the answers to these questions depend in part on whether or not investment managers actually have the *ability* to anticipate major turns in the stock market.

Because a mutual fund's performance in each succeeding year is readily measured, widely published, and easily compared with that of other mutual funds, managers in this industry are perhaps particularly sensitive to the effect on their funds' performance of a market decline or market rise during the year. We believe that our findings may have significance not only for mutual fund managers, but also for pension, trust, and endowment fund managers—despite the fact that their objectives vary widely. If it is generally true that investment managers cannot outguess the market, then it may be necessary to revise certain conceptions about the responsibilities of investment management across the board.

ANALYTICAL APPROACH

It is well known that there is a definite tendency for the prices of most common stocks to move up and down together. Because this tendency exists, it is meaningful to talk about fluctuations in the "market." It is also well known that some common stocks are more volatile (i.e., sensitive to market fluctuations) than others.

Thus, when we talk about investment managers outguessing the market, we mean anticipating whether the general stock market is going to rise or fall and adjusting the composition of their portfolios accordingly. That is, if they think the market is going to fall, they shift the composition of the portfolios they manage from more to less volatile securities (including bonds). If they think the market is going to rise, they shift in the opposite direction. The result of such shifts is a change in effective *portfolio* volatility. (A simple graphical measure of portfolio volatility was developed by one of the authors in a previous HBR article,[1] and is reviewed in some detail later in this article.)

In order to test whether or not a mutual fund manager has actually outguessed the market, we ask, in effect: *Is there evidence that the volatility of the fund was higher in years when the market did well than in years when the market did badly?* This is the question that was applied to the 57 funds we studied. Of course, we did not know that *all* of them were trying to outguess the market, but that does not matter. Unquestionably, some of them were trying to do this and thought they had the ability.

---

[1] Jack L. Treynor, "How to Rate Management of Investment Funds," HBR January-February 1965, p. 63.

Performance Data Used

Data for the mutual funds in our sample were obtained from *Investment Companies* 1963, by Arthur Wiesenberger Company.[2] For open-end investment companies, Wiesenberger employs the following formula to compute rate of return: "To asset value per share at the end of the period, adjusted to reflect reinvestment of all capital gains distributions, add dividends per share paid during the period from investment income, similarly adjusted; divide the total by the starting per share asset value."[3]

The resulting rate-of-return figure is only approximate, since it disregards subtleties relating to (1) the timing within the period of dividend distributions and (2) the relative after-tax value to the shareholder of market appreciation, on the one hand, and of dividend-interest income, on the other. We feel, however, that the measure is probably adequate for our purpose, even though these effects are disregarded.

The Characteristic Line

If, year by year, the rate of return for a managed fund is plotted against the rate of return, similarly defined, for a suitable market average—such as the Dow-Jones Industrial Average or the Standard & Poor's 500-Stock Index—the result is the kind of patterns shown in Exhibit I. A line fitting the pattern is called the characteristic line. If the line has the same slope for years in which the market goes up as for years in which the market goes down, the slope of the line is constant; the line is straight. When this is so, a single number—the tangent of the slope angle of the line—is sufficient to characterize the sensitivity of the fund in question to market fluctuations, and we can talk meaningfully about "the" volatility of the line.

The fund shown in Part A of Exhibit I has kept a constant volatility over the years included in the sample. For such funds, the degree of scatter around the characteristic line is a measure of how well diversified the fund is. The more nearly perfect the diversification of the fund, the less scatter around the characteristic line, because the more accurately the fund reflects the stocks in the market average.

Outguessing the Market

What happens, however, if a fund management tries continually to outguess the

---

[2] Port Washington, New York, Kennikat Press, Inc., 1963.
[3] *Ibid.*, p. 99.

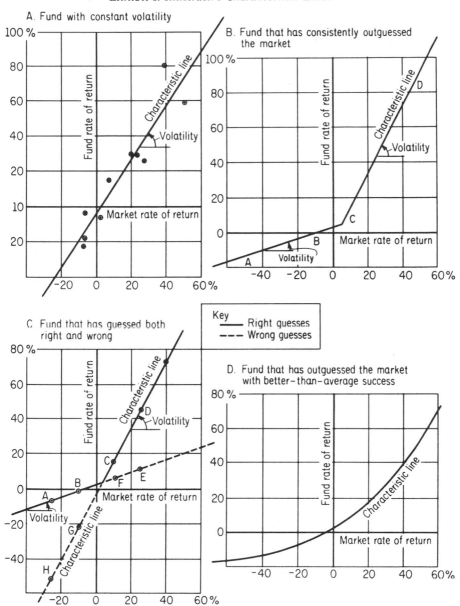

Exhibit I. Illustrative Characteristic Lines

market by oscillating between two characteristic lines, one of which has a high volatility and the other, a low volatility?

Part B of Exhibit I illustrates the extreme case in which management is able to outguess the market at every turn. Whenever management has elected the highly volatile composition demonstrated by characteristic line C-D, the market has risen; whenever management has elected the low-volatility line A-B, the market has fallen. It is clear in this case that the characteristic line is no longer straight.

If, on the other hand, fund management guesses wrong as often as it guesses right, then we have the kind of picture shown as Part C of Exhibit I. Here the fund's performance traces out the undesirable points H, G, F, and E as frequently as it traces out the desirable points A, B, C, and D. The result is considerable scatter in the characteristic-line pattern, *but no curvature.*

Probably no fund management would claim to be able to anticipate the market perfectly. Let us assume, however, that management has some prediction powers. Then, the better the market performs, the more likely management is to have anticipated good performance and to have increased fund volatility appropriately; and the larger, on the average, the chosen volatility is likely to be. The result will be a gradual transition of fund volatility from a flat slope at the extreme left of the characteristic-line diagram to a steep slope at the extreme right, with the slope varying more or less continuously in between, producing a smoothly curved characteristic line pattern with a certain amount of scatter resulting from management's bad predictions (see Part D of Exhibit I) rather than the kinked pattern associated with the policy illustrated in Exhibit I-B.

The key to our test for successful anticipation is simple: the only way in which fund management can translate ability to outguess the market into a benefit to the shareholder is to vary the fund volatility systematically in such a fashion that the resulting characteristic line is concave upward, as in Exhibit I-D. If fund management has correctly anticipated the market more often than not, then the characteristic line will no longer be straight. (And we can add, for the more mathematically inclined reader, that whether the characteristic line is smoothly curved or kinked, a least-squares statistical fit of a characteristic line to the performance data for the fund will be improved by inclusion of a quadratic term in the fitting formula.)

Choice of Funds

If the management of a balanced fund elects to change the fund's volatility, it can shift the relative proportions of debt and equity, or change the average volatility of the equity portion, or both. However, stock funds and growth funds, which are commonly considered to consist primarily of equity securities, are obviously not free to alter their volatilites by shifting the relative proportions of debt and equity (although they can alter the average volatility of the common stocks held). For this reason, it is sometimes argued that a balanced fund is more likely to make frequent changes in fund volatility. To allow for this possibility, we divided our sample in roughly equal proportions between balanced and growth funds.

In addition, it is sometimes argued that smaller funds will have less difficulty in changing their portfolio composition quickly when a change in volatility is desired. To account for this, we included in our sample of 57 mutual funds a wide range of fund sizes. Exhibit II shows the distribution of our sample among fund sizes and between balanced funds and growth funds.

Exhibit II. Breakdown of Sample By Size and Type of Fund

Market Value of Assets	Number of Funds		
	Growth	Balanced	Total
Less than $20	7	10	17
$20–$99	7	13	20
$100–$500	10	7	17
More than $7,500	1	2	3
Total	25	32	57

*In millions of dollars as of December 31, 1962.

Time Period Studied

The period covered in the study includes the ten years beginning in 1953 and ending in 1962. One may ask if our findings would have been different if another time period had been selected for study. We do not think so. Subject to the various sources of random scatter in characteristic-line patterns discussed previously, the characteristic-line pattern remains invariant over time, regardless of the behavior of the market, unless and until basic management policies or abilities change. (In fact, management policies and abilities are probably drifting slowly as individual men in the management team mature and as the composition of the management team changes, but these effects are usually small, compared to the effects on the year-to-year rate of return caused by market fluctuations.)

As mentioned earlier, if management is right more often than wrong in its attempts to outguess the market, the characteristic-line pattern will be curved. The degree of curvature depends on how heavily management bets on its expectations—that is, the degree to which management changes fund volatility when its expectations regarding the market change. So long as management policy continues roughly constant in this regard, the degree of curvature manifested in the characteristic line will remain unchanged.

The only criterion for the time period selected for a curvature study is that during the period the market should have exhibited wide and frequent swings both upward and downward, so that the characteristic-line data are not confined to a segment in the middle of the pattern which, because of its shortness, is indistinguishable from a straight line.

The period 1953-62 contains one year in which the Dow-Jones Industrials demonstrated a rate of return of 50%, and three years in which the return was negative by substantial amounts. We feel that this is a suitable period for our study because it is long enough to cover a variety of ups and down in the general market, short enough to avoid serious problems resulting from the gradual drift of fund policies over time, and recent enough to reflect modern mututal fund management practices and policies. The fact that the market was generally rising throughout the period has no effect on the characteristic line, and hence in no way invalidates our findings.

We have used yearly data because we feel that even the smaller mutual funds would be reluctant to make the changes in portfolio composition necessary to change fund volatility much more often than once a year. Based as it is on yearly data, however, the study cannot detect any success that fund managements may have had with more frequent changes in volatility.

FINDINGS

What does the study show? It shows no statistical evidence that the investment managers of any of the 57 funds have successfully outguessed the market. More precisely, we find no evidence of curvature of the characteristic lines of any of the funds.

Here are some of the more technical aspects of our study:

• In order to test for the presence of curvature, we used the methods mentioned earlier. (A least-squares regression technique was employed to fit characteristic-line data for the 57 open-end mutual funds in our sample. That is, for each of the funds we calculated the constants for the equation which "best" describes the performance data of the mutual fund for the Standard & Poor's Composite Price Index as a quadratic function of the performance.)

• Exhibit III summarizes our results. The value of the F statistic, plotted along the horizontal axis, is a measure of the degree of curvature of the fund (and is normalized to allow for variations in the amount of random scatter observed). The vertical axis shows the number of funds which had F values equal to the F value given on the horizontal axis. As the magnitude of an F value increases, the higher the probability that the amount of curvature seen for the fund is real, i.e., is greater than we would expect by random chance. The vertical dotted line marks the F value (5.6) corresponding to the amount of apparent curvature which even those funds that have no real curvature would display one time in twenty. A fund should show an F value greater than 5.6 in order to be considered to have real curvature.

Exhibit III. Distribution of Funds According to F Value

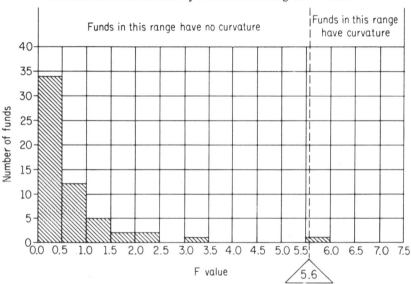

In our sample of 57 managed funds, only one displayed even an F value of 5.6. This fund's curve and also the actual data points are given in Exhibit IV.

In other words, our findings show that for the mutual funds in our sample, at least, it is safe to assume that their characteristic lines are straight. Actual funds tend to resemble the fund in Exhibit I-A rather than the funds in Exhibits I-B and I-D. Our results suggest that an investor in mutual funds is completely dependent on fluctuations in the general market. This is not to say that a skillful fund management cannot provide the investor with a rate of return that is higher in both bad times and good than the return provided by the market averages, but it does suggest that the improvement in rate of return will be due to the fund manager's ability to identify underpriced industries and companies, rather than to any ability to outguess turns in the level of the market as a whole.

The fact that only one of the 57 mutual funds in our sample has a

*Exhibit IV. Characteristic Line
of the Fund Which Has the Greatest* F *Value*

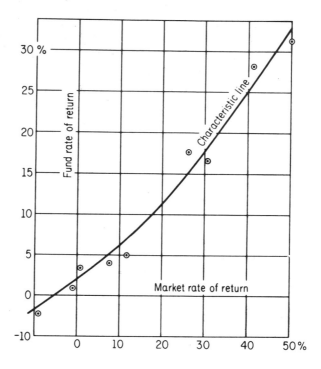

characteristic line suggesting curvature indicates that perhaps no investor—professional or amateur—can outguess the market. This finding has clear significance for the man in the street managing his own portfolio, for the man with fiduciary responsibility for a private estate, for the president of a manufacturing company responsible for its pension fund, and for a college treasurer managing an endowment. It means that probably the best assumption they can make is that investment managers have no ability to outguess the market and should not try to. It also means they should not hold fund managers responsible for failing to foresee changes in market climate.

> Profits on the exchange are the treasures of goblins. At one time they may be carbuncle stones, then coals, then diamonds, then flint-stones, then morning dew, then tears.

> > —*Joseph de la Vega,*
> > *Confusion de Confusiones* (1688)

17
RELATIVE PERFORMANCE — NONSENSE*

ALBERT YOUNG BINGHAM, C.F.A., is senior financial vice president of the Chicago Title and Trust Company in Chicago. He was one of the founders of the Financial Analysts Federation, and is a past president of The Investment Analysts Society of Chicago.

After years of effort financial analysts have managed to raise themselves to the status of a profession. Fine. But of what type? Are we to be judged as doctors, lawyers, accountants, scientists on the one hand—or as baseball and hockey players? Learned or commercial?

Who asks the surgeon what percentage of his operations have been successful? No one. The more able the surgeon, the more difficult the operations he is apt to perform. In medical meetings, where fellow surgeons review results with care, the questions asked are: "Were the right procedures used?" "Did he use good judgment?" Is Haskins & Sells a better firm than Arthur Andersen? Both use the best methods obtainable and the accounting journals do not compare batting averages. Why was Einstein a great scientist? Not because of any score card, but because he immensely advanced knowledge. A professional man's prestige is usually based upon the judgment of his peers and his contribution to the advancement of the art.

Article after article appears in the *Financial Analysts Journal* on how best to judge comparative performances of financial analysts or portfolios. Elaborate statistical techniques are employed, but the fact remains that the valuation is concerned with a unique period—the longest stock market rise and the longest bond market slide in history. Typical of long-term investor significance? Nonsense!

Started by the mutual funds, followed by the pension trusts, and spreading fast to the trust companies, we are rapidly developing a "performance kick" that has probably never had an equal. If the statistical exercise were harmless—so much for that—but it is likely to have a severe penalty.

*From *Financial Analysts Journal,* Vol. 22, No. 4 (July-August 1966), pp. 101-4. Reprinted by permission.

Possibly more important than these factors, however, is the modern fetish among mutual funds on "growth." It is no longer enough, that is, that a mutual fund can show prospective shareholders a respectable, long-range growth record that equals—or betters—the Industrial Average over the past 10 or 15 years. It is now considered necessary that the fund be able to advertise a rate of growth that is *dramatically* better than the Average on a relatively short-term basis. What this means is that the competitive scramble among some of the mutuals is leading them into highly speculative ventures of a short-term nature simply for the purpose of being able to show dramatic short-term gains as a means of attracting new shareholders. . . . .Last year the turn-over rate on the Big Board moved up only to 16% while the turn-over rate for the mutuals jumped to 19%. There is even valid reason for believing that a large measure of the erraticism of the market in recent weeks has been traceable to the mutual funds, themselves, in trying to "play the market" in the traditional style of the fast-buck, individual speculator. In a recent study of the situation, in fact, some of the newer, flashier, funds are admitting to such practices as using computers for harboring short-term swings, buying on credit, and even engaging in short-selling. One growth fund turned over a whopping 31% of its assets in the final quarter of 1965.—Schaefer's "The Dow Theory Trader."

In the middle 1920's Edgar Lawrence Smith published a small book, "Common Stocks as Long Term Investments." It was widely read and added considerable fuel to the then great bull market. To this day, it has been badly misquoted. It is universally believed that he maintained that common stocks are always better investments than bonds—over the long term. It is always forgotten that he qualified the thesis: *If* yields on stocks were notably better than bond yields. Quite a caveat.

Today, we have studies such as those by the University of Chicago which are probably as misinterpreted and doing as much damage. Critical studies have already appeared in this *Journal*. For the purpose of this article, suffice it to say that the *investor* does not put as much money in a stock at 3/8 as he does in another at 200. Further there is a fundamental fallacy in judging results purely by *percentage* of rise or fall. More of that later.

A true investment yardstick probably should use a completed cycle, but the difficulty is that such a period tends to recur infrequently; but does that justify the ending date being the highest in history to that point?

The worst cut of all—"figures prove"—the professional investor, mutual funds, or what have you, does not do as well as random selection. And why should they? Any professional investor who loaded his portfolio with the type of stock produced by random selection, wouldn't have his job long enough to have the record evaluated. And properly so. His duty is to recognize risk as well as return.

Behind the ever more elaborate formulae for measuring rate of return—and they will become more elaborate as computers become more used—there is one vital problem: How much risk was incurred? By hindsight, it makes no difference. More important, it is impossible to quantify. But that vital part in the equation exists and there is no point sweeping it under the rug.

In the March-April issue of this *Journal* is an article, "Risk and Performance" by Frank E. Block, C.F.A. This should be required reading for anyone who endeavors to set up standards for analyst or portfolio performance. I agree with almost all he says, even though he has stolen some of my best thunder. A particularly fine section is entitled, "What is risk?" He states, and I wholeheartedly agree: "We regret that we are unable to present an acceptable definition of risk."

Later in the same article, Mr. Block seems at times to substitute volatility for risk, although he does say: "There is no certainty tnat volatility . . . should be considered as being the same as risk. Volatility is a characteristic of a security or a groups of securities, *at a given time*."

Volatility is measured by percentage. So back we come to the attempted measure of performance which is usually if not always by "per cent." "Percentage" is perhaps the worst trap in which we analysts fall. To put it one way, in the early thirties I made some quite substantial gains—measured in "per cent" of my meager funds. But I never found a store where I could buy with "per cents" instead of dollars.

In the early thirties, Frederick R. Macaulay suggested that stock prices tend to fluctuate equal increments on their square roots. This is a rather complicated way of saying that in a given stock market move, stocks do not rise or fall an equal number of points or by an equal percentage. Obviously, if the general market doubles, a nine dollar issue is not going to advance as many points as a hundred dollar issue. Nor will the $100 stock rise as large a per cent as the $9 stock. What Macaulay said is that in a given rise the $100 stock,   10, [i.e., $\sqrt{100} = 10$] goes up an increment of 2 or 12^2, or $144; the $9 stock, $\sqrt{9} + 2$ will rise to [5^2, or] $25.

To judge performance by percentage is to use a rubber yardstick. It is part of the reason random selection turns out so well. In any substantial upward move a group of low priced stocks—regardless of merit—will outperform higher priced but better companies.

Or take the widespread believers in the formulae for the present worth of the future stream of earnings or dividends discounted at $X\%$. A mighty thin reed. Anyone with a large number of corporate files at his command should take the time to look through the analyses of Brunswick, S. & L.'s, etc., even *after* the collapse was well under way. Continued prosperity was still universally to be expected. Reliably predictable corporate earnings are rare indeed. This applies to a very short range, let alone the twenty or thirty years the formulae encompass.

About 1933, Robert Rhea advanced the thesis that trends in individual stocks, as in the market itself, tend to perpetuate themselves for a long period. In effect, he said that if in a low market, one bought five stocks that were acting better than the market, four of the five would continue to do so. And so was born the concept of "relative action"—too popular today. A perfectly sound

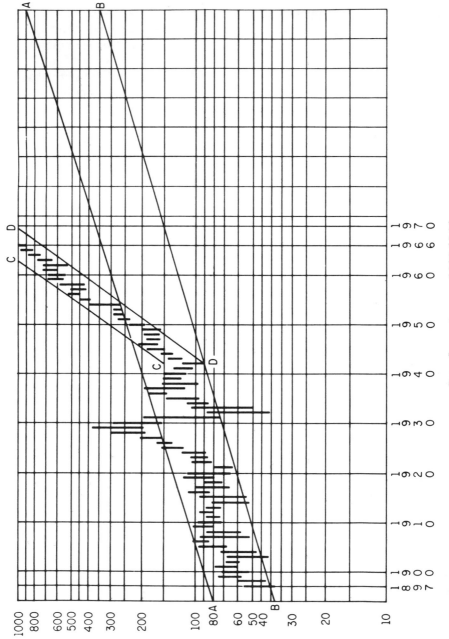

Dow-Jones Average 1897-1966

thesis when applied by the few, but very dangerous or self-defeating when widely popularized.

Today, followed by mutual funds, pension funds, etc., it means we are all in the same place at the same time. It writes "finis" to the idea of stabilization by the big funds. If evidence is needed, consult the action of the mutual funds in 1954 in the tobacco stocks as revealed by the Fulbright Committee, or even the very recent action of the funds after the threatened investigation of A. T. & T. by the FCC cushion. The more the large funds are made to be performance-conscious, the less of a cushion they become.

Later, in 1937, Alfred Cowles and Herbert E. Jones published an important article in *Econometrica*. They were accomplished econometricians. They showed that forecasts of the stock market were right just about 50% of the time. So true, but it misses the point. The investor or the speculator is not and cannot, *unfortunately* for him, be engaged in a gambling operation. If you or I match pennies or play roulette over a sufficiently long period, the law of probability says we will come out even—forgetting the house percentage. No such law of probability comes to the aid of the investor or the speculator. When it comes to matters of judgment, and that is crucial to investing, there is no law that says the investor can't be wrong 100 or 1,000 times in a row—or right, for that matter. In any case, I'll be happy with a 50% ratio—short losses and long profits—50/50. Croesus couldn't ask for better.

But have we not heard it said, at least daily. "the long-term trend of stock prices is upward"? And so it is, and has been, and hopefully will be. However, it has not been so ordained by the Deity. More likely, it is a combination of secular growth in the economy and the compounding of retained earnings in an expanding economy.

Just what is the long-term uptrend in stock prices? By linking such stock price averages as we have, we can compile a long-term picture going back for one hundred years. The farther back, the less accurate, but there appears to be little change in trend. This picture of a century, in the chart on the preceeding page, seems long enough.

The long channel A-B has been the long upward trend in prices—about 3% per year. This is roughly in accord with what we know of the growth in the economy.

Anyone who chooses to believe that C-D is the long-term trend is entitled to his belief, however expensive it may turn out to be.

Let's return to the present "performance kick." A very large, but unmeasurable part of the investing fraternity does not even *want* the greatest short-term or possibly long-term appreciation. As examples, I'll take a few cases from funds under the supervision of my own institution, simply because these are the cases I know best.

In our own corporate protfolio, we have for years had a substantial investment in bank stocks. These were not bought for maximum appreciation, but because we could, in effect, buy bond income, but with the 85% exclusion from tax. As a matter of fact, the entire corporate portfolio is invested with income as a first consideration, although capital gains have been a most welcome addition. However, it is only through income and rising income that we can pay such handy things as dividends and salaries.

This is even more the situation in the majority of our Trust accounts. Almost always the income beneficiary takes precedence over the remaindermen. In your own case would you want it otherwise?

This is even more true in the usual Common Trust Fund. Typically, the usual account must be around $50,000. In many, if not most of these accounts, the income is important to live on. Is such a fund any place for a Polaroid or a Xerox?

CONCLUSION

I have tried to show:

1. In almost all measurements of investment results—the factor of risk is not adequately recognized.

2. Percentage measurements are a rubber yardstick.

3. By no means do all accounts desire maximum performance—even if they don't realize it.

4. To the extent that we as analysts strive for maximum appreciation, over the short-term in particular, we are asking for future trouble.

18
THE S.E.C. SPECIAL STUDY AND THE   EXCHANGE MARKETS*

DAVID K. EITEMAN is part of the Graduate School of Business Administration, University of California at Los Angeles.

Publication of *The Report of Special Study of Securities Markets of the Securities and Exchange Commission*[1] in the Summer of 1963 was both a

---

*From *Journal of Finance,* Vol. XXI, No. 2 (May 1966), pp. 311-23. Reprinted by permission.

[1]88th Congress, 1st Session, House Document No. 95, Parts 1 through 5, released between April 3, 1963, and September 17, 1963. The Report is commonly referred to as the *Special Study.*

statement of confidence in the basic structure of the securities markets of this country and a well documented analysis of such weaknesses as remained within the system. Since publication of the *Study,* many changes have been made in operational procedures within the securities markets. It is the purpose of this paper to review those changes which have affected the operations of members of the New York Stock Exchange. Particular attention is given to new procedures for floor trading, specialist activities, and odd-lot operations.

FLOOR TRADING

The Special Study [2]

A "floor trade" is a transaction initiated on the floor of the Exchange by a member for his own account or for an account in which he or his member organization has an interest. Certain such transactions carried out by specialists or odd-lot dealers in their official capacities are excluded from the definition of a floor trade. "Floor traders" was a designation applied to certain members of the New York Stock Exchange whose primary activity was floor trading. Thus a floor trader was a member who bought and sold for his own account, taking profits where he could find them and running the risk that the market might suddenly turn against him.

The *Special Study* pointed out that floor traders were the only type of exchange member not assigned and in no way responsible for the execution of public orders. Rather their presence on the floor was motivated only by a personal desire to trade profitably for their own account—a motivation, it was nevertheless conceded, that was in the best tradition of the free enterprise system.

Criticism of floor trading did not originate with the *Special Study.* Indeed, floor trading had been attacked many times previously, usually as a vestige of a bygone era when the Exchange conceived of itself as a private club operating for the benefit of its members rather than as a public market serving the well-being of the nation as a whole.[3]

The *Special Study* raised two major objections to floor trading. Its first objection was the floor traders possess an unwarranted competitive advantage over the investing public. By virtue of their physical presence on the floor, floor traders avoid paying even a minimal floor commission and are in addition so

---

[2] Floor trading is treated in Part 2, pp. 203-42 of the *Special Study.*

[3] Among the previous studies of floor trading are: S.E.C., "Report on the Feasibility and Advisability of the Complete Segregation of the Functions of Dealers and Brokers" (1936); S.E.C., "Report to the Commission by the Trading and Exchange Division on Floor Trading," January 15, 1945; and Cole, Hoisington & Co., "Report to the New York Stock Exchange on Floor Trading" (May 3, 1945).

situated as to observe and act upon market developments faster than the investing public.

The *Special Study* estimated that a floor trader could make a profit buying 100 shares of a $25 stock to resell later the same day if the stock rose by as much as 8 cents a share. Members trading from off the floor, and thus paying a floor brokerage fee would need a price rise of 15 cents to break even, and the public at large would need a price rise of 68 cents to break even.[4] Because of this cost advantage, the *Special Study* argued, floor traders could trade on smaller fluctuations in price than could the general public.

The *Special Study* further argued that a floor trader's location on the floor of the exchange provided a "feel for the market" not available to the general trading public and that this "feel" constituted an unwarranted competitive advantage. Changes in market activity could be observed moments before they appeared on the ticker tape, and the floor trader could react with split-second speed. His intuitive reaction to sudden developments was further sharpened by his ability to listen to the observations and opinions of other members on the floor and by his ability to become familiar with the trading techniques of particular specialists or brokers.

The second main objection raised by the *Special Study* was that floor trading was inimical to the orderly function of the market as a whole because it accentuated price fluctuations both for the market as a whole and for individual securities; i.e., floor trading was alleged to be a significant destabilizing factor within the stock market. The *Special Study* reviewed numerous past studies of stock price movements and conducted additional analyses of its own. It concluded that floor traders tend to trade with the price trend in the market as a whole, especially when the market is moving in a pronounced direction. Other tests showed that floor traders followed the trend of price movements to an even greater degree in individual stocks. The *Special Study* also found that floor traders concentrated the bulk of their share volume at any one time in a relatively small number of stocks.

Subsequent Developments—The Registered Trader

In response to the criticism of floor trading, the New York Stock Exchange engaged the management consulting firm of Cresap, McCormick and Paget to

---

[4]The S.E.C.'s cost estimates included, where applicable, brokerage fees, clearance fees, New York and Federal Transfer taxes, and the S.E.C. fee. The costs did not include a return to the floor trader on his investment in a seat on the Exchange, which in 1961 would have represented an investment worth from $147 to $225 thousand, or his investment in Exchange dues, floor privilege fees, initation fee, or other incidental costs. However, the *Special Study* estimated that on the average these additional fixed costs would amount to less than 2 cents per share. *Special Study,* Part 2, pages 208-9.

conduct a separate study of floor trading and to review the *Special Study's* findings.[5] After four and a half months of study, Cresap, McCormick and Paget submitted a report which recommended continued floor trading on the Exchange on a modified basis to preserve the constructive aspects of floor trading while eliminating the defects. Their report observed that a need exists for mobile capital ready and willing to flow toward market imbalances if this capital can be channeled in a responsible and properly controlled manner. This need, they found, is likely to increase. They found that irreparable harm could come to the auction market from failure to devise an effective means of employing the speculative risk-taking talent and capital on the floor to beneficial ends. In their report, Cresap, McCormick and Paget also took issue with the *Special Study's* criticism of floor traders concentrating on active stocks, pointing out that it was in just such stocks where imbalance of buying and selling most frequently occur. Thus it was in these cases in particular where constructive floor trading was most needed.

Cresap, McCormick and Paget suggested that a new category of member be created to replace those members referred to as floor traders. Such a new category of member would preserve speculative risk-taking and capital mobility, for the new type of member would be available to help maintain continuity and price stability by providing additional support to the specialists when the latter's particular stocks were subject to major imbalances of supply and demand.

Specific recommendations on floor trading in the Cresap, McCormick, and Paget report were as follows:

(1) Traders in the newly established category would be registered by the Exchange to deal in all stocks generally after meeting specific qualifications, including (a) familiarity with performance requirements for their classification, attested to by passing an appropriate examination, (b) expressed intent to engage in risk-taking for the objective of improving the continuity and stability of the market, (c) acceptance of an obligation to engage in only such trading practices as are consonant with a fair and orderly market, and (d) possession of a minimum amount of trading capital to ensure adequate performance of their function. Any member or member firm would be eligible to register for such a trading account by meeting the above qualifications, including the capital requirement over and above the amount of capital required for any other activities of the member. Trading accounts established under this new classification would be required to meet minimum performance standards, including a certain percentage of their trading volume being against the trend as

---

[5] Cresap, McCormick and Paget, *Study of Floor Trading,* February 1964.

measured by the Exchange's "tick test."[6] This percentage would have to be met bi-weekly.

(2) Trading accounts would be governed by a number of specific regulations, including a requirement that all purchases, whether on the bid or the offer, would be limited to prices below the previous day's high except on minus or zero-minus ticks, on transactions closing out or reducing short positions, on arbitrage transactions, and on transactions intended to correct errors. The effect of this rule would be to remove the possibility that floor trading purchases could contribute to a prolonged or significant rise in the price of the stock. Under already existing rules of the exchange, short sales at minus or zero-minus ticks are illegal.

(3) Public orders would receive preferential treatment over floor trading orders by rules denying parity based on time or price, or precedence based on size to a floor trading order over a public order.[7]

(4) Members of the Exchange who have no specifically registered to engage in floor trading would not be allowed to initiate orders or effect transactions for their own account while on the floor, except to correct transactions made in error or upon the express invitation of a floor official to assist in a difficult market situation.

Submission of the Cresap, McCormick and Paget report was followed shortly by the approval of a new class of membership to replace the former floor traders. The term, "registered trader" was applied. The registered trader classification followed the general recommendation of the Cresap, McCormick, and Paget recommendations enumerated above. In addition, registered traders

---

[6]The "tick test" measures performance in the market in terms of the relationship of a transaction to the last preceding transaction at a different price. A transaction at a price above the last price is a "plus tick," and a transaction at a price below the last price is a "minum tick." A transaction at a price equal to the preceding price but above the last *different* price is a "zero-plus tick," and a transaction at a price equal to the preceding price but below the last different price is a "zero-minus tick." A trader's activities would be regarded as stabilizing if he bought predominantly on minus or zero-minus ticks and sold predominantly on plus or zero-plus ticks. The *Specail Study* objected to this measure of stabilization on the grounds that it measured only the relationship of a price to its preceding price, rather than to the longer-term price trend. The *Special Study* also pointed out that whenever the quoted market straddles the last transaction price all purchases on the bid and all sales on the offer are by definition stabilizing. See *Special Study,* Part 2, pages 102-4 for an evaluation of the "tick test."

[7]When two or more bids are made at the same price, the bid to be made first is entitled to priority. If no bid is entitled to priority, then the rules of precedence apply. If all the bids are for amounts of stock less than the amount offered, the bid for the largest number of shares has precedence over the others and will be filled first. Bids for quantities of stock greater than the amount offered have precedence over bids for amounts of stock less than the amount offered. If several bids are made for an amount of stock greater than the amount offered, these bids are considered to be on a parity, i.e., to have equal claim, and the issue is settled by matching a coin.

were required to possess at least $250,000 minimum capital by January 1, 1965, and to maintain a stabilization performance, as measured by the "tick test," of 75 per cent, on a monthly basis. The new rules also forbid a registered trader from effecting transactions for his own account while holding an executable order. Any transaction initiated off the floor by a registered trader is regarded as an on-floor transaction if the trader has already been on the floor during that day, and registered traders are required to file daily reports of their trading activities.

The Exchange also clarified existing rules with regard to congregating in or dominating the market in a particular stock by expressly stating that no more than three registered traders could be in the trading crowd for one stock at the same time unless written permission was obtained from a floor governor.

THE SPECIALIST

The Special Study[8]

In a "continuous" market, public customers place market orders to buy or sell shares of stock with the understanding that such order will be executed immediately on reaching the floor. Public customers furthermore expect that the price at which such orders are filled will be nor more than a small variation away from the last previous transaction price. The alternative to a continuous market is for market orders to wait on reaching the floor until a counterpart order arrives—perhaps minutes later but conceivably hours or even days later. A second alternative would be to have a system under which an immediate sale could be achieved only at a substantial reduction from the last price, or under which an immediate purchase could be achieved only by paying a substantial premium.

The New York Stock Exchange provides a continuous market in which investors may expect quick execution of market orders at reasonable prices. The specialist is at the heart of the market mechanism which ensures immediate and reasonable executions when public counterpart orders are not instantaneously available. Buying and selling for his own account and risk, the specialist assumes the responsibility for quoting at all times both a bid and an offer, while at the same time limiting his transactions in support of his quoted bid and ask in so far as practicable to those reasonably necessary for the maintenance of a fair and orderly market. When buying or selling for his own account, the specialist acts as a dealer, and his profit comes from the difference between the price at which he buys and the price at which he sells.

---

[8]Specialists are treated in Part 2, pages 57-171 of the *Special Study*.

Specialists combine dealer activities with additional duties as brokers who fill orders left with them by commission brokers for execution. These orders normally arise from price limit orders which must be held for days or weeks before execution is possible. The customer expects his limit order to be filled when the stated price can be obtained, yet a commission broker could not cover the floor with an accumulation of such orders and still expect to be at the right post at the instant the limit price is first attainable. Limit orders are handed to specialists to hold and execute when the opportune moment arrives. In filling such orders the specialist assumes the position of a fiduciary subagent; his responsibility is to the customer and his remuneration comes from sharing a portion of that customer's commission.

The *Special Study* recognized that the specialist must compromise between his self-interest as a dealer and his fiduciary obligations to the customers of commission brokers. The specialist system itself constitutes a compromise between a desire for a completely free market and a market given continuity and orderliness by a professional market maker.

The *Special Study* concluded that the specialist system "appears" to be an essential mechanism for maintaining continuous auction markets and, in broad terms, appears to be serving its purpose satisfactorily. However, the *Study* did set forth a number of specific improvements in specialist practice, concept, and method which it believed should be adopted to better the market mechanism.

Subsequent Developments

Publication of the *Special Study* was followed by an evaluation of the specialist system by a special Exchange committee of specialists and then by several months of conferences and discussions with S.E.C. staff members. The announced goal of these undertakings was to modify the specialist system so as to improve the over-all liquidity, strength, and vitality of the market for the purpose of serving the public interest, improving the quality of the Exchange market, and strengthening the specialist system. The result of the various meetings, announced in September, 1964, was twofold: a new S.E.C. rule dealing with the specialist system, and a number of modifications of Exchange rules, policies and procedures as they pertain to specialist activities.

The new S.E.C. Rule 11b-1 for the first time embodied formal acknowledgement by the S.E.C. of the dual broker/dealer function of the specialist. The new rule provided for the Exchange establishing rules on capital requirements for specialists, on defining in a positive manner specialists' obligations to maintain a fair and orderly market, on restricting specialists' activities to those reasonably necessary for the maintenance of such a market, on defining the responsibilites of specialists acting as brokers, and on improving methods for the effective and systematic surveillance of the specialist system. Under this S.E.C. rule, the Exchange could alter its own rules without prior approval of the Commission, but the Commission would have 30 days within which it could initiate action intended ultimately to disapprove any Exchange rule changes. The new S.E.C. rule also provided that the S.E.C. could order the suspension or cancellation of a specialist's registration in one or more of his specialty stocks if that specialist were found to have violated any Exchange rules.

As a result of its studies and discussions with the S.E.C., the New York Stock Exchange modified existing rules, policies, and procedures in twelve areas. Four of these modifications, representing the establishment of entirely new procedures, were as follows:

(1) In establishing, increasing, liquidating, or reducing positions in specialty stocks, existing Exchange policy was made explicit by additional rules requiring that a specialist's transactions be consistent with his market-making function. The new rules limited a specialist's acquisition of more than 50 per cent of any substantial block of stock offered at the last sale price and further limited his reoffering or rebidding for the stock in the market. Additional limitations were imposed on specialists' liquidating all or substantially all of a position by selling stock at prices below the last different price, or by purchasing stock at prices above the last different price. Specialists were additionally required to avoid failing to re-enter the market, where necessary, after effecting such transactions, and to avoid failing to maintain a fair and orderly market during liquidation of their inventory.[9]

The general tenor of these changes is to put more severe restrictions on a specialist's buying or selling for his own account when such transactions might run counter to the best interest of the market as a whole. The changes were in keeping with a *Special Study* recommendation that specialist participation to maintain a fair and orderly market be stated in a more positive manner than previously so that more even standards of performance could be expected from the various specialist units.[10]

(2) The *Special Study* recommended that specialists be prohibited from granting "stops" at any price at which the specialist holds an unexecuted customer's order capable of execution.[11] The recommendation was implemented by a new rule affirming that a specialist may "stop" stock for his

---

[9] These changes were incorporated into Exchange Rule 104.10(5) and (6).
[10] *Special Study,* Part 2, Page 168, recommendation 3.
[11] *Special Study,* Part 2, Page 169, recommendation 7(c).

own account when there is no executable order on his book at the stop price, but that he may not stop stock against the book or for his own account at a price at which he holds an order capable of execution.[12] Exceptions to this rule may occur at an opening or reopening, if there is a competing order in the crowd, and under certain conditions in response to an unsolicited request from a broker that a stop be granted.

(3) At certain times a specialist will "clean up" a large block of stock by buying the remainder of the block at a price fractionally lower than the going bid. Under new rules, the specialist is now uniformly required to allocate the purchased stock to all executable buy orders in his book. The only portion of the block which need not be so allocated is those shares which would have been acquired at the current bid, either for the account of the specialist or for orders held by him.[13] A similar rule applies in the event of an order to purchase a block of stock for which the specialist supplies all or a portion.

(4) The *Special Study* recommended that explicit prohibitions be placed on specialists' servicing accounts of public customers.[14] This recommendation was adopted by the Exchange in the form of a new rule that no specialist may accept a buy or sell order for any stock, in which he is registered directly, from (a) the issuing company; (b) any officer, director, or 10% stockholder of that company; (c) any pension or profit sharing fund; or (d) any financial institution such as a bank, trust company, insurance company, or investment company.[15] In making this change the Exchange noted that it had no indication that specialists had given preferential treatment to their own public customers and that the proposed revision was designed merely to provide additional safeguard against the remote possibility of preferential treatment being given in the future.

In addition, orders given to specialists on the floor may not indicate the account of the originating customer. Exchange rules were also modified to incorporate already existing policy to the effect that it is contrary to good business practice for a specialist to "popularize" the stocks in which he specializes.

The remaining eight changes in specialists' procedures consisted of modification or codification of already existing Exchange rules and policies. These were:

(1) Capital requirements for specialists were increased so that each specialist would have the ability to carry 1,200 shares of each 100-share unit

---

12Exchange Rule 116.30.
13Exchange Rule 104.10(7) and (8).
14*Special Study*, Part 2, page 170, recommendation 7(f).
15Exchange Rule 113.

stock and 120 shares of each 10-share-unit stock,[16] and the Exchange announced its intention of reviewing specialist capital requirements periodically in the light of price levels, volume and other market conditions. The increased capital requirements were set at the minimum level recommended by the *Special Study.*[17]

(2) The Exchange reaffirmed existing policy that, in normal situations, specialists' participation in opening and reopenings should not have the effect of upsetting the public balance of supply and demand, but that nevertheless specific situations may develop when exceptions to this principle are required. This existing Exchange policy was incorporated into rules of the Exchange, along with an affirmation of the specialists' right to buy or sell stock as a dealer to minimize the disparity between supply and demand at an opening or reopening.[18] This addition to the rules followed a *Special Study* recommendation.[19]

(3) Exchange rules have long required specialists to maintain continuity in the stocks in which they specialize. Continuity has usually been interpreted to mean that the price of succeeding transactions in a changing market should vary no more than 1/8 or 1/4 point from the price of the preceding transaction. In accordance with a request of the *Special Study,*[20] the concept of market continuity was broadened to include the requirement that reasonable depth be maintained; i.e., a reasonable volume of shares should be traded at each variation in price.[21] The term "reasonable" is a subjective concept which will vary with conditions in each stock—price range, volume, etc.—and with over-all market conditions.

In conjunction with this change, the Floor Department of the Exchange distributed a circular to all specialists calling attention to Exchange policy requiring that specialists' quotations for their own accounts "bear a proper relation to preceding transactions and to anticipated succeeding transactions."

maintaining two or more trading accounts in stocks in which they are registered, the purpose of these trading accounts being to segregate purchases and sales for tax purposes. [22] The *Special Study* reported receiving testimony that on occasion specialists trade to adjust inventories kept on a LIFO basis. The Exchange's response to this recommendation was to modify its rules to state

---

[16]Exchange Rule 104.20 and 104.23.
[17]*Special Study,* Part 2, page 168, recommendation 4.
[18]Exchange Rule 104.11.
[19]*Special Study,* Part 2, page 168, recommendation 5(a).
[20]*Special Study,* Part 2, page 169, recommendation 5(c).
[21]Exchange Rule 104.10 (1), (2), and (3).
[22]*Special Study,* Part 2, page 169, recommendation 6.

that transactions made for the purpose of adjusting LIFO inventory may not be made except as part of a course of dealings reasonably necessary to assist in the maintenance of a fair and orderly market in that stock.[23] The Exchange rejected the *Special Study's* recommendation that specialists should be allowed to maintain only one trading account and went on record strongly favoring the right of specialists to maintain long-term investment accounts in addition to their short-term trading accounts because of the favorable tax considerations involved.

(5) The *Special Study* objected to Exchange practice in not printing transactions in "stopped stock" on the ticker tape when a member requested that the print be omitted.[24] The Exchange decided to retain its policy for the present, but to print all such omitted sales on the tape at the end of the day and to include their volume within the total volume reported for the day.[25] The Exchange also agreed to review this decision, with the idea of including all transactions in stopped stock on the tape at the time of transaction after the Exchange's new "900 Ticker" system becomes fully operative.

(6) Under Regulations T and U of the Board of Governors of the Federal Reserve System, a member acting as a specialist may finance his transactions on a basis mutually satisfactory to the specialist and the creditor. Exchange rules were revised to require immediate notification by telephone and subsequent confirmation in writing of any intention to terminate or change an existing financial arrangement or to issue a margin call to a specialist.[26] This change, which incorporated an existing Exchange request to specialists into a formal rule, was designed to provide the Exchange quickly with any information relevant to a specialist's ability to maintain a fair and orderly market in the stocks assigned to him. Should it appear that the specialist could not continue in business because of his inability to make satisfactory financial arrangements or to meet a margin call, the Exchange is to notify the S.E.C. The change followed a recommendation of the *Special Study*.[27]

(7) In response to *Special Study* requests for the availability of more statistical information on specialist operations,[28] the Exchange amended its rules to require that each specialist and specialist organization maintain records showing the breakdown of its income as between commission income and dealer profit and loss in each specialty stock.[29] This information would be available for

---

[23]Exchange Rule 104.12.
[24]*Special Study*, Part 2, page 169, recommendation 7(d).
[25]Exchange Rule 125A.16.
[26]Exchange Rule 104.30.
[27]*Special Study*, Part 2, page 170, recommendation 10.
[28]*Special Study*, Part 2, page 170, recommendation 11.
[29]Exchange Rule 104.50.

the confidential use of the Exchange on request. The exchange further agreed to conduct studies to determine the feasibility of using Exchange computer equipment in conjunction with surveillance of the specialist system and to explore the development of more objective standards of price continuity and market depth in assessing the quality of specialists' performance.

(8) Lastly, the Exchange codified existing policy to the effect that any substantial or continued failure by a specialist to engage in a proper course of dealings is grounds for the suspension or cancellation of that specialist's registration in any or all of his specialty stocks.[30]

ODD-LOT OPERATIONS

The Special Study [31]

The *Special Study* made two major recommendations in relation to odd-lot operations on the New York Stock Exchange. The *Study* recommended (1) that the Exchange accept the responsibility for regulating odd-lot differentials, and, as a first step, initiate a cost study of the odd-lot business; and (2) that the Exchange study the feasibility of automating odd-lot operations. As will be seen, these two recommendations are interconnected.

For many years the odd-lot differential was established by the odd-lot houses themselves in conjunction with the commission brokerage firms. The *Special Study* described negotiations between the odd-lot firms and the several regional exchanges at the time of the 1951 increase of the odd-lot differential to 1/4 point on stocks priced at $40 and above to illustrate how pressure by New York odd-lot firms could compel the various regional exchanges to raise their odd-lot differential to the same level.[32] The *Special Study* concluded that the odd-lot investor was not in a position to influence the magnitude of the differential because of a lack of price competition in the odd-lot business, and added that if odd-lot firms could reduce some of their costs which were incurred more for the benefit of the commission brokerage firms than for the odd-lot public, a reduction in the size of the differential would be justified.

The *Special Study* also reviewed a 1956 proposal by Ebasco Services, Inc., to automate odd-lot operations. In one plan suggested at that time, data-processing equipment would have been used to match odd-lot orders with reports of round-lot transactions. The computer would then execute the odd-lot

---

[30]Exchange Rule 103.
[31]Odd-lot operations are treated in the *Special Study,* Part 2, pages 171-202.
[32]*Special Study,* Part 2, pages 181-186.

order and fill out and route the necessary paper work. The essence of the proposal involved the concept that because the execution of most odd-lot orders (certain unusual types excepted) was an automatic procedure not involving human judgment, the number of associate brokers employed by the odd-lot firms could be reduced. After commenting on the 1956 Ebasco Services, Inc., report, the *Special Study* recommended that the Exchange proceed to make further studies of the feasibility of automating the execution of odd-lot orders and of the impact such automation would have on the costs of the odd-lot business.

The *Special Study* also made recommendations dealing with rules regulating the triggering of round-lot sales by odd-lot dealers, with setting up improved reporting and surveillance procedures, and with disclosure of the odd-lot differential in customers' confirmation of odd-lot transactions.

Subsequent Developments

On June 1, 1964, the New York Stock Exchange formally assumed jurisdiction over the amount of the odd-lot differential to be charged, thus in effect complying with the first recommendation of the *Special Study.*

The Exchange also employed the public-accounting firm of Price Waterhouse to conduct a cost study of the odd-lot business covering the entire year of 1964. At the present writing this study is not available to the public; however, the impact of the various factors enumerated in the recommendations are being evaluated by the Exchange and by the Securities and Exchange Commission. The odd-lot houses report they believe that progress has been made by the Exchange and by the Commission in arriving at a clearer understanding of the principles involved in the odd-lot houses' borrowing of stock and informational services. Possibly as a result of this study and possibly because the odd-lot dealers found themselves in competition with their own commission house customers, the odd-lot dealers withdrew on October 1, 1965, from the practice of arranging stock borrowings between member firms.

Subsequent to the *Special Study*, odd-lot dealers have met with Exchange officials many times to discuss problems inherent in computerized execution of odd-lot orders. In October 1965 the Exchange announced a limited test of off-floor handling and pricing of odd-lot orders to be conducted in early 1966 by Merrill Lynch, Pierce, Fenner and Smith and the major odd-lot houses. Leading up to the ability to conduct this test was the installation by Merrill Lynch of 7740 switching equipment and the advent of post round-lot sale print-out machines on the floor of the Exchange. The 7740 switching machines enable Merrill Lynch to divide odd-lot orders into post categories and to print them at any point deemed desirable. Meanwhile the Stock Exchange print-out machines record round-lot sales at the instant they are recorded at each post in a computerized reading device.

The proposed test will determine if the combined use of these two machines will enable the execution of odd-lot orders at some physical location other than on the floor.

More tests along the same line are contemplated for later in 1966 with additional commission brokerage firms participating. Only after these tests are completed will a final decision be made on automation. Full automation of the odd-lot operation will involve development of additional communication facilities between the auxiliary post and the odd-lot associate brokers for the purpose of informing the associate brokers of odd-lot orders awaiting execution and of the inventory postion of the odd-lot firm. The Exchange emphasized in its announcement that odd-lot associate brokers will continue to be required to execute round-lot offsetting transactions for the odd-lot firm.

The Exchange has moved to comply with other recommendations of the *Special Study*. Trading rules covering the execution of odd-lot orders and offsetting round-lot transactions were adopted. At certain times the odd-lot associate broker will find himself holding, say, customers' sell orders totalling more than 100 shares and at the same time wanting to sell against these orders in the round-lot market. If the associate broker's round-lot sale would automatically trigger the execution of odd-lot orders in number greater than the number of shares sold in the round-lot market, the associate broker is now required to deliver his round-lot sale order to the specialist for execution at the highest possible price. Thus the round-lot sale is made by an agency whose interest is identical with that of the odd-lot sellers.

If this new rule were not in effect, a conflict of interest situation would arise because the odd-lot firms' profit would be maximized by having the offsetting and triggering round-lot sale priced as low as possible—the odd-lot firm would then make its same differential on the first 100 shares purchased from odd-lot customers, but would make additional profit on that portion of the odd-lot sell orders acquired for existing odd-lot firm inventory. A similar rule applies on the buy side of the market.

The last recommendation of the *Special Study* requested the disclosure to odd-lot customers of the amount of the odd-lot differential paid. At present, practice is to show only the net transaction price (which includes the differential) on the customers' confirmation of transactions, plus or minus appropriate commissions and taxes.

The odd-lot firms maintain that it is a debatable question of fact as to whether or not the odd-lot customers actually bear the cost of the differential. In many cases it is possible that odd-lot market orders will be executed at prices more favorable to the odd-lot customer than would a round-lot market order submitted at the same time.[33] The matter of "disclosure" of odd-lot differentials is currently under study by the Exchange.

CONCLUSIONS

The *Special Study of the Securities Markets of the Securities and Exchange Commission* represented the culmination of the most detailed scrutiny of the American securities markets since the 1930's. Unlike many other governmental investigations of economic institutions, the *Special Study* was undertaken at a time of prosperity for both the country and for the institution under study. The decision to make the study was not preceded by major economic, financial or political scandal; and the study was made and reported with a minimum of recrimination by the parties involved. This timing was probably an excellent thing, for it permitted an invaluable analysis of the American security markets to be made in an atmosphere conducive to unrushed and thorough contemplation of the many interacting complexities in such a market.

In the broadest sense the *Special Study* reached two conclusions, One, it found no major defect in the operations of our securites markets, and two, it found room for continued improvement in a myriad of operational detail. Through the sincere and honest effort of both the Special Study staff, the Securities and Exchange Commission, and the Stock Exchange community, it has been possible in the years since 1963 to improve many aspects of the securities markets without at the same time causing a set-back to confidence in the integrity of these markets.

The importance of the creation of the new registered trader classification to replace the older floor trader grouping is primarily conceptual: the primary obligation of the registered trader to help maintain a sound public market now clearly has legal precedence over his self-interests should the two conflict, and rules have been devised and implemented to ensure the fulfillment of this obligation. The benefits which traders do impart to the auction market appear to have been preserved, while the dangers appear to have been removed.

The specialists' dual function of both broker and dealer in the heart of the price-determining mechanism has been officially recognized by a new S.E.C. rule, and many existing Exchange policies and procedures have been incorporated into the official rules of that institution. Greater surveillance of

---

[33]See Eiteman, W. J., Dice, C. A., and Eiteman, D. K., *The Stock Market.* 4th edition (N.Y.: McGraw-Hill, 1966) pages 250-53, for an example of circumstances in which odd-lot customers pay less (or receive more) per share than would have been paid or received on round-lot market orders submitted at the same time.

specialists in the light of the new rules should provide for most specialist units achieving the optimal performance attained in the past by the best units; and future market crises should not lead, as they have so often in the past, to a few specialist units being found to have acted other than in accord with the best interests of the investing public.

Implementation of *Special Study* recommendations on automation and cost cutting for odd-lot firms has moved slower than other reforms. However much effort is currently being put into research, and the investing public has every reason to expect significant changes within the next year or so.

PART **IV**
INVESTMENT ANALYSIS

INTRODUCTION TO PART IV

In the following eight essays various aspects of investment analysis are discussed from the future of financial analysis through some of the problems of security analysis and technical analysis. Whether one is viewing portfolio policy from a conservative or an aggressive viewpoint, or whether one is an individual investor or an institutional investor, the success of his efforts will in large part be determined by the effectiveness of his investment analysis. In these essays, only an introduction to various analytical problems and approaches is presented and a much more extended investigation of investment analysis is worthy of consideration; but a number of the problems an investor or an analyst must face are presented by the respective authors with the hope that these analyses may illuminate, if not reduce, the risk that every investor assumes.

In the first selection in Part IV Benjamin Graham discusses the growth in number and influence of financial analysts and the increased responsibility that accompanies such a growth. He suggests that the main problems facing the analysts are competition and the speculative element. Looking into the future, the author sees three main problems and suggests a course of action to overcome them. He concludes positively, noting that from record-keeping to computers the future should offer highly satisfactory rewards for the men and women who have the ability to make financial analysis their career.

In the second article Paul Wendt presents seven techniques for evaluating growth stocks. After a description of each technique, a calculation is made using General Motors data for illustrative purposes. The techniques are then compared and contrasted with accompanying comments by the author.

In the third essay Edward Renshaw makes a case for a statistical approach to security analysis. He reviews the past and present work that has been carried out in the field of central value or intrinsic value for individual securities and averages. The idea that security analysis can obtain the objectivity of a science is not agreeable to all members of the profession, but Renshaw suggests that statistical analysis is a step toward the scientific approach. He also notes the limitation of statistical security analysis, but concludes that statistical analysis may be a useful tool in decision-making.

In the fourth selection Douglas Hayes critically examines some of the current dimensions in the selection of securities, particularly common stocks. Specifically he looks at the role of the computer, appraising potential economic value, mathematical models, and price performance. He notes that the weight of short-run performance should be evaluated in the light of corporate performance, not the market performance of the security.

In the fifth article Robert Levy sets forth the principles underlying technical analysis, noting that technical analysis does have conceptual and theoretical foundations. He also presents a critique of the intrinsic value approach and a statement on the implications of the random walk theory.

In the sixth essay Harry Sauvain notes that in the earlier years of security analysis the concept of financial risk held more importance than interest-rate risk in relation to safety of principal with emphasis on the highest-grade securities. Sauvain examines the area of interest rates relative to grades of securities and maturities and the increased importance of interest-rate risk. He concludes that the portfolio manager is faced with a paradox in evaluating different portfolios of money-rate type securities and that he must decide whether stability of income or stability of principal is the more important in his particular circumstances.

In the seventh selection John Clendenin discusses the increased importance of inflation risk in the post World War II economy and notes that the existence of price-level variations has led to the selection of common stocks, especially "growth stocks," as high-grade investment vehicles. Clendenin examines the general economic trends that may be expected in the future and the suitability of common stocks as high-grade investments. He suggests seven tenets that must be considered in evaluating the desirability of a common stock investment program.

In the last selection Robert Mayer discusses financial risk through an analysis of internal risk in the individual firm, a fundamental concern of both the financial manager and the investment portfolio manager. He examines financial risk through its major indicators—activity, efficiency, business productivity, leverage and cost of borrowed capital. These are related to show their interrelation by reference to risk theory, the probability, expressed as a fraction not exceeding unity, that the firm will fail.

19

THE FUTURE OF
FINANCIAL ANALYSIS*

*BENJAMIN GRAHAM, author, lecturer, and
university professor, lives in Beverly Hills,
California.*

Judged by its record in the past twenty-five years, a career as a
financial analyst should have nothing to fear from the future. For thinking back,
it was a quarter of a century ago that The New York Society had only 82
members and today it totals 2,945 members—some of whom are assigned to
financial tasks in South America, Europe, and the Far East.

Moreover, there are now 29 constituent societies which comprise *The
Financial Analysts Federation.* And if we measured our expansion in dollar
terms by annual dues collected, we might well claim to be one of the leading
"growth industries" of the country.

Our growth in numbers has been accompanied by a corresponding advance
in our financial influence. Would it be an exaggeration to say that the greater
part of security transactions today are based to some degree on work done by
Financial Analysts—ranging from perhaps the tangential influence of a brokerage
house circular to full direction of portfolio changes?

With this growth of numbers and influence there should have come a
somewhat corresponding increase in responsibility. But until recently there had
been few visible signs of such a development. Now, with the foundation in 1959
of *The Institute of Chartered Financial Analysts,* and with arrangements
completed to award the CFA designation, we may celebrate a *major* milestone in
our progress towards a true professional status, accompanied by *truly*
professional obligations to the public.

This move has been made none too soon to meet a rising demand for
changes in Wall Street's ways of doing business. The recent decision of the

---

*From *Financial Analysts Journal,* Vol. 19, No. 3 (May-June 1963), pp. 65-70. Reprinted
by permission.

Securities and Exchange Commission—in the "Rockville Center case"—indicates that Financial Analysts will be held to new accountability in the areas of fraud, and possibly beyond. Putting on a prophet's mantle I might foresee a perhaps distant time whan all printed material that analyzes and/or recommends a security (and is distributed to the public) will have to appear over the signature and with the responsibility of a Chartered Financial Analyst.

For our profession I think the broader term "Financial Analyst" is preferable to "security analyst," because most senior analysts must now be prepared to go beyond the impersonal study of securities and to consider the requirements of the individual client. Examination III for the Chartered Financial Analysts designation covers "Investment Management," including the construction of porfolios suitable for various types of investors (and speculators). There is thus double function of the Financial Analyst, related in part to securities and in part to people. As portfolio adviser he prescribes for the financial health of his "patient" in much the same way as a doctor does for his physical or mental health.

It is my basic thesis—for the future as for the past—that an intelligent and well-trained Financial Analyst can do a useful job as portfolio adviser for many different kinds of people, and thus amply justify his existence. Also I claim he can do this by adhering to relatively simple principles of sound investment; e.g., a proper balance between bonds and stocks; proper diversification; selection of a representative list; discouragement of speculative operations not suited for the client's financial position or temperament—and for this he does not need to be a wizard in picking winners from the stock list or in foretelling market movements.

But regardless of my minority opinion on this point, Financial Analysts will undoubtedly continue to pursue as their chief activity the attempt to pick the stocks "most likely to succeed." And even though it is now fashionable to decry the various averages as misleading or meaningless, most will still tell you—without having their arms twisted—their opinion whether these averages are going up or down. Can we expect the Financial Analysts to do a good job in these two key areas in the future?

My views on the validity of stock-market forecasting have been unfavorable for about half a century. This may entitle me to a high mark for consistency, but it hardly qualifies me as an impartial student of the subject. Let me make only a guarded prediction here. It is more than just possible that the investigations of Wall Street's practices in the future will include a really comprehensive study of the claims and accomplishments of the leading approaches to market forecasting. (I think of something resembling the articles that appeared last year in Fortune, but more extensive in coverage).

If the Securities and Exchange Commission comes to grips with this intriguing problem the results might be quite interesting, along one of at least two divergent lines. The first would argue: (a) market analysis is an important part of security analysis; (b) Financial Analysts must be fully responsible for their work; hence (c) every published market prediction will have to be made over the name and with the responsibility of a Chartered Financial Analyst. The opposite possibility is merely that all such prognostications will be required to bear in large type the legend: "For entertainment purposes only. Do not take seriously."

Passing on to the work of the Financial Analyst as the selector of the most promising common stock, I see two major obstacles here to brilliant success for the average Analyst or for Analysts as a whole. The first grows out of competitive developments, the second from the large element of speculation that newer investment concepts have injected into common stocks of superior quality.

Analysts' Problems: Competition

Let us consider first the matter of competition—not from outside sources but from the very growth in numbers and the intensified training of those inside our profession. My basic point here is that neither the Financial Analysts as a whole nor the investment funds as a whole can expect to "beat the market," because in a significant sense they (or you) *are* the market. It should be clear that if *all* market operations were Analyst-advised then the average Analyst could not do better than the "outside public" because there would be no outside public. Thus, to beat the market he would have to beat himself—an impossible bootstrap operation. Hence the greater the over-all influence of Financial Analysts on investment and speculative decisions the less becomes the mathematical possibility of their over-all results being better than the market's.

This overlooked fact explains, I think, a phenomenon which has aroused unnecessary controversy. I refer to the much-attacked comparisons that indicated that mutual funds have not outperformed the Standard—Poor's 500-stock Composite in the past decade. The figures themselves cannot be challenged on the grounds that the funds are more conservative or less risky than the general market, for they suffered about the same average percentage decline in 1956 and again in 1962 as did the S-P 500 index. But it is a completely valid answer and defense that the funds perform a valuable service for innumerable people who could not or would not do as well as the general market. I, for one, have no doubt that the funds have amply justified their existence for many years past and will continue to do so.

Analysts' Problems: Speculative Element

I come now to the second obstacle in the way of successful stock selection by Financial Analysts—which is the increased injection of the speculative element in the valuation of high-grade issues. I spoke at some length on this subject at a Financial Analysts Federation dinner as far back as 1958, under the heading of "The New Speculation in Common Stocks." My basic point then was that in the old days most stocks were speculative because of weaknesses and risks associated with the particular concern or business, but in the new days the common stocks of strong companies were becoming increasingly speculative because their price levels were discounting future growth more and more liberally. That tendency continued unchecked from 1958 to May 1962.

This new type of speculative risk can best be illustrated by reference to the stock issue which sold in 1961 at the highest aggregate value for any industrial company—just about $17 billion—and which was undoubtedly the best regarded from the standpoint of financial strength and future prospects. The company of course is IBM, which for a number of years has carried the highest quality rating given by Standard & Poor's. Yet the stock of this truly marvelous enterprise dropped in price from 607 in 1961 to 300 at its low of 1962—a loss of over 50% and of more than $8 billion in market value *in less than six months*. That loss was proportionately about 1¾ times the decline suffered by the Standard-Poor's 500-stock index from its all-time high to its 1962 low.

This comparison brings out sharply the relatively new tendency for high quality and high risk to go together in the field of common stock. Whether we like it or not—and I for one consider it an unfortunate development—it has every appearance of being a permanent characteristic of the stock market. I am reminded here of Marcel Proust's casual reference to "love and the suffering that is inextricably connected therewith." The public's love affair with common stocks is not likely to be any more sorrow-proof. It seems to me that the larger the speculative component in the price of the typical common stock—whether derived from internal weakness or a vulnerable market multiplier—the less dependable must become the work of the Analyst in choosing one against another.

A word should be added here about technology. Most of the high-multiplier stocks have been "technological issues"—e.g., computers, photographic processes, electronics. But technological change is one of the *most speculative* elements in the valuation picture. What it gives to one company it is likely to take away, at least in part, from others, which may have been last year's technological favorites. The high multipliers can be justified only by very long-term projection of future growth and maintained earnings; but technology itself, with the rapid changes it brings about, implies the opposite of dependable long-term expectations for any of its products or processes, and even for any enterprise largely controlled by technological factors.

It is worth spending another few minutes to consider the problem of stock selection from another angle. You are all familiar with the fact that over any span of years there has been a remarkable divergence in the relative price movement of the 30 stocks in the Dow-Jones Industrial Average, as well as in almost any other representative list.

Many will say that these great variations in performance indicate clearly the opportunities for exceptional profits that are open to expert Analysts who can identify the most promising issues. The contrary implication is that Analysts as a group are incapable of evaluating the future of individual companies with reasonable accuracy; for if they were, the market prices would have discounted much more closely the actual developments in the ensuing years.

In this connection it is interesting to note the comments of a Wiesenberger Manual on its tabulation. The authors state that their figures show: (1) the wisdom, if not the necessity, of diversification in modern markets; (2) how unrealistic can be the impression created by any market "average;" (3) how "selective" have become modern markets. To my over-critical eye these remarks seem to partake of the copious confusion into which we have plunged ourselves in recent years. To begin with, the greater the wisdom and necessity for diversification, the more realistic for actual investment results become these much maligned market averages.

The fact is that, despite the wide difference in the composition of the Dow-Jones 30 and the Standard & Poor's 500, the year-by-year changes of these two indexes have been remarkably close, and these in turn have been approximated by the over-all performance of the mutual funds. Contrariwise, the quoted reference to the selective nature of modern markets seems to support Wall Street's favorite claim that good Analysts can select the best stocks, in such manner that those they advise can prosper even when the averages decline. But basically, of course, the concept of selectivity is opposed to that of wide diversification. If Financial Analysts as a whole could really be good selectors the diversification policies followed by the funds would be quite illogical.

What I have been saying undoubtedly sounds highly unflattering to the pretensions of security analysis in its cherished activity of common-stock selection. Is the case really as bad as I have made it? Well, there are at least two large grains of comfort to consider. But even these involve a paradox. The first is that the Analysts do in fact render an important service to the community in their study and evaluation of common stocks. But this service shows itself not in spectacular results achieved by their individual selections but rather in the fixing at most times and for most stocks of a price level which fairly represents their comparative values, as established by the known facts and reasonable estimates of the future. These comparative valuations may not be highly dependable when judged against subsequent developments; but they are probably the best that can be made by any process and as such are of real utility to those buying and selling stocks.

To bring this subtle point home, let us imagine for a moment that some ukase from Washington resulted in banishing Financial Analysts from the Wall Streets of America much as Plato would have banished all poets from his Republic. What would happen? Common stock prices would become much more irrational than they have been in recent years—a state of affairs a little difficult for some of us to imagine. Financial Analysts would still ply their outlawed trade in secret—meeting perhaps in dank cellars instead of in more plush surroundings to exchange their findings; a black market for their services would soon spring up, and they might even be paid more than their present munificent salaries, because their work would be illegal and attended by more serious risks than the familiar one of being wrong.

The fact that the combined work of Financial Analysts tends to bring about reasonably defensible relative prices is greatly to their credit, but generally escapes recognition and proper appreciation. Conversely—and here is the paradox—the Analysts have been able to claim credit for good over-all results for their clients over a span of many years, but this achievement must be admitted (in private) to be not so much the result of their superior abilities as of the long bull market that began in 1949. Going back much farther, these satisfactory investment results may be ascribed to an underlying tendency of common stocks for the past 80 years to yield a return of some 7½% compounded, in dividends plus price appreciation. Most of our "advisees," if you had merely kept them from doing foolish things, should have realized an excellent annual return over the years. Nor is there reason to fear for the long-term future in this regard, if we can assume that common stocks will continue to fluctuate about some price curve that tends upward.

No Tinge to Speculation

My long-held concern about the growth of the speculative element in common-stock prices leads me to consider the subject now from quite a different angle. The great and praiseworthy campaign of Wall Street in the past decade has been directed at creating "a nation of investors." But to accomplish this, Wall Street has insisted more and more on the investment character of common stocks generally and on the pleasing concept that everyone who came into the stock market is engaged in investment operations. Speculation was in no way prohibited by the SEC legislation, but it seems to have been virtually outlawed by the new semantics of Wall Street. Some of you may recall some rhetorical questions I posed in a letter to The Wall Street Journal last June apropos of their front-page headings: "Many Small Investors Bet on Further Drop; Step Up (odd-lot) Short Sales." This was about as far as one could possibly go in distorting the proper meaning of the term "investor."

In my view the financial community has followed the wrong policy—in both its own and the public's interest—in trying to eliminate the idea of speculation from our language and thinking. If common stocks and speculation must go together—now as much as in the past, in the future as much as now—it is essential that this fact be recognized clearly, taken fully into account by Analysts and others, and made adequately clear to the public. In the past, the New York Stock Exchange very sensibly contended that there was nothing wrong in speculation if carried on by people who knew what they were doing and could afford the risks involved. Furthermore, the Exchange pointed out that speculation differs inherently from gambling, because speculative risks—such as attach to common stocks—are pre-existing and must be taken by someone, whereas the typical risks of gambling are created by roulette or horse players as they place their bets.

I haven't the slightest doubt that nine people out of ten who have margin accounts with brokers are *ipso facto* speculators. My only quarrel with this picture is that they have all been encouraged to believe that they are investors, which simply isn't true. Wall Street has no reason to be afraid of the term "speculation"; it is at least as likely to attract the public as it is to repel them. What the financial community may have to fear is the politically potent complaints of a comparatively small number of persons who have taken much greater losses than they could afford, and can with some justice place the chief blame on "account executives" who had told them they were "investing in America." Nor have the Financial Analysts been without blame here, because of their own insistence on calling nearly every purchase an investment.

LOOKING INTO THE FUTURE

The point I have just tried to make is not a digression from my main theme but ties in closely with my concept of the future role and activities of Financial Analysts. In our textbook we have held consistently to the thesis that Financial Analysts cannot deal successfully enough with basically speculative situations, and that they should try to limit their activities as far as possible to commitments they may consider justified by well-established investment criteria. Recent reflection on the matter leads me to advance some modification of that view.

Financial Analysts in general will not be able to turn their backs on the pervasive speculative elements in common stocks. It will be only at infrequent bear-market levels that representative issues will be obtainable on what I should term a pure investment basis, with nothing significant paid for their speculative component. At other market levels—such as the present, for example—it will be only the exceptional common stock that can be bought on such attractive terms.

It is unrealistic to think that 8,000 or more Financial Analysts can confine their activities mainly to choosing safe bonds, to getting up more or less mechanical portfolios of leading common stocks, or even to hunting down bargain issues, of which there could not possibly be enough to go round. No, the Analyst of the future must continue his studies in depth of numerous companies; plus his endeavors to appraise management competence, technological possibilities and risks, and overall prospects; plus his comparative valuations among similar companies and against the general market level. He must then make his choices, submit his individual recommendations, and be prepared to stand or fall by his own over-all record—judged, let us hope, with a reasonable degree of leniency.

But the change I suggest, in all earnestness, is that the Analyst give full and formal recognition to the speculative factors in the common stocks he deals with. This recognition might well express itself in a studied effort to present separately for each issue analyzed the investment value—as a kind of "minimum true value" —and then the additional speculative component of value. This is not the place for me to spell out how this separation of value components should be made: it is perfectly proper for different Analysts to take different approaches to this question, which may vary widely as between more or less conservative practitioners. But each of them its proponent should be prepared to defend in some intelligible and plausible manner.

May I suggest in this connection that Analysts consider the technique of developing a single-figure comparative valuation for the issue studies, based solely on the past records—including, of course, the past rate of growth—and that this "past-record value" be used as a point of departure for the "present value" which will take all new and relevant factors into consideration. This present value should then have its investment and speculative components delimited as clearly as possible. (Incidentally, my "past-record value" may be termed the actual value of the stock if one could assume that the past factors would continue unchanged into the future).

In November 1957 the *Financial Analysts Journal* published a paper of mine entitled "Two Illustrative Approaches to Formula Valuations for Common Stocks" in which I developed a concrete method for determining the "past-record value" of a common stock, and worked it out for the 30 issues in The Dow-Jones Industrial Average. The silence that greeted this effort was deafening and disappointing. However, this same article has been reprinted in a book just published by The Institute of Chartered Financial Analysts. The book is titled "Readings in Financial Analysis and Investment Management". I have renewed hope now that other Financial Analysts will be moved to do some work along the same lines and perhaps develop one or more "single figure" formulas that may be widely adapted.

Let me illustrate what I have in mind generally by a comparison between IBM and International Harvester (which occurs next on the NYSE list.) At the end of 1961 the price of IBM was 579 against about 50 for Harvester. Both were sound and important companies, but IBM was undoubtedly the better enterprise. Did this make IBM both a more promising and a safer purchase than the other? Here was what might be called the standard type of problem for the Financial Analyst. If he tried to deal with it along the lines of my suggested procedure he might have set the investment component of IBM as low as $200—a valuation of some $6 billion for the entire concern.

The speculative component he would have valued in accordance with his own method, which in turn would reflect his temperament as much as his detailed study of future possibilities. His figure might have been higher or lower than the $380 difference between the market price and his investment value; the important point here is that he would have made clear to himself and his clients the combination of opportunity and risk that is inherent in so large a speculative component of market price or total value. Quite differently, the Analyst might well have found an investment component of say, $40 per share for Harvester—based on its average earnings, its dividend record, its asset value (about $55), and of course his conviction that the company's earning power was not likely to deteriorate in the long-term future. This would have left a speculative component of only $10, or 20% of the market quotation, from which he may or may not have concluded that the issue was attractively priced.

I am far from urging, with the ready aid of hindsight, that the much lower speculative component of Harvester proved it to be a better purchase than IBM at the end of 1961. But I do urge that the risk component—hence the actual risk—was proportionately much smaller, and that this element was worth isolating and paying close attention to, in the work of financial analysis.

Putting the matter another way, let me state my conviction that the competent Financial Analyst can do a more expert and worthwhile job in the field of delimiting investment and speculative areas of value than in drawing the bald conclusion that Company A's shares are a better buy than Company B's.

This rather modest estimation of what financial analysis may reliably accomplish leads me to suggest a procedure by which the senior Analyst may combine his work as a portfolio-creator and supervisor with his penchant for selecting the most of present practice, and run somewhat as follows: The Analyst would start with a representative group —more or less equivalent to the Dow-Jones 30 stocks—which is calculated to give the buyer a future experience very close to that of the various averages. He should not reject this list out of hand as too easily put together and thus unworthy of his talents. Indeed he should treat his own "private" choices as competitive with this basic list, in the sense that each such choice would require a clear-cut demonstration of superior attractiveness (say 20% in his valuation against market price) to warrant inclusion in the portfolio as an addition or substitution.

This approach could be carried down to the level of an industry Analyst in a large organization, who studies a relatively few companies in depth. He, too, would either accept direct responsibility for the conclusion that an issue he recommends has the required 20% "margin of indicated value" (as I call it), or else present his analysis in a form to enable his superior to make such a finding.

Returning now to my outline-treatment of the future of financial analysis I should like to touch briefly on three more points. The first two may be called crusades of my own, which I have carried on for years with an outstanding lack of success, but on which I am not yet ready to concede defeat. Perhaps the future is on my side. My first demand is for comprehensive and objective record-keeping by Financial Analysts, in a form which would permit themselves and others to judge of the validity of various investment approaches in terms of their actual working out for many cases and for many years.

To my mind such compilations are essential to any true advance of our membership towards self-understanding and a professional viewpoint. The investment funds are ideally suited for the gathering and careful evaluation of this material, based on their standard forms, procedures and record. Such evaluations of various analytical approaches could also be reported on, at proper intervals, in the *Financial Analysts Journal* and elsewhere, as a service to our profession and the public.

My second crusade has been to urge that the Analysts use their judgment and their influence in the area of managerial efficiency—not only towards avoiding the shares of poorly-managed companies (which in Wall Street is often carried too far), but more positively in the support of efforts from stockholders outside the management to improve unsatisfactory results. The present method of accomplishing this is by permitting the price to decline to an intrinsically absurd level, at which point new people often acquire a controlling interest and then make the necessary changes. This is hardly the best way for existing owners to protect their investments. Whether the future will bring any improvement I hesitate to say—but I may hope so.

I did, in fact, recently get a brainstorm or nightmare on this subject that may amuse you. After all, the largest equity owner of nearly every American corporation is the U. S. Government, with its present 52% share of the profits. Suppose our young President brought his famous vigor to bear on the problem of poorly-managed companies, insisting that the interest of the Treasury Department required them to make more money or else. You may enjoy playing a bit with that bizarre idea.

My final point relates to the possible use of computers in various aspects of financial analysis. Lloyd S. Coughtry's article in the January-February issue of the *Financial Analysts Journal* shows how a computer may be used to project future operating results in the public utility field, which is better suited than others for such elaborate calculations. Much more controversial is the question whether computers may be of major assistance in working up portfolios or in deciding on individual purchases and sales.

Skeptical as we may be of such a prospect it would be unwise to dismiss it out of hand. I believe there is theoretical merit in the original Markowitz concept of "efficient portfolios." This seeks to find by a computer program the portfolio that offers the largest expected return compatible with a given acceptable risk, or, conversely, the least risk associated with a required or expected return. Under this approach it would be up to the Analyst to estimate the degree of risk as well as the expectable return for each issue in the large group from which the portfolio would be drawn. Perhaps the development of techniques to identify the speculative component in individual issues may aid the Financial Analyst in supplying reasonably dependable material for the computers to work their magic upon.

Be all this as it may, of one thing I am certain. Financial analysis in the future, as in the past, offers numerous different roads to success. Many will gain it by way of an intensive knowledge of one or more industries; others by specializing in technology; others by an outstanding ability to evaluate the management factor; still others by a flair for the public's psychology—perhaps even specializing in fantasy; others, again, will have a good nose for bargains and be experts in special situations of all sorts. For men and women with real ability in one or more of these many directions, financial analysis (or security analysis) will continue to offer highly satisfactory rewards.

20
CURRENT GROWTH STOCK VALUATION METHODS*

PAUL F. WENDT is professor of finance in the Graduate School of Business Administration at the University of California at Berkeley. Prior to World War II, the author was associated with Goodbody and Co., members of the New York Stock Exchange.

Most modern stock valuation techniques are based upon the present value theory, which was first set forth in detail by John B. Williams in his *Theory of Investment Value.* Building on the earlier theoretical foundations found in Marshall, Bohm Bawerk and Irving Fisher, Williams argued that the present value of a share of stock is equal to the summation of all dividends expected to be received from it, discounted to the present at an appropriate rate

*From *Financial Analysts Journal,* Vol. 21, No. 2 (March-April 1965), pp. 91-103. Reprinted by permission.

of interest.[1] He argued that tangible income to the investor, dividends, were the only appropriate base for consideration in the valuation of stocks. More recently, others have argued that it does not matter whether one capitalizes dividends or earnings, since price changes in stocks would discount earnings and potential future dividends and since investors could elect to receive income either as dividends or by the sale of stock.[2]

Although most recent writers on the theory of stock valuation have continued to favor the capitalization of future dividends, they have accorded increasing attention to capitalization of earnings for rapidly growing enterprises.[3] The purpose of this article is to describe briefly some of the current growth stock valuation techniques and to illustrate the differences in methods, assumptions and resultant valuations by reference to the valuation of General Motors common in mid-1964.

The three methods described briefly in the first part will not be illustrated because of lack of data, similarity to other techniques, or because of other limitations. The seven techniques illustrated in the second part, for which published information is available in sufficient detail to permit calculation, have been selected to provide indication of the range of values which result from alternative assumptions and objectives.

PART I

Building directly on Williams' theoretical foundations, Walter developed the following formula for valuation of the future dividend stream expected from a stock, and illustrated its application to growth, intermediate and so-called creditor stock categories. By his definition, a growth stock is one for which the rate of return on marginal investment (after adjustment for preferential tax treatment of capital gains) was larger than the company's cost of capital or capitalization rate.[4]

$$V_c = \frac{D + \dfrac{R_a}{R_c}(E - D)}{R_c}$$

[1]Alfred Marshall, *Principles of Economics,* 8th Edition (London, 1925), Vol. 5, Chapters IV, VI, XV. Irving Fisher, *The Nature of Capital and Income* (New York, 1906). John B. Williams, *The Theory of Investment Value* (Cambridge, 1938).

[2]F. Modigliani and M. H. Miller, "Dividend Policy, Growth and the Valuation of Shares," (*Journal of Business,* October 1961).

[3]James E. Walter, "Dividend Policies and Common Stock Prices," (*Journal of Finance,* March 1956, pp. 29-42). B.G. Malkiel, "Equity Yields and Structure of Share Prices," (*The American Economic Review,* December 1963), pp. 1004-1031. See also *AER,* December 1964, "Comment and Reply," pp. 1029-51.

[4]Walter, *op.cit.*

Where:

D = Annual cash dividends expected per share
E = Earnings per share
R_a = Rate of return corporation will earn on additional investment
R_c = Market capitalization rate
V_c = Value per share

Malkiel, writing in *The American Economic Review* for December 1963, sets forth a formula for calculating the present value of future dividends which is closely similar to the methods employed by Williams and Walter, and to some of the techniques illustrated below. His formula implies the use of the reciprocal of a standard multiplier as a discount rate.[5]

$$P = \frac{D\ (1+g)}{1+r} \quad \frac{D\ (1+g)^2}{(1+r)^2} \quad \frac{D\ (1+g)^N}{(1+r)^N} \quad \frac{M_s E\ (1+g)^N}{(1+r)^N}$$

Where:

M_s = Standard earnings multiplier S&P averages
D = Dividend in dollars
g = Company's growth rate as a percentage
E = Earnings in dollars
r = Standard rate of growth S&P averages or the apparent marginal efficiency of the representative standard share
N = Number of years forecasted
P = Present value of future stream of receipts

The *Value Line Survey*, which might be credited with initiating the econometric analysis of the relationship between stock prices, dividends and earnings at the practitioner level, is based upon a multiple regression analysis of dividend payments, earnings and lagged market prices for a large sample of individual issues. Arnold Bernhard, President, describes the evolution of techniques employed by his firm in his book *The Evaluation of Common Stocks.* Revisions in technique are published in the "Commentary" to the financial service. The Value Line technique seeks to establish a so-called Quality Rating for each of 1,100 individual issues, a Potential Value five years hence and a Current

---

[5]Malkiel, *op. cit.* See also Sanford L. Margoshes, "Present Value Techniques of Common Stock Valuation," (*Financial Analysts Journal,* March-April 1961), pp. 37-42.

Value. Using General Motors common stock as an illustration, the author illustrates the technique for establishing these value concepts (pp. 61-76). The most recently published analysis of General Motors common stock published on July 24, 1964, indicated an expected potential value in 1967-69 of $90 based upon an estimated eight-year growth rate of 6.3%. This valuation appears to be based upon the equation $V = 8 \times 5$-year moving average Cash Earnings. (See the "Commentary" of April 3, 1964, describing the revised method of ranking stocks for the next three to five years.)

The estimated normal current value in July 1964 was $70 per share based upon estimates of earnings of $5.75 and dividends of $4.10 for the year ending September 1965. The regression formula used in order to obtain the above normal value was:

$$\log \text{Normal Value} = 1.168 + 0.750 \log (0.68 \text{ Earn.} + \text{Divd.})$$

The constant (1.168) incorporated General Motors' long-term trend and logged price factors.

PART II

The earnings per share of General Motors (shown in Chart I), have been growing at an annual rate of about 5.3% for the last ten years. The dividend growth, however, was almost 9% per annum. Why this difference? In the early years of the last decade the pay-out ratio was only about 50%. In 1963 General Motors reported earnings of $5.56 per share and paid a dividend of $4.00, equivalent to a pay-out ratio of approximately 70%. It is to be expected that future dividend growth will be more in line with earning growth. In the following illustrations, the assumption is made that dividend and earnings growth will be about 5.3% for the next ten years.

The seven valuation techniques which follow are associated with the writings of John C. Clendenin; W. Scott Bauman, Nicholas Molodovsky, Graham, Dodd, Cottle & Tatham; Jeremy C. Jenks, Robert Ferguson, and William Kurtz. Although the author has endeavored to follow these various techniques as described in the *Financial Analysts Journal* and elsewhere, it must be emphasized that the assumptions have been made by the author, and the resultant valuations represent his interpretation of the values resulting from the application of the different techniques illustrated. Messrs. Clendenin, Bauman, Jenks, Ferguson, Molodovsky, and my colleague, Prof. M. J. Keenan, made many helpful comments and suggestions on the final draft of this article.

Chart I. *General Motors: Earnings, Dividends, Cash Generated, and Price Range Per Share, and Price/Earnings Ratio Actual 1954-1963; Estimated 1964-1973*

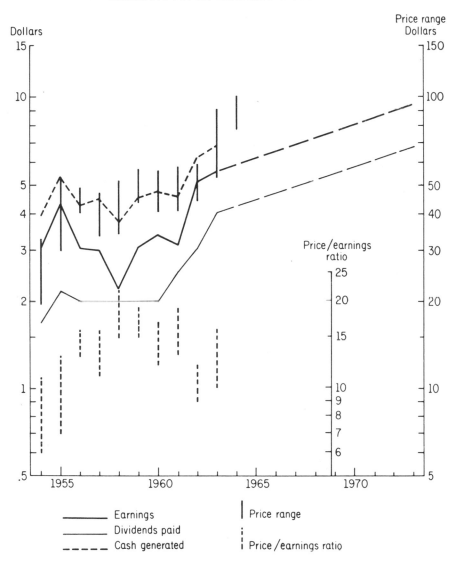

Source: Actual 1954-1963, Standard and Poor's Corp., *Standard Listed Stock Reports,* General Motors, November 10, 1964. Estimates 1964-1973, estimated by the author, see text.

Technique #1—Clendenin

John C. Clendenin has developed a method for determining the justifiable price-dividend multiplier for a growth stock, given alternative assumptions as to rates of growth, duration of growth, and discount rates. He presents a series of present value tables (see Appendix A) which can be used either to determine the assumptions concerning growth rate and duration which are implicit in the current market value of a stock, or for determining the investment value of a stock, given certain assumptions about growth and appropriate discount rates.

Following Williams' theory, Clendenin states:

> Basic theory asserts that the value of a share of stock to a long-term investor is contained entirely in the future dividends the share (or its successors following mergers, stock dividends, or spin-offs) may pay, plus the value of occasional rights or small miscellaneous distributions which do not dilute the basic equity.[6]

In describing the use of his technique, Clendenin shows that it can be applied to short-term investment as well. A person who plans to hold a share of stock for only three years, for example, will arrive at today's value by discounting to its present value (a) the dividends he expects to receive during the next three years, and (b) the price he expects to receive at the time of sale, which will be determined by all future dividends the stock is expected to yield from year 3 to infinity.

Three factors are basic to Clendenin's valuation method: (1) the rate of dividend growth, (2) the duration of the growth trend, and (3) the discount of capitalization rates (or yield rates as he calls them). Cautioning investors concerning over-optimism about growth rates and duration, he advocates a system of progressively higher discount rates (with a maximum of 7%) to be applied to expected dividend returns in the distant future. (See Appendix A)

Clendenin suggests that twenty years are "not beyond the scope of reasonable estimation in the case of well-established concerns." Beyond that time he advises caution, but illustrates that the largest part of the value of any stock attaches to the dividends of the first twenty years because of the increasing effect of discounting as time progresses. He also suggests application of the method to groups of stocks rather than single issues, to obtain greater reliability in long-term projections.

The analyst using Clendenin's method of growth stock valuation still faces a major task, namely that of deciding what values to assign to Clendenin's basic three factors: growth rate, duration, and discount rates. The author offers limited help on how to estimate future growth rate duration. He arrives at a

---

[6]John C. Clendenin, "Theory and Technique of Growth Stock Valuation," Occasional Paper No. 1' (Bureau of Business and Economic Research, UCLA, 1957).

discount rate by checking what the norm is among high-grade stocks, adds 1% to expected real-terms growth rate to take into account average inflationary forces, and suggests a discount rate which depends on the quality of the corporation whose stock is considered. Clendenin avoids being any more specific in assigning values to his factors because "in all instances the investor has a subjective analysis to make. . . . "

Application of Technique #1 to General Motors Common Stock

Reading from Clendenin's Table I in Appendix A (extrapolating to 5.3% growth rate) and assuming that growth will continue for only 10 years, and that earnings remain stable for the ensuing 90 years; General Motors stock is worth:

Multiplier Dividend
25.40   X $4.00   = $101.60
Its closing price on July 17, 1964 was 94 3/8.

It can be seen from Appendix A that the multipler rises rapidly as the growth rate and growth period assumed increase. It is interesting to observe from Appendix A that at the July 17, 1964, price of 94 3/8, General Motors common appeared to discount an approximate 4% growth rate for 10 years capitalizing future dividends at the rates shown (i.e., 23.04 X $4.00 = $92.16).

Technique #2—Bauman (Variable Discount Rate Method)[7]

Bauman uses, as did Clendenin, the present value concept of arriving at a stock value by discounting at an appropriate yield rate all future cash incomes or dividends. He spells out the factors that determine future dividend income; namely, the growth rate and the growth duration, and argues that a company with a growth rate in excess of the average shown in an industry will sooner or later find its growth rate declining to the average level. How long this "transitional" period lasts depends on the company, the industry, product, competition, etc. A guide to follow is to determine the probable position of the company in its life cycle. For example, if a company has been experiencing an abnormally high growth rate, Bauman suggests," . . . unless there is sufficient evidence to the contrary, the best earnings and dividend projection is probably one based on a decreasing rate of growth," until it eventually approximates the

---

[7]W. Scott Bauman, "Estimating the Present Value of Common Stocks by the Variable Rate Method," Michigan Business Reports No. 42 (Bureau of Business Research, University of Michigan, 1963).

secular growth rate for the majority of companies in the economy. This secular growth rate of dividends and also earnings plus non-cash charges was found to have been about 4% during the last 36 years. For reasons of convenience, and for lack of evidence to the contrary, Bauman makes the assumption in his model that the growth rate will decline by equal amounts over the span of the transitional period.

According to Bauman, therefore, in order to make a good estimate of future dividends, the investor must ascertain (a) the current growth rate of dividends (and earnings), and (b) how long will it take until the growth rate has declined to the 4% growth rate average typical for the majority of corporations.

Once the investor has determined the pattern for future dividend incomes, he must discount them to arrive at a present value. What shall be the discount rate? Bauman offers guidelines of from 6 to 10% depending on the risk involved.

The discount rate applied to the first year's expected dividends is usually the lowest, and it increases with time as incomes of more distant years become more and more uncertain. That is, the risk premium added to the discount rate increases with time. Although he does not advise the investor exactly on how much higher future discount rates should be than initial rates, he gives a very strong clue by showing what rates were representative for a majority stock average. The Standard and Poor's Index was shown to be comprised mainly of large companies with medium to high quality. An initial discount rate of 6.5% was held to be reasonable. The average price-dividend ratio for the period 1949-1962 was 24.2, giving an average dividend yield of 4.13% with a 4% annual growth rate. Based on these relationships and using trial-and-error method, it was mathematically consistent to have the first year's dividend income discounted at 6.5% followed by the second year's dividend income discounted at 6.54875%, the third year's by 6.59750%, with each succeeding year's discount rate increased in a linear manner by the amount of 0.04875 percentage points.

Bauman relies heavily upon historical data, and believes this action is justified by absence at present of any indicators which point to large changes ahead. He reminds the investor, however, to be on guard constantly to recognize signs of changes.

Application of Technique #2 to General Motors Common Stock

How is the present value actually determined by Bauman's method? The same figures for General Motors are applied with the following assumptions:

1. According to Bauman, a discount rate of 6% is applied to the dividend in the first year for a company with a high quality rating. Consequently, this rate is used for General Motors in the first year. Because the discount rates applicable to dividend income in succeeding future years are higher, the average discount

rate over the first ten-year period applicable to dividend income is actually 6.2%.

2. The transitional period should be 10 years, since dividends grow at 4% per year beyond the 10 years.

3. Bauman's tables assume that the annual growth rates during the transitional period gradually decrease to 4%. Since we assume that the average annual growth rate over the ten years is 5.3%, a weighted average of approximately 5.3% is obtained if an initial growth rate of 6% is selected.

4. The residual growth rate used will be 4% (as Bauman recommends).

From Variable Rate Table B-6 in Appendix B, the price-dividend ratio applicable for General Motors is found to be 29.9. The present value of General Motors is then $4.00 × 29.9 = $119.60.

Again, it would appear that the stock is underpriced at 94 3/8. Based on Bauman's Table B-6, shown in Appendix B, if the assumed initial dividend growth rate of 6% declines to 4% over a ten-year period, and if an initial discount rate of 7% is used, General Motors would provide an approximate average yield from dividends of 7.24% at the price of 94 3/8 (i.e., 23.8 × $4.00 = $95.20).

Technique #3—R. Ferguson[8]

Robert ·Ferguson presents a method of determining justifiable price/earnings ratios for growth stocks as compared with some standard. His objectives are to answer the following questions:

(a) How many years of the present high growth rate are assumed by today's market price before the growth rate of the company will drop to the "standard" rate?

(b) What price/earnings ratio is justified, given a certain rate of growth which is higher than the standard rate for a certain number of years?

---

[8]Robert Ferguson, "A Nomograph for Valuing Growth Stocks," (*Financial Analysts Journal,* May-June 1961), pp. 29-34. A similar technique was presented by W. Edward Bell in "The Price Future Earnings Ratio—A Practical Guide to Stock Valuation," (*Analysts Journal,* August 1958), pp. 25-28. The author contends that his Nomograph is not intended as a "theory of value," but simply as a means of determining current price/earnings ratios which are consistent with assumptions about earnings growth and going market P/E ratios. The author also rejects my view that an adjustment for dividends would represent double counting. My colleague, Professor Michael Keenan, to whom I am indebted for his careful review of this and other points, has pointed out to me that this does not exactly involve double counting, but rather a *very important difference* as to what the price of a share does and does not incorporate. He says, "It seems much more likely to me that the current market price does not incorporate some notion of dividend payments but my empirical evidence is not very strong here."

The standard can be of any sort, depending upon the kind of company analyzed. The Dow-Jones Industrial Average and Standard and Poor's serve as good examples.

Ferguson takes the market price as a base and then tries to determine what estimates of the basic factors (growth rate and growth duration) the market makes. He then leaves the investor to decide whether these estimates are too low or too high in his judgment. Ferguson develops a nomograph which eliminates the need for complicated calculation on the part of the investor (see Appendix C). The nomograph is a graphical solution to the equation:

$$\frac{P_a}{P^1{}_a} = \frac{(1 + R_a)^n}{(1 + R_b)^n}$$

Where:

P_a = Some standard price/earnings ratio
$P^1{}_a$ = Growth stock price/earnings ratio
R_a = Standard growth rate assumed
R_b = Rate of growth assumed for growth stock

Although it appears that Ferguson ignores the discount rate, closer examination reveals that the use of a standard growth rate in the denominator of his equation (as in Malkiel referred to above), implies that investors will apply uniform discount rates to all common stock earnings, and that differences in price/earnings ratios arise *only* from differences in assumed growth rates and duration.

A further assumption is made implicitly that the quoted growth rates stay on the same level until period T and then drop off suddenly to a rate equivalent to the "standard rate." An analysis based on the foregoing assumption differs, of course, very strongly from Bauman's Variable Rate Method, which assumes evenly declining growth rates and increasing discount rates for incomes with longer futurity. Molodovsky's most recent techniques also assume evenly declining growth rates, as will be observed elsewhere in this Journal.

In the last paragraph of his article describing the nomograph, Ferguson states:

> We have not considered the fact that many stocks pay dividends which are an important source of profit, in addition to price appreciation. This is especially true in situations where the growth rate is of the same order of magnitude as the dividend yield. In these instances, the neglect of dividends may well result in an incorrect calculation. An approximate adjustment for dividend income, useful in many instances, would be to add the yield to the per share earnings growth rate and use the resultant figure in place of the growth rate.

This implicitly assumes that the current market price of stocks completely disregards dividend payments. In my view this procedure would represent double counting and overstate justifiable price/earnings ratios for growth stocks, since dividend payout, in my opinion, is already implicitly reflected in the standard price/earnings ratio used in his equation. (See note 8.)

Application of Technique #3 to General Motors Common Stock

1. To determine length of "transitional" period we use 4% as the standard DJIA growth rate, and assume a standard P/E ratio of 15. For General Motors the P/E is 17, and the growth rate is, of course, 5.3%.

The following instructions are used in the application of the nomograph in Appendix C:

(a) Locate the columns marked "standard growth rates." Choose the one with a growth rate equal to that of the standard, in this case, the R = 4% column (by interpolation).

(b) Go up this column until you come to the rate of growth of the company being analyzed, in this case, 5.3% (by interpolation). Then, move horizontally to the right until you reach the vertical "R line." Mark this spot.

(c) Locate the columns marked "standard price/earnings ratios." Choose the one with the price/earnings ratio equal to that of the standard, in this case, the P/E = 15 column.

(d) Go down this column until you come to the price/earnings ratio of the company being analyzed, in this case, 17. Then, move horizontally to the left until you reach the vertical "P/E line." Mark this spot, too.

(e) Connect these two marks with a straight line and read the number where the line intersects the diagonal "time line," in this case, 9. This is the length of time, in years, discounted by General Motors' price/earnings ratio (17).

General Motors' present market price therefore assumes the current 5.3% growth rate to continue for at least nine years, before it will drop to the 4% average rate as evidenced by the DJIA.

2. To determine the maximum price/earnings ratio which should be paid for the 5.3% growth rate of General Motors as compared with the DJIA rate of 4% if maintained for 10 years:

(a) Locate the number 10 on the "time line." Mark this spot.

(b) Locate the columns marked "standard growth rates." Choose the one with a growth rate equal to that of the standard, in this case R = 4% column (by interpolation).

(c) Go up this column until you come to the rate of growth of General Motors, in this case 5.3% (by interpolation). Then, move horizontally to the right until you reach the vertical "R line." Mark this spot, too.

(d) Connect these two marks with a straight line and extend the line until it intersects the "P/E line." Note the point of intersection.

(e) Locate the columns marked "standard price/earnings ratios." Choose the one with a price/earnings ratio of P/E = 15.

(f) Move horizontally to the right from the point noted in (d) until you come to the standard price/earnings ratio column chosen in (e). Read off the price/earnings ratio, in this case 18.5. This is the maximum price/earnings ratio that should be paid for General Motors.

Since the earnings base assumed is $5.56, the maximum price one should pay for General Motors currently (under the growth assumptions stated above) is 18.5 X $5.56 = $102.86.

It can be noted that the alternative selection of a standard price/earnings multiplier of 20 would have resulted in a price/earnings ratio for General Motors of approximately 23 and a resultant value of approximately $128.

Technique #4—Molodovsky[9]

Nicholas Molodovsky has written several articles on the subject of growth stock valuation. He has made a comprehensive historical analysis of the Standard & Poor's and Cowles Commission indexes, and used them as the standard with which to compare all stocks. From the figures of the above-mentioned stock indexes (which were carefully adjusted to make them as representative as possible for the 1871-1959 period studies) the author developed basic historical parameters. The historical growth rate of dividends and earnings has been about 2.5%. The average yield for the period as evidenced by the "Stock Averages" has been about 5%. These two figures combine to show a total effective yield per year of 7.5%, which Molodovsky consequently used as the discount rate in the present value formula in studies contributed to the *Financial Analysts Journal* through 1960. Including later years through 1963, the above parameters respectively changed to about 2.7%; 4.9% and 7.8%.

Molodovsky always took great pains to emphasize that any standardized selections of future periods, such as ten years, for instance, could serve illustrative purposes only. He stressed that in actual analytical practice, projections of future earnings trends of different stocks would have to be made for whatever varying periods might be specifically indicated. Such characteristics of appropriate valuation parameters were already noted, in no uncertain terms, in his 1959 and 1960 studies. He developed his thinking a bit further in his later papers. His article "The Many Aspects of Yields," which appeared in the

---

[9]Nicholas Molodovsky, "Valuations of Common Stocks," (*Analysts Journal,* February 1959), "Stock Values and Stock Prices—Part I," (May-June 1960), and "Dow-Jones Industrials—A Reappraisal," (March-April 1961).

March-April 1962 issue of the *Financial Analysts Journal*, contained the following statement:

> It is clear that the nature of the industry to which a given company belongs—as well as that corporation's particular characteristics—should in reality determine both the length of the period for which earnings are projected into the future and also the delicate process of the "splicing" with an overall historical rate. Depending on each individual case, such a transition may well take the form of mathematical curves with very different gradations of diminishing rates of growth.

Such gradual transitions can be easily performed by a computer, which could also carry out the valuation formula's requirement of an infinite time horizon. According to Molodovsky, this latter condition can be easily met by combining the compound interest formula used for computing a bond's yield to maturity with the expression of a geometric progression for an infinite number of terms which constitutes a mathematical description of a common stock's natural *habitat*. The requisite formulae may be found in any high school textbook of algebra.

It so happens that this issue of the *Financial Analysts Journal* carries an article by Molodovsky and two of his associates discussing the valuations of the DJIA and of its thirty component stocks.[10] Since General Motors is one of the prominent members of this club, I shall let Molodovsky and his associates speak for themselves regarding the valuation of GM.

Technique #5—Graham, Dodd, Cottle, and Tatham[11]

Messrs. Graham and Dodd, in the most recent edition of their text also get on the "present-value-bandwagon" which by now seems to be "*the*" basic principle in all major stock valuation models.

The authors are probably the most conservative of all the writers mentioned in this study so far because of the limitations placed on growth projections. The maximum growth period which they consider in any of their techniques is ten years. In one method they even bring the limit down to seven years.

The authors present two methods of their own described below and in their text (pp. 536-538). Following Molodovsky, they assume a single discount rate of 7.5% for all companies no matter whether high, medium, or low quality, an assumption criticized by Bauman. The authors also follow Molodovsky in

[10]Pages 104.23.

[11]B. Graham, D. L. Dodd, and S. Cottle, *Security Analysis* (New York: McGraw-Hill Book Co., 1962), Chapter 39.

assuming a normal price/earnings ratio. The authors assume a normal payout ratio of 60%. They mention, however, that this ratio is fairly high for good growth companies. The higher the growth rate the smaller the pay-out ratio usually becomes. For this reason, the authors do not follow the other writers in capitalizing dividends. Dividends become almost meaningless for good growth stocks, and they consider earnings as much more representative of such a firm's current and future income potential.

METHOD A

This approach, referred to as their "preferred method," projects earnings growth for only the next seven years. A multiplier is applied to the average of the next seven years' earnings, that is to the fourth year's earnings. The multiplier, of course, depends on the expected rate of growth for the next seven years, but will lie within the range of 13 to 20 because of the limits on the growth rate from 3½% to 20% set by the authors.

The following table, illustrated in their text *Security Analysis,* was developed on the basis of the above parameters:

Table 39-4

Expected Rate of Growth (Four Years	Multiplier of Average (4th Year Earnings)	Multiplier of Current Earnings
3.5%	13X	15X
5.0	14X	17X
7.2	15X	20X
10.0	16X	23½X
12.0	17X	27X
14.3	18X	31X
17.0	19X	35½X
20.0	20X	41½X

METHOD B

Graham and Dodd advance two other formulas which yield similar results.

(B-1) Value = $8.6T$ plus 2.1, where T is the tenth-year compound amount of $1.00 of present earnings growing at any assumed rate. The reader may be reminded that we still work under the assumption of 0.60 pay-out and 7.5% discount rate. The growth period in this method is assumed to be 10 years.

A 2.5% growth rate will yield $T = \$1.28$, and here the multiplier

is $\qquad$ (8.6 × 1.28) + 2.1 = 13.1
and a 10% growth rate will show a multiplier of 24.4 times
$$(8.6 \times 2.59) + 2.1 = 24.4$$
(B-2) Value = current "normal" earnings × (8.5 + 2*G*), where *G* is the average annual growth expected for the next 7 to 10 years. "Normal" earnings are those as they would appear on a smoothed-out earnings curve or "trend line." The authors have arrived at this formula from the finding that a multiplier of 8.5 is appropriate for a company with zero expected growth, and a 2 1/2% growth rate calls for a multiplier of 13.5

A 10% growth rate will show a multiplier of 8.5 + (2 × 10) = 28.5 as compared with 24.4 in the first formula.

As mentioned before, Graham and Dodd's methods for valuing growth issues bear evidence of extreme conservatism in recommending the use of short periods of anticipated growth and relatively low residual growth rates and multipliers. Other writers express conservatism in different ways. Clendenin and Bauman assign a higher discount rate to years in the distant future, rather than limit estimates to 10 years. Graham and Dodd, on the other hand, disregard any higher than "average" growth rate later than 10 years hence.

As with other analysts cited, Graham and Dodd do not advise the reader on how to select the proper growth rate. Whereas past trends definitely are an important factor to consider, they should not be the sole factor. Simple projection of past trends can also lead to results far too optimistic.

Application of Technique #5 to General Motors Common Stock

METHOD A

A 5.3% growth rate calls for a multiplier of about 14.2 to be applied to the fourth year's earnings, or a multiplier of about 17.4 applied to current earnings (according to Table 39-4 shown above).

$$17.4 \times \$5.56 = \$96.74 \text{ is the intrinsic value}$$

METHOD B

(B-1) 8.6*T* + 2.1
$\qquad$ 8.6 (1.68 + 2.1 = 14.45 + 2.1 = 16.55
$\qquad$ Value = 16.55 × $5.56 - $92.02 Value

(B-2) Current earnings × (8.5 + 2*G*)
$\qquad$ (I assume that $5.56 is the current normal earnings figure)

$5.56 \times (8.5 + 10.6)$
$5.56 \times 19.1 = \$106.20$ Value

Technique #6—Jeremey C. Jenks[1,2]

Jeremey C. Jenks, associated with C. J. Lawrence and Sons, a New York Stock Exchange member firm, criticizes existing methods of comparative valuation because they are either based on price/earnings ratios or on price/dividend ratios. He argues that "no *one* approach will give satisfactory results in a wide variety of common stocks . . . because there are *two* 'investment' reasons for owning common stocks . . . dividend income and hope of capital appreciation if the company grows." Thus there really is no sharp dividing line between an "income stock" and a "growth stock."

In this technique, two different multipliers are computed (as in Walter), one to be applied to the dividend from one set of factors, and another multiplier from another set of factors, to be applied to the earnings retained in the business. The two resultant values are added together in order to obtain "the value" of the stock.

The dividend multiplier is based on the assumption that the value of a dividend is a function of:

(1)   The yield on high grade, money rate, taxable bonds (Lawrence uses governments)
(2)   The quality of the dividend

For quality classifications, the author uses rating scales from A to F (similar to ratings of bonds) applied as follows:

The best dividend is worth 1% current return basis less than long-term Government bond yields. Each graduation in quality is marked down an additional 1/2%. (Page 9 of booklet.)

A dividend's quality is determined by the following five factors:

(1) Debt + Pref. as % of Capital
(2) Debt + Pref. as % of Working Capital
(3) Pay-out (in %)
(4) Drop in the Net Earnings in 1958 from the 1956-57 peak
(5) Total Plow-back as % of Equity

[1,2]C. J. Lawrence, "Comparative Valuation of Common Stocks" (a booklet published by Cyrus J. Lawrence & Sons, New York, 1959).

For the ratings which are assigned by these five factors the author has developed tables (see page 5 of C. J. Lawrence booklet).

The price/earnings multiples used at various levels of yields for long Governments are as follows:

Yield Long Governments

Rating	3%	3½%	4%	4½%	5%	5½%
A	27.5	25	22.2	20	18.2	16.7
B	25	22.2	20	18.2	16.7	15.4
C	22.2	20	18.2	16.7	15.4	14.3
D	20	18.2	16.7	15.4	14.3	13.3
E	18.2	16.7	15.4	14.3	13.3	12.5
F	16.7	15.4	14.3	13.3	12.5	11.8

He used an average of several of the long Government issues. The following bonds seemed representative to him at the time of his writing:

		Yield	
	12/10/58	10/23/59	1/7/60
3¼% May 1985	3.73	3.92	4.39
3½% February 1990	3.83	4.05	4.43
3% February 1995	3.59	3.81	4.11

The Retained Earnings Multiple is based on the growth prospects of the business. Lawrence employs three measurements:

(1) The historic rate of growth in earnings. Any large fluctuations are corrected by sales trends.

(2) The 3-year average plowback as a % of equity is designed to show the company's ability to finance growth internally.

(3) The 3-year average expansion factor is intended to measure the company's efforts to grow.

By averaging these three factors, the authors hope to get some indication of the growth potential of a company.

The following table of multipliers is derived, which corresponds to certain growth rates:

Growth Factor and Price-Retained Earnings Multiples

0	8.9 X	8%	14.0 X	16%	22.1 X
1%	9.5 X	9%	14.8 X	17%	23.4 X
2%	10.0 X	10%	15.7 X	18%	24.8 X
3%	10.5 X	11%	16.7 X	19%	26.2 X
4%	11.1 X	12%	17.6 X	20%	27.8 X
5%	11.7 X	13%	18.6 X	25%	37.0 X
6%	12.4 X	14%	19.6 X	30%	48.0 X
7%	13.2 X	15%	20.9 X	35%	90.0 X

Jenks develops retained earnings multiples by use of compound interest tables but making a 2% negative adjustment.

The Jenks (Lawrence) method employs a final adjustment factor to each valuation, based largely upon the size and relative importance of the company in its industry. In the illustration below, it can be seen that the adjustment factor for General Motors was 130%.

Application of Technique #6 to General Motors Common Stock

An application of the Jenks valuation approach to the stock of General Motors follows: The following valuation can be compared with a 1961 valuation of General Motors by Cyrus J. Lawrence & Sons, which, using a dividend multiplier of 18.1 and an earnings multiplier of 8.6, and applying these to estimated annual earnings of $3.11 for 1961 and $4.00 for 1962 resulted in estimated valuations of $50.50 and $58.10 before adjustment and $65.70 and $75.50 after adjustment.[13]

		Government Yield Basis	
Dividend Rating	*%*	*Rating*	*4%* *Multiple*
Debt is pfd. % cap. (1963 figure)	7.6	B	20
Debt is pfd. S.C. (1963 figure)	14.6	B	20
Current payout—(1963)	72.2	E	15.4
Drop in net '61–'62 to '63	0	A	22.2
Average plowback % equity	6.0	D	16.7
AVERAGE			18.9

[13]C. J. Lawrence and Sons, *General Motors Corporation in the World Automobile Market* (New York, May 1962).

Growth Rating	%	Multiple
Growth in earnings	5.3	11.9
Average plowback % equity	7.0	13.2
Average expansion factor	7.9	13.9
Average		13.0
Consistency factor		70
Adjusted multiple		9.1

No. of shares (12/31/63) — Total 286,653,007 shares

Earnings	Actual 1963	Estimated 1964
Gross plant	7,967 mil.	7,967 mil.
Sales to gross plant	2.08	2.26
Sales	16,495 mil.	18,000 mil.
Net income	1,592 mil.	2,140 mil.
Pfd. div.	13 mil.	13 mil.
Net for common	1,578 mil.	2,127 mil.
Net per share	$5.56	$6.00
Div. per share	$4.00	$4.80
Retained per share	$1.56	$1.50
Div. cap. at *18.9*	$75.60	$85.05
Retained cap. at *9.1*	14.2	13.65
Estimated values	89.8	98.70
Adjusted est. values*	116.7	129.30

*Net income over 200 million. The estimated values are multiplied by 130%.

It can be seen that the application of the Jenks' technique results in an adjusted value for General Motors of $129.30.

Technique #7—William Kurtz

William Kurtz, of Hemphill Noyes and Co., has developed a somewhat different adaptation of the present value method described in a company memorandum entitled "Valuation Standards for Investments," which involves three steps:

(1) A price/earnings multiple of 14 as a normal ratio for a non-growth stock.
(2) A growth rate adjustment (five-year compound interest factor at the assumed growth rate) which is multiplied by the standard (14).

(3) An investment quality rating which rates issues as Premium quality (1.33), Standard (1.00), and Discount (.67) and permits intermediate quality rating multipliers.

Application of Technique #7 to General Motors Common Stock

Based on these elements, the value of General Motors common, assuming a 5.3% growth factor (for five years as the maximum growth period allowed) might be estimated as follows:

14.0 X 1.28 (compound amount of $1 for 5 years at 5.3%) X 1.10 (quality adjustment factor for General Motors) = $109.58.

This technique has the simplifying advantage of eliminating the selection of a growth period, assuming a standard maximum of 5 years. Its disadvantage, of course, lies in this very assumption, and in the subjective determination of a quality rating. Others may take issue with the assumed normal price/earnings ratio of 14 for a non-growth issue.

SUMMARY

Virtually all the techniques examined have been directed toward the estimation of "intrinsic" value, although some of the methods were more directly aimed toward the determination of price/earnings or price/dividend ratios. Most of the methods require that the analyst make a separate and in most cases a subjective estimate of future growth rates. Jenks' technique is somewhat distinctive in that he relies entirely upon historical data and short-run estimates of current earnings.

A wide range of growth assumptions are illustrated in the several techniques discussed, in many cases without providing any guidance for the analyst as to the method of selecting a growth rate to be applied to a particular issue. So-called residual or normal growth rates range from 2.5% to 4% and residual multipliers vary from 13. to 17.1. These differences are frequently the principal factors accounting for the relatively wide range of valuations established by using the various methods shown in Table A, which provides a review of the assumptions and valuation results.

The highest valuations resulted from the methods of Bauman, Jenks and Kurtz, whereas the Value Line approach and the Graham and Dodd methods resulted in the lowest estimated values. Bauman's high figure is a result of three factors, a long "transitional" period, a not very high (the second lowest) discount rate, and a high (the highest of all methods) residual growth rate. A 10-year transitional period with an initial growth rate of 6% was used in order to have a 5.3% average growth rate as in the other methods. A relatively high normal, non-growth price/earnings ratio and the subjective quality rating multiplier account for Kurtz' high estimate.

Two of the techniques (Clendènin and Bauman) are based upon the use of

Table A. Comparison of Assumptions
and Valuations for Seven Growth Stock Valuation Techniques

Technique	Growth Rate	Growth Duration	Discount Rate	Residual Growth Rate	Value
1. Clendenin	5.3%	10 years	4%, 5%, 6%, 7%	None	$101.60
2. Bauman	5.3%	10 years (trans. period)	6.2%	4%	$119.60
3. Ferguson	5.3%		Current market P/E multiplier		$102.86 (maximum)
4. Molodovsky	See text of Molodovsky's article in this issue*				
5. Graham & Dodd Method A	5.3%	7 years	7.5%	3.5%	$96.74
Method B-1 (8.6T+2.1)	5.3%	10 years	7.5%	2.5%	$92.02
Method B-2 (8.5+2G)	5.3%	10 years	7.5%	2.5%	$106.20
6. Lawrence (Jenks)	5.3%		Variable rates for dividends and retained earnings		$129.30
7. Kurtz	5.3%	5 years	Basic market multiplier of 14 x earnings		$109.58

*Financial Analysts Journal, March-April 1965, pp. 104-23.

a multiplier applied to future dividends, three methods are based on earnings, while the third, Jenks', uses a combination of earnings and dividends. The techniques examined reveal an implied pay-out ratio in the dividend multipliers similar to that for General Motors (70%). It is obvious that the differences in the resultant valuations would have been greater if the pay-out ratio on General Motors were subsequently different. The important question appears to be, not whether a multiplier should be applied to earnings or dividends, but whether it can anticipate the relative weight which will be given to dividends and earnings in the market.

It should be pointed out that the discount rates shown in Table A are not strictly comparable, since in some cases (Molodovsky, Graham and Dodd), they apply to both dividend income and price appreciation, while in others (Clendenin and Bauman), they apply only to dividend income. In the case of the Ferguson and Kurtz models, the multipliers are applied to total earnings and represent the reciprocals of discount rates.

The Ferguson technique makes no explicit assumptions about growth rate, growth duration, or discount rates. Ferguson merely examines the growth rate and duration inherent in the current market price and compares them with the components contained in a standard such as the DJIA. By his method, relative to the standard, General Motors' growth potential warrants a maximum price of $102.86, slightly more than $8 over the current market price. Much depends, in his method, upon the so-called standard growth rate assumed.

Jenks' method also does not lend itself to a simple check on the basic assumptions as the majority of approaches do, since it is largely based on historical data. Since his technique is not based upon long-term projections, the method does not employ present value techniques. It can be noted that the so-called adjustment factor used in the Lawrence technique adds $25 to $30 to the resultant share value. This factor adds an important element of subjectivity to Jenks' technique. Mr. Jenks reports that new simplified valuation methods have been developed by his firm using Standard and Poor's Compustat tapes.

CONCLUSIONS

It is apparent that widely differing values can be assigned to growth stocks by varying the assumptions concerning future growth rates and duration of growth and by applying different discount rates to future dividend returns. None of the valuation techniques discussed provide any accurate method for estimating future growth rates or duration.

What then is the operational usefulness of these techniques? It can be argued that the application of these valuation methods will provide rough guidelines to a "range of values" for growth stocks under consistent assumptions. Assuming that an analyst is prepared to establish his own discount rates and time horizon for estimating future growth, the range of indicated values will be relatively narrow, as can be noted in Table A. The values for General Motors assuming a ten-year growth period at 5.3% per annum and a 7.5% discount rate are in a very close range. The differences noted are due to the varying assumed residual growth rates, which will influence the multipliers applied to earnings at the conclusion of the growth period. This element of prediction involves a high degree of uncertainty, since it not only requires judgment with respect to long-term growth, but also implies that the analyst can forecast price/earning ratios which will prevail in the distant future. Graham and Dodd maintain that the use of a short-growth period and a long-term average multiplier for residual earnings adds a "safety factor" to security analysis, which by its very nature involves a high degree of uncertainty.

Viewing the difficulty of forecasting long-term future corporate earnings, it would appear that the weight of evidence should favor the use of growth periods of 10 years or less. This has the further advantage that it should make less uncertain and difficult any forecast of residual growth rates and multipliers, since it brings them closer. The assumption of a gradual rather than an abrupt decline in growth rates, as Bauman and Molodovsky recommend, also seems warranted. It must be recognized, however, that adherence to these relatively conservative assumptions leaves the more distant future to be eyed with varying degrees of optimism by professional and amateur crystal gazers, and thus leaves the final judgment as to over-or under-valuation to the market place.

The recent availability of Standard and Poor's Compustat tapes has opened up new horizons for multiple regression analysis of stock market data. Economists at the Bank of New York and Trust Company have assumed a leading role in cross-section multiple regression analysis of stock prices, earnings and dividends based on the Compustat tapes. Whitbeck and Kisor describe this analytical technique in the *Financial Analysts Journal* for May-June 1963[14]. Regressing current average market price/earnings ratios on estimated growth rates, dividend pay-out (supplemented by indexes of stability and marketability), they derive an average multiple regression equation for 135 representative issues. Using the coefficients from this equation, they derive theoretical price/earnings ratios for individual issues, based upon their current estimates of growth, dividend pay-out, etc. By comparing these with actual prevailing price/earnings ratios (assuming "normalized" earnings), they derive indexes of relative under- or over-pricing in the market for individual stocks.

The most significant potential for stock valuation techniques embodied in this cross-sectional multiple regression analysis of stock prices (and price/earnings ratios) lies in the comparison of changes over time in the relative weights accorded in the market to expected growth in earnings and dividend pay-out. It is of further consequence, of course, to examine the relationship between price/earnings ratios, estimated growth rates and dividend pay-out by individual industries or groups of industries to shed further light upon the diversity of investor expectations over time and among different stock groups. This should provide a test of the validity of the valuation technique described above. Such analysis may pave the way to greater insight into the behavioristic characteristics of security investors over time and shed more light on the never-ending academic discussions concerning the relative weight attached by investors to dividends versus earnings.

---

[14]Volkert S. Whitbeck and Manown Kisor, Jr., "A New Tool in Investment Decision Making," (*Financial Analysts Journal*, Volume 19, No. 3, May-June 1963), pp. 55-62. The authors illustrate the derivation of a theoretical price/earnings ratio and an estimated value for General Motors Common Stock ($51), based upon estimated market parameters as of June 8, 1962, page 58.

APPENDIX A

Table I.   Approximate Present Values of All Future Dividends on a stock now paying $1.00 per annum, if the dividend is expected to increase at the indicated compound rate for the indicated period of years and then remain stable until 100 years from today, and if the payments of the first decade are discounted at 4%, those of the second at 5%, those of the third at 6%, and those of the 70 years at 7%.

Growth Period	Annual Growth Rates				
	5%	4%	3%	1%	0%
None	$17.01	$17.01	$17.01	$17.01	$17.01
10 years	24.05	23.04	21.37	18.37	17.01
20 years	31.21	27.51	24.27	19.12	17.01
30 years	35.97	30.55	26.08	19.51	17.01
40 years	39.65	32.67	27.22	19.69	17.01
50 years	42.63	34.23	27.99	19.80	17.01

Table II.   Approximate Present Values of the Future Dividends on a stock now paying $1.00 per annum, if the dividends are expected to grow at the indicated rates for 20 years and then remain stable for the next 80 years, and if the dividends of the first decade are discounted at 4%, those of the second at 5%, those of the third at 6%, and those of the remaining 70 years at 7%.

Growth Rate Per Year	Present Values				
	First Decade	Second Decade	Third Decade	Next 70 Years	Total
6%	$10.85	$11.36	$ 7.36	$ 5.96	$35.53
5%	10.35	9.84	6.09	4.93	31.21
4%	9.87	8.53	5.03	4.08	27.51
3%	9.40	7.37	4.14	3.36	24.27
2%	8.96	6.39	3.41	2.76	21.52
1%	8.53	5.52	2.80	2.27	19.12
0%	8.11	4.74	2.30	1.86	17.01

NOTE: These tables and similar appendix tables are calculated on the assumption that each year's dividend is received at the year end, and that it contains the full year's growth element. The short-cut calculation methods which were used may underestimate some of the values by as much as 1½ per cent. Slide rule computations were used.

APPENDIX B

Variable Rate Table B-6.   10-Year
Transitional Period Price-Dividend Ratios

Initial Growth Rates (Per Cent)	Initial Discount Rates							
	5%	6%	6½%	7%	8%	9%	10%	12%
Depressed								
0	29.6	22.4	20.0	18.1	15.1	13.0	11.4	9.1
1	31.1	23.6	21.0	18.9	15.8	13.5	11.9	9.5
2	32.6	24.7	22.0	19.8	16.5	14.2	12.4	9.9
3	34.3	25.9	23.1	20.8	17.3	14.8	12.9	10.3
Constant								
4	36.0	27.2	24.2	21.7	18.1	15.5	13.5	10.8
High								
5	37.8	28.5	25.3	22.8	18.9	16.2	14.1	11.2
6	39.7	29.9	26.5	23.8	19.8	16.9	14.7	11.7
8	43.6	32.8	29.1	26.1	21.6	18.4	16.0	12.7
10	48.0	36.0	31.9	28.6	23.6	20.1	17.4	13.7
12	52.7	39.4	34.9	31.3	25.8	21.9	19.0	14.9
14	57.9	43.2	38.2	34.2	28.2	23.8	20.6	16.1
16	63.4	47.3	41.8	37.4	30.7	26.0	22.4	17.5
18	69.5	51.7	45.7	40.8	33.5	28.2	24.3	18.9
20	76.1	56.5	49.9	44.5	36.5	30.7	26.4	20.5
25	95.1	70.3	61.9	55.2	45.0	37.8	32.4	24.9
30	118.2	87.1	76.6	68.1	55.4	46.3	39.6	30.3
35	146.1	107.4	94.3	83.7	67.8	56.6	48.2	36.6
40	179.9	131.8	115.5	102.4	82.8	68.8	58.5	44.2
50	268.7	196.0	171.3	151.6	121.9	100.9	85.3	63.8
60	394.8	286.7	250.2	220.8	176.9	145.8	122.7	91.1
70	570.7	413.2	359.8	317.1	253.1	207.9	174.4	128.6

APPENDIX C

Growth Stock Nomograph

Standard price/earnings ratios

Standard growth rates

21
FOUNDATIONS OF
SECURITY ANALYSIS*

*EDWARD F. RENSHAW is a member of the
faculty of the University of North Carolina.*

In his book *The Scope and Method of Political Economy,* John
Neville Keynes distinguishes between "a positive science . . . a body of
systematized knowledge concerning what is; a normative or regulative
science . . . a body of systematized knowledge discussing criteria of what ought
to be; and an art . . . a system of rules for the attainment of a given end;" and
comments that, "confusion between them is common and has been the source of
many mischievous errors."

An examination of the voluminous literature that has been written on the
subject of stock market behavior indicates that "security analysis," as distinct
from "market analysis," is largely a normative science; it is concerned primarily
with the problem of determining the "true or intrinsic" value of securities.
According to its leading proponents, Graham and Dodd, the security analyst
should only be concerned with those fluctuations in security prices which create
opportunities to buy at less than the "true" value and to sell at more than such
value.

Market analysis, on the other hand, is largely a positive science; it is
concerned with the identification of trends and relationships which are internal
to the market itself and can be used to forecast the direction of price
movements.

The limitations of both approaches to the over-all problem of investment
decision has been clearly recognized. While in the long run average prices
probably do not deviate far from true investment values, it is nevertheless a
disturbing fact that "undervalued" securities can remain undervalued for
uncomfortably long periods of time and "overvalued" securities can become
even more overvalued. As Graham and Dodd have pointed out:

---

*From *Analysts Journal,* Vol. 14, No. 1 (February 1958), pp. 57-61. Reprinted by
permission.

In actual practice the selection of suitable buying and selling levels becomes a difficult matter. Taking the long market cycle of 1921-33, an investor might well have sold out at the end of 1925 and remained out of the market in 1926-30 and bought again in the depression year of 1931. The first of these moves would later have seemed a bad mistake of judgment, and the last would have had most disturbing consequences. In other market cycles of lesser amplitude such serious miscalculations are not so likely to occur, but there is always a good deal of doubt with regard to the correct time for applying the simple principle of "buy low and sell high."

On the other hand, it can be demonstrated, on paper at least, that while any number of forecasting systems would have worked well during certain periods in the past, it is generally possible to find periods in which each system would not have functioned satisfactorily. The Cowles Commission's studies and others have demonstrated that stock market forecasters have been rather unsuccessful at forecasting. Indeed, since to be correct in forecasting a substantial change in price implies that the general market has made an error in buying and selling at existing prices, a serious question can be raised as to whether it is reasonable to expect forecasting to ever be generally successful.

These words of caution are not meant to be disparaging of either approach to investments. At least to the non-extremists, both approaches have a certain relevance—security analysis as a guide to the selection of the best buys, and market analysis as a guide to the most appropriate timing. At this stage in the development of security analysis and market analysis, however, one is almost forced to conclude that both approaches are in practice largely arts; the science of either, as denoted by the existence of a large body of systematized knowledge, is relatively undeveloped. It is to the task of assembling such a body of knowledge with respect to security analysis that this paper is addressed.

A CASE FOR DEVELOPING THE SCIENCE OF SECURITY ANALYSIS

The study of what would or "ought" to occur in a rational economy has more importance for him who would understand in order that he might change and improve the "rules of the game" than for him who merely desires to win under the existing rules. The normative aspects of security analysis have much greater appeal to the reformer than to the speculator. It would be absurd for the individual speculator to base his operations naively on an attempted analysis of how the social present should be adjusted to the social future; he would stand to lose his shirt if the market did not eventually adjust to the future in the way he predicted that it "ought" to.

From the standpoint of the average investor and the security market as a whole, however, there is a strong case for systematically developing the normative aspects of security analysis; the hope is that by rigorously defining and publicizing intrinsic values, irrational deviations between what is and ought to be with respect to the level of security prices will be minimized. Since intrinsic values are inherently more stable than actual market prices, a minimizing of the variance of actual prices around intrinsic values would result in increased price stability.

The social value of greater price stability in the security market practically goes without saying. Fluctuations in security prices that are unrelated to the economic fortunes of the business which they represent or the substitution possibilities which exist in other investment markets, narrow the market for securities by increasing unnecessarily the risk of committing funds to it. The supply of risk capital is consequently restricted. Fortunes are made and lost without sufficient economic cause, and the market place loses its respect as a necessary intermediary between saving and investing in a complex society. Johnson, in commenting on the problem of unstable agricultural prices, has noted:

> The effectiveness of prices as directives in inducing appropriate allocation of resources is greatly impaired by violent fluctuations in prices and incomes such as those experienced in the interwar period.

His observation is not without relevance to the security markets. One has merely to look at the extent to which the Federal Government is and has been involved in the direct stabilization of other markets to obtain an inkling of a social desire for greater price stability.

If the irrationality of past disturbances is not to contain the seeds of similar disturbances in the security market of the future, it would seem imperative that objective standards be formulated and agreed upon for determining the intrinsic value of securities, individually and collectively, and further that these values be made widely known to the public at regular intervals so that investors and speculators, who have neither the time nor the technical training and equipment for making highly complex valuation studies, may have a firmer bench mark upon which to gauge their purchases and sales.

In the words of Frederick Macaulay, "The chief reason for the deviations of the actual from the 'rational' is the inability of human beings to foresee the future, let alone adjust the present to it . . . . To the extent that the future can be foreseen it can be prepared for." The science of security analysis, as envisaged herein, would entail making the best possible use of historical information so that it may aid us in peering into the future. Again quoting Frederick Macaulay:

> Lack of knowledge of the future is a fundamentally disturbing factor

but the effects of inability to handle logically the facts of the present must not be underestimated. Indeed, if that inability were less, our knowledge of the future would be greater.

It is to the task of assembling and utilizing the information at our disposal, so that we may better understand not only how the market has behaved in the past but how it ought to behave in the present in order to prevent unnecessary adjustments in the future, that this article is directed.

THE CONCEPT OF CENTRAL VALUE

The most important single factor determining value is now held to be the indicated average future earning power. Intrinsic value would then be found by first estimating this earning power and then multiplying the estimate by an appropriate "capitalization factor."

As Graham and Dodd have suggested, the problem of determining intrinsic or central value can be broken down into two distinct aspects, estimation of average future earning power and finding a suitable capitalization factor. Except for relatively new businesses which have no established earning power and businesses which on other grounds are expected to have a radical change in fortune, it is pretty well agreed that the best estimate of future earnings is some weighted function of past earnings. If transitory factors which cause unusually high or low earnings in any one year are to be partially balanced out or eliminated, it is necessary to attach weight to earnings which have accrued in more than one year. At the present time there does not seem to be agreement as to the kind of weighting system that should be used: should estimates of future average earning power entail the use of a ten-year moving average, a five-year moving average, a system of declining weights, or a set of weights modified by a trend factor? Choice of a weighting system, however, is not a crucial matter as far as the over-all analysis of central value is concerned; from a statistical point of view, the best set of weights can be found as an incidental matter to the process of determining capitalization factors.

The most crucial aspect of central value is the determination of suitable "capitalization factors." Another way of looking at the same thing is to ask what are the determinants of an appropriate price-earnings ratio as distinct from actual price-earnings ratios that can be computed directly from current prices and earnings. One of the greatest weaknesses of security analysis at the present time is the off-hand and unreasoned manner in which capitalization factors are obtained. In valuing the Dow Jones industrial average, Graham arbitrarily assumes that the appropriate capitalization factor can be taken as the reciprocal of twice the interest rate on Moody's all-corporation AAA bonds. In the second edition of *The Intelligent Investor,* he comments:

The multiplier should reflect prospective longer-term changes in earnings. A multiplier of 12 is suitable for stocks with neutral prospects. Increases or decreases from this figure must depend on the judgment and preferences of the appraiser. In all but the most exceptional cases, however, the maximum multiplier should be 20 and the minimum should be 8.

As opposed to an approach to the determination of capitalization factors which is either very arbitrary or largely objective, the view that will be taken by this analyst is that capitalization factors should be obtained by relating multipliers observed in the market to plausible economic variables. In this manner behavior in the stock market over long periods of time can be used to obtain capitalization factors. This approach to the problem is not at all out of line with what might be regarded as the underlying assumption implicit in security analysis:

> This field of analytical work may be said to rest upon a twofold assumption: first, that the market price is frequently out of line with the true value; and, second, that there is an inherent tendency for these disparities to correct themselves. (Graham and Dodd.)

> Prices and values cannot indefinitely move in opposite directions. It can be demonstrated statistically that over reasonably long periods average prices do not deviate far from the true investment values. If a coefficient of correlation between them was computed, it would probably be very high. (Nicholas Molodovsky.)

Critics of security analysis have been prone to point out that the "intrinsic value suffers from an inadequate formulation of its own central concept and, therefore, cannot be accepted for precise, unambiguous scientific use." According to Pickett and Ketchum:

> The "true" or intrinsic value of a share of stock is a much more intangible concept. The par, book, and market values can be obtained from published data relating to the corporation, and these amounts are definite. The intrinsic value, on the other hand, is dependent upon subjective valuations and personal opinion.

If security analysis is ever to obtain the objective status of a science, it will be necessary: to specify the variables that determine suitable capitalization factors, to decide upon statistical measures which represent the impact of these variables, and to agree upon an objective procedure for measuring quantitatively the impact of a change in each variable upon the capitalization factor.

Before proceeding to a discussion of how statistical analysis can be used to aid in obtaining capitalization factors, it is desirable to dicotomize security analysis.

Murphy has noted that "perhaps the greatest need is for a method of valuing equity earnings in relation to (1) other investment media, and (2) gradations of value within the equity field." On this basis the science of security analysis can be broken down into two distinct but not necessarily separable phases. One phase is concerned with the problem of establishing a central value for a representative list of securities in relation to other types of investment media, such as bonds, savings accounts, real estate, commodities and money; these media can be viewed as constituting alternative investment opportunities outside the security field. The implication of a central value for a representative security index that is lower than the market price is that securities are priced high in relation to at least one other investment medium, and that investors "should" endeavor to substitute these media for securities until the market price of securities converges with its central value.

A second phase of security analysis is essentially concerned with the problem of establishing a central value for individual or groups of similar securities. The implication of a central value for an individual security that is lower than its market price is that the market price is too high relative to other securities and that investors should substitute "high" for "low" priced stocks up to the point at which prices and values converge.

PHASE I.   THE DEVELOPMENT OF CENTRAL VALUE IN RELATION TO REPRESENTATIVE AVERAGES

A great deal of unintegrated statistical work has been done in an endeavor to strike central values for stock averages. The work has ranged from the naive to the very sophisticated. Some concept of central value is usually an integral part of all but the simplest formula plans. In recent years these plans have gained favor with institutional investors as a means of regulating the purchase and sale of common stocks.

One can classify the work that has been done under two categories: the price trend approach and the capitalized earnings approach. Most attempts to establish a central value for a representative average have concerned themselves with the problem of estimating an underlying trend in stock prices around which the average can reasonably be expected to fluctuate. The kind of price trends used have ranged from a linear trend, as is the case with Oberlin College, or a logarithmic trend, as is the case with the Keystone Seven Step Plan, to a ten-year moving average, as is the case with the F. I. Du Pont Institutional Index. Templeton, Dobbrow & Vance have developed a somewhat more complicated normal price based on previous normals. The most complicated estimate of central price is undoubtedly that of Zenon Szatrowski. His method essentially involves a correlation between the logarithm of the annual average of Standard and Poor's index of industrials for each year and the arithmetic mean of the logarithms of the annual averages for the preceding years beginning with 1871.

The capitalized earnings approach to central value has several adherents. It includes Graham's concept in which he states that the central value of the Dow Jones industrial average is equivalent to the reciprocal of twice the rate of interest on Moody's AAA bonds times a ten-year moving average of earnings. Oglebay Norton uses a variant to this approach. Average conditions are assumed to exist when average earnings on common stocks are 1 2/3 times the yield on long-term high-grade bonds; Oglebay Norton make their own forecast of earnings for the Dow Jones industrial average, rather than resort to a moving average of past earnings. Robert Storer has normalized the earnings of Standard and Poor's 50 industrials by deflating the series and computing its logarithmic trend; the trend in earnings is then reinflated and multiplied by the factor 12.9—which represents the average historical relationship between normal earnings and the particular index of stock prices employed—to obtain a central value for the index.

Nicholas Molodovsky has used two different procedures in determining what might be regarded as central values for indexes of his own construction. His price orbit involves the capitalizing of a twelve-year moving average of earnings by a constant multiplier (14.8) derived from an average price earnings relationship that has existed since 1937. Recently he has fitted an equation to quarterly data on price, earnings, dividends, and lagged price which essentially combines the price trend approach with the capitalized earnings approach by including lagged price as a variable.

From the standpoint of practical formula planning, the inclusion of lagged price in the formula appears to have the advantage of increasing the number of transactions that could be made under the plan. On normative grounds, however, there is little reason to believe that last quarter's price should bear a particular relationship to the "true" value of the index. The use of confidence intervals as a means of controlling stock purchases and sales has considerably more statistical merit than an arbitrary range of operation established by guess.

An analysis of price trends seems to ignore the underlying determinants of price which are prospective earnings and the alternative return which can be obtained by investing in other assets. From an economic point of view, it is somewhat difficult to imagine why stock prices should trend upwards at a rate which might be relied upon to establish plausible normal values for security averages. In a general way, we do know that businesses retain earnings and that this retention eventually reflects itself in higher stock prices; but this knowledge does not in itself provide firm grounds for assuming that business saving will increase stock values at a discernible rate that will maintain itself in the future.

In light of the theoretical and conceptual difficulties involved in the price trend approach to central value, it is truly amazing that the results which would have been obtained by price trend formulas, at least on paper, are often so striking. The question remains as to whether these results are the product of fortuitous circumstance or the product of underlying forces which can reasonably be expected to maintain a similar trend in the future. These doubts are not necessarily meant to disparage the price trend approach to central value, but to raise the question, on what rational economic grounds is it justified?

At this juncture the most appealing approach to central value is the capitalized earnings approach. Further research should be undertaken, however, to refine and improve the work that was initiated by Graham. High-grade bonds are not the only substitute for securities. One might well wish to ascertain the effect of changes in the rate of return/price of real estate and commodities. Monetary factors might also be taken into account. In addition to substitution possibilities, one would want to test the significance of earnings trends, the variability of earnings around the trend, and of price variability. These suggestions are meant only to be illustrative of what might be done to improve our knowledge of the determinants of central value. The inclusion of any variable in the central value model must ultimately rest on its being both statistically significant and theoretically plausible.

PHASE II.   THE DEVELOPMENT OF CENTRAL VALUE THEORY IN RELATION TO INDIVIDUAL EQUITIES

There are essentially two methods of establishing a central value for individual stocks. The first method is identical to the way in which a central value can be struck for any stock average; one simply endeavors to determine, by means of time series analysis, whether the individual security is over- or under-priced in terms of historical relationships. The New England plan is an example of the price trend approach (based on a ten-year moving average) applied to individual common stocks. The work of Arnold Bernhard in his Value Line Studies is an example of the capitalized earnings approach applied to individual stocks, although it should be noted that his use of a lagged price really makes his work fall partially into the price trend category. The Burlingame plan and the Howe method might also be mentioned as constituting attempts to measure the central value of individual securities in terms of relationships that are internal to the historical behavior of each security.

The usefulness of these approaches is somewhat limited. While they serve to indicate whether a stock is over- or under-valued in terms of its own historical price and earnings, they do not necessarily answer the question: Is an individual security over- or under-valued relative to other securities? The most fruitful approach to this latter question is cross-sectional analysis.

Two cross-sectional studies of different industries can be mentioned as leading in the direction of relative price analysis. The first is a study by George Cresson. In 1943 he correlated the mean high and low price of 32 leading oil companies with proven reserves per common share, dividends, and undistributed earnings. Recently John Collins has correlated the price of 37 bank stocks with operating earnings, dividends, book value, and net profits, and has suggested that:

> There is implicit in this method a prediction that if the market, generally, remains fairly constant, the stocks found to be below normal will tend to rise to normal, and that if the market, generally, rises, those below normal will tend to rise more than the others, and that if the market, generally, declines, the subnormals will tend to decline less than the others. For those above normal, the converse should be true. And these tendencies should persist until there is an appreciable change in the values of the determinants.

While Mr. Collins makes no attempt to subject the foregoing assertion to an empirical test, the idea that over- and under-valued stocks can be detected by observing the difference between actual market prices and those prices which are indicated by (or calculated from) cross-sectional correlation analysis, is nevertheless suggestive of a fundamental approach to security analysis.

Perhaps the finest statistical work that has been done in this direction of isolating the determinants of capitalization factors has been carried out under the auspices of the Public Finance Workshop in the Department of Economics at the University of Chicago. In a study of the "Determinants of Risk Premiums on Corporate Bonds," Larry Fisher has subjected the following hypothesis to a comprehensive empirical test involving several hundreds of observations which were taken during various periods of time:

> (1) The average risk premium on a firm's bonds depends on the risk that the firm will default on its bonds and on their marketability. (2) This "risk of default" can be estimated by a function of three variables: the coefficient of variation of the firm's net income over the past nine years (after all charges and taxes), the length of time the firm has been operating without forcing its creditors to take a loss, and the ratio of the market value of the equity in the firm to the par value of the firm's debt. (3) The marketability of a firm's bonds can be estimated by a single variable, the market value of all the publicly traded bonds the firm has outstanding. (4) The logarithm of the average risk premium on a firm's bonds can be estimated by a linear function of the four variables just listed.

Haskel Benishay has recently launched a study of the "Determinants of the Differences in Rates of Return on Corporate Equity." His hypothesis is as follows:

> The rate of return on stocks is a function of (1) the expected variability of the future income stream, (2) the liquidity of the stocks,

(3) the equity-debt ratio of the firm, (4) "age," the time lapsed since last period of major down-turn in the firm's fortunes (reorganization), and (5) some relevant measure of the trend in a company's ups and downs.

Since interest and the rate of return are nothing more than the reciprocal of capitalization factors existing in the market, a study of their economic determinants is of great value to security analysis. If the important economic determinants of capitalization factors can be isolated by means of cross-sectional correlation analysis, they can be used to aid the analyst in making statements with regard to the question of how a stock ought to be priced relative to other stocks.

CONCLUDING REMARKS

It is to be expected that a suggestion to rest security analysis on a statistical foundation will be met with mixed opinion and emotion. On one hand, those analysts who are statistically oriented are apt to applaud the suggestion without recognizing its limitations. On the other hand, those who find it difficult to think in terms of algebraic relationships and probabilities are apt to meet the suggestion with suspicion and hostility. It is only fitting that my concluding remarks be dedicated to those analysts who place their faith in "intangibles" and variables which are peculiar to individual firms and, hence, do not lend themselves readily to quantitative analysis. Paradoxically as it may seem, it is this group which stands to gain the most from the development of security analysis as an applied mathematical science. If a correlation of security prices with the more important economic determinants should disclose, for instance, that a particular stock or group of stocks in under- or over-valued, it is for the trained and experienced analyst to search for variables, such as factors of account, which have been excluded from the more general model, but might justify a discrepancy between price and indicated value.

It would surely be naive to assume that any statistical model is an infallible indicator of "true" value. Its indications must always be interpreted in light of the possibility of biased observations and of plausible relationships that were excluded from the model for practical reasons and for want of generality. To the extent, however, that other reasons cannot be advanced in support of deviations, they serve as evidence of irrational pricing and forewarn of price adjustments that may be in the offing at some future time. Models of the security market can be looked upon as providing a frame of reference from which to initiate more intensive studies of individual situations; the model's residual deviations can be looked upon as indicating directions in which further study may be warranted.

BIBLIOGRAPHY

Graham & Dodd: Security Analysis.
G. A. Drew: New Methods for Profit in the Stock Market.

Cowles & Jones: Econometrica, Vol. 5.
L. C. Wilcoxen: Journal of the American Statistical Association, Vol. 37.
J. Timbergen: The Review of Economics and Statistics, Vol. 21.
Zeon Szotrowski: Journal of the American Statistical Association, Vol. 40.
Justin Barbour: Analysts Journal, 4th Quarter, 1948.
Irving Sitt: Analysts Journal, 2nd Quarter, 1956.
N. Molodovsky: New Tools.
J. Mindell: The Stock Market.
F. R. Macaulay: The Movement of Interest Rates.
Pickett & Ketchum: Investment Principles and Policy.
D. Gale Johnson: Forward Prices for Agriculture.
Lucile Tomlinson: Practical Formulas for Successful Investing.
Dewey & Dakin: Cycles.

22
THE DIMENSIONS OF ANALYSIS: A CRITICAL REVIEW*

DOUGLAS A. HAYES, C.F.A., is professor of finance, Graduate School of Business, University of Michigan. He has been a member for several years of the Council of Examiners for the Institute of Chartered Financial Analysts and of the Committee on Professional Ethics and Education.

The process of selecting individual securities, and particularly common stocks, for investment portfolios has several dimensions. But while the basic structure of the portfolio selection process is fairly well established, considerable controversy seems to exist as to the means by which these dimensions should be implemented. It is our purpose to review critically a few

*From *Financial Analysts Journal,* Vol. 22, No. 5 (September-October 1966), pp. 81-83. Reprinted by permission.

major areas of conflict currently extant in investment analysis. Hopefully, this might enable practicing analysts to identify more clearly the issues involved and the possible implications of the alternative points of view.

For example, it is generally agreed that the process should be oriented to and conditioned by specific portfolio objectives, such as growth, income requirements, quality limitations, and diversification targets. But as these matters are essentially in the domain of overall portfolio strategy rather than security analysis per se, they are regarded as outside the scope of this review. However, it might be noted that considerable controversy currently exists in this area as to the usefulness of computer programs to suggest and delineate the characteristics of efficient or optimum portfolios. It is my tentative opinion that existing models for portfolio structures are likely to be of very limited practical use as they seem to involve some highly questionable assumptions in order to obtain required quantifications, such as that the entire spectrum of risk factors can be adequately measured by the relative price volatility of individual issues.

A second crucial dimension of security selection is concerned with appraising the potential economic values (primarily prospective earnings and dividend flows and the risks surrounding their achievement) embodied in the industries and related companies that appear eligible to meet the portfolio requirements. The content of most of the literature, as well as of our series of C.F.A. examinations, suggests that mastery of this broad area is considered to be of prime importance to the professional development of financial analysts and portfolio managers. And rightly so. For while the random-walk theory of security prices may be convincing with respect to the problem of obtaining short-term trading results, this theory does not conflict with the proposition that long-term investment returns will largely be a function of the long-term economic performance of particular industries and companies.

Although the concept that investment results are likely to be heavily related to corporate performance in a long-term sense is generally accepted, some recent contributions to the field have alleged that the implementation methodology should be completely revolutionized. For example, Lerner and Carleton allege that a critical investigation of the past financial statements to reveal potential problems of consistency and comparability of reported income and balance sheet data can be largely discarded because accounting and disclosure standards have improved to the point where the underlying data require no critical review.[1] Moreover, they allege that financial risk factors no longer require appraisal because of the greatly improved stability features of the economy; in lieu thereof, they suggest elegant mathematical techniques to develop the theoretical effects of assumed patterns of various management decisions and economic data on security values. [2]

---

[1] Lerner and Carleton, *A Theory of Financial Analysis,* Harcourt, Brace, and World, Inc., New York: 1966, pp. 3-4.
[2] *Ibid.,* pp. 37-126.

However, the empirical evidence would suggest that these allegations are seriously in error. Largely because of recurrent tinkering with the tax rules for national economic policy reasons, a strong case can be made that the reported incomes of many, if not most, corporations have become subject to increased problems of consistency and comparability rather than less.[3] Again, while there is no doubt that general economic stability has been greatly improved through the development and vigorous application of modern fiscal and monetary concepts, individual industries and companies continue to record wide variations in revenues and net income. The earnings collapse of the cement companies despite generally favorable conditions in the construction industry can be cited as a case in point. In a dynamic and highly competitive private economy, it is entirely possible for a condition of general stability and growth on a macro-economic basis to be accompanied by wide fluctuations and divergent trends on a micro-basis. Therefore, the position that techniques designed to estimate potential risks arising from potential earnings instability are entirely obsolete because severe general depression conditions are highly unlikely appears open to serious question.

In short, the argument that a large portion of conventional analysis techniques should be discarded in favor of elaborate mathematical models does not appear convincing for practical purposes in the present stage of the arts. However, continued experimentation with such models undoubtedly will continue. Moreover, it is entirely possible that they will prove to be valuable supplements in the complex process of appraising the relative investment merits of individual companies. But at the same time it is doubtful if they will completely replace orthodox techniques because of the necessity to introduce highly simplifying assumptions in order to reduce the models to manageable proportions.

A third dimension involved in investment decisions consists of placing some estimate of value on the potential stream of earnings and dividends. The various concepts and techniques for implementing this task have probably been explored more widely in recent years than any other phase of investment analysis. The result has been both a proliferation of techniques and serious differences in fundamental veiwpoints. Because of space limitations, only a few of the conflicts can be cited herein; a worthwhile research project would certainly be a critical comparative analysis of this entire area.

First, a fundamental difference exists as to whether values should be established in absolute or relative terms. The "absolutists" hold that multipliers or capitalization rates should have a firmly established range which should change only slowly through time, if at all.[4] Only in this way, it is argued, can

---

[3]For documentation see the symposium issue of articles on "Uniformity in Financial Accounting," *Law and Contemporary Problems,* Duke University, Autumn, 1965 and particularly my own article entitled "Accounting and Investment Analysis," pp. 752-71.

[4]Graham, Dodd, and Cottle, *Security Analysis,* 4th edition, McGraw-Hill, New York, 1962, Chapter 37.

commitments be restrained at over-valued market levels and encouraged at more attractive price levels. The "relativists" on the other hand hold that investment decisions essentially represent a choice among the alternatives available at any existing point in time. The relative levels of bond and stock prices, along with other considerations (the estimated inflationary bias of the economy for example), are the basis for determining the proportions of the portfolio within each area. But once this decision is reached, the multipliers on individual stocks should relate only to those currently prevailing in the market as represented by a general index of stocks or a qualified list of alternatives.[5] Otherwise, it is argued, the valuation process may decide not *which* stocks to buy but whether *any* stocks should be bought, and thus cancel out the basic portfolio strategy already presumably determined.

A second area of conflict relates to the usefulness of present-value theory and related techniques in determining common stock values. One group holds that such techniques are highly desirable to provide a more rigorous framework for making selection decisions and that their use may also sharpen greatly comparative value estimates. On the other side, it is argued that because of recurrent dynamic changes within the economy and individual industries, the long-term earnings forecasts required under the present-value approach have little actual validity. As a consequence, it is concluded that what appears to be a scientific and precise method of valuation is merely a theoretical exercise at best and misleading at worst.[6]

An intermediate position here would seem desirable. Certainly, the use of these techniques to obtain comparative *estimates* of *relative* values can be defended. The tables of growth yields, constructed by Soldofsky and Murphy, and the series of iso-yield curves, developed by David Eiteman, are fairly recent technical contributions incorporating present-value theory which appear to have considerable promise in this connection.[7] On the other hand, when present-value techniques are used to compute *precise* values for given stocks without qualification, then they may render a misleading impression of accuracy. Moreover, used in this way they may lead to a decision to reject most qualified stocks unless flexibility in the choice of discount and growth rates is maintained.

While the need to consider portfolio objectives, prospective earnings and dividend flows, and to estimate appropriate values for such flows are generally

---

[5]For a more complete discussion of this view, see Bing, "Appraising our Methods of Stock Appraisal," *Financial Analysts Journal,* May-June, 1964, pp. 118-24.
[6]The exchanges between Messrs. Molodovsky and Bing in the *Financial Analysts Journal,* May-June, 1964, pp. 118-28 and continued by Bing in the July-August issue, pp. 109-ll are representative of the differences here.
[7]Soldofsky and Murphy, *Growth Yields on Common Stocks: Theory and Tables,* Bureau of Business Research, State University of Iowa, Iowa City, 1961; and David Eiteman, "A Graphic Framework for Growth Stock Selection," *California Management Review,* Winter, 1965, University of California, pp. 39-50.

accepted dimensions of security selection, there is a fourth dimension which is highly controversial as to whether it should have any role at all. Reference here is to an analysis of the prospective price performance that might be anticipated over the following year or so.

The arguments in favor of considering this factor seem to be primarily based on pragmatic and operating considerations rather than on investment theory and principles. First, it can be observed that highly favorable portfolio returns in recent years could often have been obtained by acquiring stocks which had a strong visible following among investors and speculators. The results on stocks in the airline and color television industries cannot easily be ignored. Second, some portfolio managers, like it or not, operate in a competitive environment, and the quarterly or annual relative market results may be quite significant in obtaining (or retaining) clients. As is well known, mutual funds and some pension funds seem to be particularly exposed to competitive price performance criteria over fairly short time periods. Therefore, they may correctly argue that even if in principle this dimension should be secondary to long-term value criteria, as a practical matter they cannot afford to disregard it.

On the other side, it is clear that the analytical factors in this area are often really behavioral in character rather than economic or financial. As the education and training of most analysts have largely been in economics and finance rather than in psychology, a legitimate question of competence to evaluate behavioral factors can be raised.

The eminent economist, John Maynard Keynes, had a lively section in his famous *General Theory* on this point wherein he concludes by observing that many professional investors become involved in the rather vague game of "devoting our intelligences to anticipating what average opinion expects the average opinion to be" rather than selecting the investments which appear to have the "best genuine long-term expectations."[8] In short, Keynes raised a fundamental question that is quite pertinent today: May not a preoccupation with prospective market popularity in reaching investment decisions detract from the desired degree of attention to the basic value elements which are most likely to be pertinent to favorable long-term results? Keynes' comments, it might be noted, were not those of a purely academic theoretician; he was known to have accumulated a sizeable fortune through investment activities. My opinion for investors not confronted by short-term competitive performance criteria is on the record as follows: "After an investment decision has been reached, subsequent review should focus primarily on the corporate performance rather than on the market action of the stock.[9]

---

[8]Keynes, *The General Theory of Employment, Interest and Money,* Harcourt, Brace and Co., New York, 1936, p. 156.
[9]Hayes, *Investments: Analysis and Management,* 2nd edition, Macmillan Co., New York, 1966, p. 81.

23
CONCEPTUAL FOUNDATIONS
OF TECHNICAL ANALYSIS*

ROBERT A. LEVY has been a member of the faculty at the School of Business Administration of The American University in Washington, D.C. He is a director of Conrad & Co., Inc., mutual-fund distributors, Hyattsville, Maryland.

The stock market fundamentalist relies upon economic and financial statistics and information. He investigates corporate income statements, balance sheets, dividend records, management policies, sales growth, managerial ability, plant capacity, and competitive forces. He looks to the daily press for evidence of future business conditions. He analyzes bank reports and the voluminous statistical compilations of the various government agencies. Taking all these factors into account, he projects corporate earnings and applies a satisfactory earnings multiplier (price-earnings ratio, capitalization rate) to arrive at the intrinsic value of the security under observation. He then compares this intrinsic value to the existing market price and, if the former is sufficiently higher, he regards the stock as a purchase candidate.[1]

The term "technical" in its application to the stock market means something quite different than its ordinary dictionary definition. It refers to the study of the market itself as opposed to the external factors reflected in the market. Technical analysis is, in essence, the recording of the actual history of trading (including both price movement and the volume of transactions) for one stock or a group of equities, and deducing the future trend from this historical analysis.[2]

From Financial Analysts Journal, Vol. 2, No. 4 (July-August 1966), pp. 83-89. Reprinted by permission.

[1]Robert D. Edwards and John Magee, *Technical Analysis of Stock Trends* (Springfield, Mass.: John Magee, 1958), p. 3.

[2]*Ibid.,* p. 5.

Various tools of technical analysis have evolved over the years. Time and space preclude a discussion of these numerous tools; rather, they will simply be identified. The interested reader is encouraged to consult one or more of the cited publications for more complete information.[3] The precursor of all technical principles was the Dow Theory, which evolved as a result of the work of Charles H. Dow, editor of *The Wall Street Journal* from 1889 to 1902, and his followers. Other technical tools or indicators include the Elliott Wave Principle, Barron's Confidence Index, odd lot statistics, short interest ratios, breadth (advance–decline) indexes, statistics on new highs and lows, upside-downside volume data, bar charts and point-and-figure charts, which picture price and volume movements, moving average trend-lines, relative strength measures, and statistics on debits and credits of brokerage balances—to name a few of the more important ones.

Technical theory can be summarized as follows:

1. Market value is determined solely by the interaction of supply and demand.

2. Supply and demand are governed by numerous factors, both rational and irrational. Included in these factors are those that are relied upon by the fundamentalists, as well as opinions, moods, guesses and blind necessities. The market weighs all of these factors continually and automatically.

3. Disregarding minor fluctuations in the market, stock prices tend to move in trends which persist for an appreciable length of time.

4. Changes in trend are caused by the shifts in supply and demand relationships. These shifts, no matter why they occur, can be detected sooner or later in the action of the market itself.[4]

The basic assumption of technical theorists is that history tends to repeat itself. In other words, past patterns of market behavior will recur in the future and can thus be used for predictive purposes. In statistical terminology, the stock market technician relies upon the dependence of successive price changes.

The assumption of the fundamental analyst is quite different. He believes that each security has an intrinsic value which depends upon its earning potential, and that actual market prices tend to move toward intrinsic values. If his belief is correct, then determining the intrinsic value of a security by capitalizing future earnings is equivalent to predicting the security's future price.[5]

---

[3]See particularly: *Encyclopedia of Stock Market Techniques,* Investors Intelligence, Inc., Larchmont, N. Y., 1963; Garfield A. Drew, *New Methods for Profit in the Stock Market* (Boston: The Metcalf Press, 1954); and Joseph E. Granville, *A Strategy of Daily Stock Market Timing for Maximum Profit* (Englewood Cliffs, N.J.: Prentice-Hall, Inc., 1960).
[4]Edwards and Magee, *op cit.,* p. 86.
[5]Eugene F. Fama, "Random Walks in Stock Market Prices," *Financial Analysts Journal,* XXI, No. 5 (September-October 1965), p. 55.

THE CASE FOR TECHNICAL ANALYSIS

Robert D. Edwards and John Magee, two outspoken advocates of the technical school, argue that:

It is futile to assign an intrinsic value to a stock certificate. One share of United States Steel, for example, was worth $261 in the early Fall of 1929, but you could buy it for only $22 in June of 1932! By March, 1937, it was selling for $126 and just one year later for $38. . . . This sort of thing, this wide divergence between presumed value and actual value, is not the exception; it is the rule; it is going on all the time. The fact is that the real value of a share of U.S. Steel common is determined at any given time solely, definitely and inexorably by supply and demand, which are accurately reflected in the transactions consummated on the floor of the New York Stock Exchange.

Of course, the statistics which the fundamentalists study play a part in the supply-demand equation—that is freely admitted. But there are many other factors affecting it. The market price reflects not only the differing value opinions of many orthodox security appraisers but also all the hopes and fears and guesses and moods, rational and irrational, of hundreds of potential buyers and sellers, as well as their needs and their resources—in total, factors which defy analysis and for which no statistics are obtainable, but which are nevertheless all synthesized, weighed and finally expressed in the one precise figure at which a buyer and seller get together and make a deal (through their agents, their respective brokers). This is the only figure that counts.

. . . In brief, the going price as established by the market itself comprehends all the fundamental information which the statistical analyst can hope to learn (plus some which is perhaps secret from him, known only to a few insiders) and much else besides of equal or even greater importance.

All of which, admitting its truth, would be of little significance were it not for the fact, which no one of experience doubts, that *prices move in trends* and trends tend to continue until something happens to change the supply-demand balance.[6]

The technical analyst justifies his activities in several ways. First, he contends that short-term market fluctuations are more important than long-term trends, where importance is judged by the profit potential in trading. Certainly the trader who buys at the bottom of each short-term movement and sells at the top will realize greater profits than the investor who benefits only from the major trend. Second, the technician contends that information on fundamental conditions comes too late for maximum profit. The fundamentalist is forced to

---

[6]Edwards and Magee, *op cit.,* pp. 5-6.

wait for statistics on sales, orders, earnings, dividends and similar factors. By the time information of this sort is made publicly available, the market may have already discounted its effect and commenced a substantial upward or downward move. The technical trader, however, can act instantaneously on any change in stock prices whether or not the news underlying the change has been made public. The technician believes that the movement of the market precedes the movement of other economic series, rather than vice-versa.[7] (In this regard, he has the support of the National Bureau of Economic Research which, in its study of business cycles, has listed stock market prices as one of twelve leading ndicators.)[8]

It is admitted by technicians that some fundamental analysts may be able to forecast the trend of business quite accurately; they may even know exactly what present economic conditions are, and what future conditions will be; moreover, they may be absolutely correct in their earnings projections for a given company. Yet, even assuming all of this to be true, their projections of stock market action could be grossly in error.[9] It is only technical analysis which can detect the buying and selling pressures caused by psychological and emotional, rather than economic and financial, factors. Only the market action itself reflects the existence of inside information not made publicly available. This important fact has been relied upon by all technicians, and written about by George A. Chestnutt, Jr., the manager of a mutual fund which depends heavily on technical methods.

There are so many factors, each having its own effect on the price fluctuations of any individual stock, that it is practically impossible to analyze them *separately* and give each its proper weight in an attempt to estimate the stock's future market action. Often the essential information is known only to insiders. It is not released to the public until it is too late to act upon it.

Fortunately we do not need to know *why* one stock is stronger than another in order to act profitably upon the knowledge of the fact. The market itself is continually weighing and recording the effects of all the bullish information and all the bearish information about every stock. No one in possession of inside information can profit from it unless he buys or sells the stock. The moment he does, his buy or sell orders have their effect upon the price. That effect is revealed in the market action of the stock.[10]

---

[7] George L. Leffler and Loring C. Farwell, *The Stock Market* (New York: The Ronald Press Company, 1963), p. 574.

[8] Julius Shiskin, "Business Cycle Indicators: The Known and the Unknown," *Business Cycle Developments* (Washington: U.S. Department of Commerce, Bureau of the Census, September 1963), Appendix H.

[9] Joseph E. Granville, *New Key to Stock Market Profits* (Englewood Cliffs, N.J.: Prentice-Hall, Inc., 1963), p. 20.

[10] George A. Chestnutt, Jr., *Stock Market Analysis: Facts and Principles* (Larchmont, N.Y.: American Investors Corporation, 1965), p. 19.

The argument of the technical analyst, in a nutshell, is that stock price moves are caused by the interaction of supply and demand, and that the flow of funds into and out of various securities is first detected by the various technical market indicators, not by the analysis of fundamental economic and financial statistics.[11]

A CRITIQUE OF THE INTRINSIC VALUE APPROACH

Technicians agree that trends and patterns evolve, for the most part, as a result of market action taken by those persons who have, or think they have, some superior knowledge of underlying fundamental factors. The obvious corollary, which fundamentalists are quick to point out, is that the possessors of this superior knowledge are in the best position to maximize their profits from stock market transactions. Since fundamental knowledge, so the argument goes, is the "stuff" which even technical analysts must ultimately rely upon to produce the trends and patterns which they study, so it must therefore be a better foundation for security appraisal.

In fact, *there is little justification for denying that properly-performed fundamental analysis is superior to technical analysis.* The technician must wait until those persons who have critical information, which others do not have, make their move in the market. Even though the technical analyst may be able to act before critical information is publicly available, nevertheless he will be later in his actions than will be the "insiders" who are first aware of the underlying fundamental factors. The conclusion must be, therefore, that investment analysis will be most successful when the analyst is among the first to gain and correctly evaluate the necessary superior knowledge.

But the technician still has a strong argument. First, it is possible that properly-performed fundamental analysis could lead to unsatisfactory investment results. The opinion of the fundamentalist regarding the intrinsic value of a given security, even if correct, must be shared by other investors who control substantial financial resources and are willing to place these resources in the market place. Only when opinions are converted into action, and only when a sufficient amount of capital is involved, will the market price move toward intrinsic value. Thus the fundamental analyst may find himself heavily invested in a security for a considerable length of time before market support develops. Of course, this lowers his rate of return by tying up funds which could have been invested elsewhere. The technician, however, purports to avoid this potential problem by delaying his investment until market support for a

---

[11]Joseph E. Granville, *A Strategy of Daily Stock Market Timing for Maximum profit, op cit.,* p. 9.

particular stock has already appeared. It is conceivable that the sacrifice in profits resulting from late selection is no greater than the opportunity cost of unproductive capital arising from early selection.

Second, and of greater importance, how many investors are able to successfully engage in fundamental analysis? How many are capable of being among the first to recognize and evaluate critical information? How many have the necessary non-monetary rescources (primarily time and reliable statistical information)?

Assume, for the sake of argument, that all investors are capable, and that they have sufficient time to analyze the economic and financial factors affecting any given security. These investors will then attempt to project the earnings of a particular company and capitalize these earnings in order to arrive at some estimate of intrinsic value. The most important of the statistical data upon which the investors will rely are the company's financial statements. Under these circumstances, how successful will the fundamentalist be in his analysis? The question could be posed in a more direct manner: How complete and reliable are the corporate financial reports which are the major source of information for the fundamental analyst?

The purpose of published annual reports is to convey information to present and prospective stockholders about the operations of the corporate entity. This information should include all that is relevant (both qualitative and quantitative) to enable the investor to make a rational and informed judgment as to the investment worth of the company. Consequently, published annual reports should be designed for the use of the skilled financial analyst. Only then can they possibly include information in sufficient volume and detail as to provide for an efficient allocation of capital resources through investment selection.

The Securities and Exchange Commission, through Regulation S-X, has prescribed the form and content of financial reports filed with the S.E.C. The Securities Acts Amendments of 1964 extended these filing requirements to most over-the-counter companies, thereby matching the requirements which theretofore had been imposed only upon listed firms. Prior to 1964 the S.E.C.'s filing requirements had only an indirect effect (through public pressure) on the form and content of published annual reports to stockholders. The published reports could, and often did, differ from the Form 10-K annual reports filed with the S.E.C. Differences were both as to dollar amounts and as to the extent of the information provided. However, in May 1964 the S.E.C. adopted Rule 14a-3 which prescribed, among other things, that any material differences between the methods of reporting to the S.E.C. and the methods of reporting to stockholders must be noted in the published annual report along with a reconciliation of the differences. Consequently, subsequent to 1964, published annual reports did not differ in dollar amount from the Form 10Ks. Nevertheless, there are still considerable differences in the extent and volume of information in the two reports. Many corporations publish no more than a summary balance sheet, income statement and statement of retained earnings for a one-year, or perhaps two-year period. Needless to say, this is unsatisfactory to the fundamental analyst.

Some of the information which is badly needed in published reports, but which is seldom available, includes: (1) production in units; (2) sales in units; (3) rate of capacity operated; (4) breakdown of operations as between domestic and foreign; (5) division of sales as between intercompany and outsiders; (6) wages, wage rates, hours worked and number of employees; (7) state and local taxes paid; (8) amount and details of selling and general expenses; (9) amount and details of maintenance expenditures; (10) details of capital expenditures; (11) details of inventories; (12) details of properties owned; (13) number of stockholders; (14) sales by product line and by consuming industry; (15) research and development costs; (16) details of long-term lease arrangements; (17) details of stock option and pension plans; (18) more complete disclosure of depreciation policies; and (19) orders booked and unfilled orders.[12] And this is by no means an all-inclusive list.

The American Institute of Certified Public Accountants has commented extensively upon the adequacy of information in published reports. Of particular importance are the remarks appearing in three of the *Accounting Research Studies,* covering the accounting ramifications of financial leases, business combinations, and pensions respectively.[13] In these studies, investigations of annual reports revealed gross inadequacy of information.

The sparse quantity of information is only one of the problems of the fundamentalists, however. Of equal importance is the question of reliability. Presumably, when the financial statements of a company are accompanied by the unqualified approval of an independent certified public accountant, investors and creditors may be assured of the fairness and integrity of the reports. The auditor's report indicates whether he feels that the financial position of the company and the results of its operations are presented fairly, in conformity with generally accepted accounting principles. The audit supposedly eliminates, or at least discloses, unintentional errors by corporate accountants, bias on the part of corporate management, deviations from generally accepted accounting principles, and deliberate falsification. The audit also determines whether the

---

[12]Benjamin Graham, David L. Dodd and Sidney Cottle, *Security Analysis* (New York: McGraw-Hill Book Company, Inc., 1962), pp. 80-82.

[13]John H. Myers, "Reporting of Leases in Financial Statements," *Accounting Research Study No. 4* (New York: American Institute of Certified Public Accountants, 1962); Arthur R. Wyatt, "A Critical Study of Accounting for Business Combinations," *Accounting Research Study No. 5* (New York: American Institute of Certified Public Accountants, 1963); and Ernest L. Hicks, "Accounting for the Cost of Pension Plans," *Accounting Research Study No. 8* (New York: American Institute of Certified Public Accountants, 1965).

financial statements have been prepared on a basis consistent with that of the prior year and whether they fully disclose all material facts.[14]

In practice, there are many reasons why the auditor's certificate is of less-than-desirable significance. First, the auditor's examination is limited to a program of tests which are not infallible in detecting errors. Second, such concepts as "fairness," "materiality," "full disclosure" and "consistency" are subjective in nature and cannot be objectively verified.[15] Third, and fortunately least frequent in occurrence, there may be outright dishonesty by the independent auditor or collusion between the accounting firm and its corporate client. Fourth, and of greatest importance, there are no truly generally accepted accounting principles. The accounting profession is in a state of flux. In some cases there are a multiplicity of acceptable procedures, while in other cases, those principles which have been applied for so many years are now being subjected to serious re-analysis and skeptical re-evaluation.

Questions as to both fairness and objectivity of financial reporting were raised in five of the *Accounting Research Studies*.[16] The specific problems included asset valuation, treatment of leases, business combinations, adjustments for changes in price level, and pensions. In each of these areas there is considerable doubt as to the propriety of presently ·employed accounting principles (particularly as to the appropriateness of historical cost valuations.)

Additional accounting problems exist in the following areas: (1) matching revenues and expenses (e.g., direct vs. absorption costing, installment sales, long-term construction contracts, stock options, depreciation, the investment credit, and deferred taxes); (2) distinguishing between several acceptable accounting methods and determining the effect of using one as opposed to another (e.g., depreciation, the investment credit, and inventory valuation); and (3) estimating various factors which are relevant to the accounting process (e.g., depreciable lives and bad debt expense).

Financial ratios, while potentially useful to the fundamentalist, can be no better than the figures from which they are derived. And these figures, in turn, are only as good as the underlying accounting principles. Year-to-year comparisons and trends are suspect because the flexibility of accounting procedures permits manipulation of the financial data. Inter-company

---

[14]Walter B. Meigs, *Principles of Auditing* (Homewood, Ill.: Richard D. Irwin, Inc., 1959), pp. 1-2.

[15]*Ibid*, pp. 14-17.

[16]Robert T. Sprouse and Maurice Moonitz, "A Tentative Set of Broad Accounting Principles for Business Enterprises," *Accounting Research Study No. 3* (New York: American Institute of Certified Public Accountants, 1962); Myers, *op. cit.;* Wyatt, *op. cit.;* Accounting Research Division, "Reporting the Financial Effects of Price-Level Changes," *Accounting Research Study No. 6* (New York: American Institute of Certified Public Accountants, 1963); and Hicks, *op. cit.*

comparisons are also unreliable because of the wide choice of permissible accounting methods.

The end-result is that the analyst, using publicly available information, has an extremely difficult task in trying to reconstruct a corporation's financial statements in order to get some picture of the company's earning power.

Nor does the analyst's problems terminate upon the evaluation of recent financial statements. This only provides his with an approximation of current and historical earnings. Now he must project these into the future. Moreover, a one-year projection is not adequate. As stated in a widely-respected text on fundamental analysis:

> Typically, these ... studies rest on a careful but too abbreviated forecast of probable future earnings for a company—covering generally only the next twelve months or less.
> ... While such a measurement is important, it is hardly sufficient for an investment recommendation, since value cannot soundly be established on the basis of earnings shown over a short period of time.[17]

And that isn't all of the fundamentalist's trials and tribulations. Determining current and historical earnings is a difficult task indeed. Projecting these earnings for a number of years into the future is even more difficult. But now comes the most difficult job of all: selecting an appropriate price-earnings multiple (or capitalization rate). The problems inherent in this last step are reflected in the following statement by Graham, Dodd and Cottle, commenting upon a 1953 estimate by the Value Line Investment Survey of the 1956-1958 prices of the stocks in the Dow Jones Industrial Average.

> ... although the earnings estimates were wide of the mark in several instances ... the aggregate earnings estimate for the 29 stocks was very close to the actual. ... By contrast, the aggregate market value estimate for 1956-1958 was significantly less accurate—missing by more than 22 per cent the three-year mean price. ... This tends to confirm our view that earnings can be predicted with more confidence than can the capitalization rate or multiplier, which to a major degree will reflect the market psychology existing at the time.[18]

Reference to the historical relationship between market price and *current* earnings is to no avail. Graham, Dodd and Cottle compared, over the 25-year period, 1935-1959, the quarterly earnings (on an annualized basis and seasonally adjusted) of Standard and Poor's 500 Composite stock group with the quarterly average stock-price index. They found that in 46 out of the 100 quarters stock

---

17Graham, Dodd and Cottle, *op. cit.,* p. 434.
18*Ibid.,* p. 439.

prices moved counter to the change in earnings (i.e., earnings increased while prices declined, or vice-versa).[19]

Granville emphasized this same important point by demonstrating the lack of correlation between prices and earnings as uncovered in his examination of hundreds of stocks. He found that price-earnings ratios fluctuated widely and that this fluctuation "dilutes the widely held belief that good earnings are a necessary accompaniment to advancing stock prices."[20]

With all of these difficulties (determining current earnings, projecting future earnings, and selecting an appropriate capitalization rate) it might be expected that even the best fundamental analysts can be far wide of the mark. This expectation would be justified by the facts. The 1965 range of the Dow Jones Industrial Average was 840.59 to 969.26, and the average of the 1963-1965 DJIA annual high-lows was 813.60.[21] But in March of 1961 Naess and Thomas projected the 1965 Average at 688; and Value Line, in January of 1961, suggested that the mean for 1963-1965 would be 705.[22] Errors of this size are not unusual. Graham, Dodd and Cottle, in the 1962 edition of their book, *Security Analysis*, stated that "careful consideration of this problem . . . led us to increase our 1951 valuation standards by an arbitrary 50 per cent."[23] Such arbitrariness certainly bespeaks unreliability.

It is clear that fundamental analysis, even when performed by so-called experts, can be quite inaccurate. The question remains as to whether technical analysis offers any better possibilities. At least one prominent author believes that it does.

There have been frequent occasions when technical analysis was the *only* thing that could possibly have given the correct answer to the future trend of the market. This was true, for example, in the spring of 1946. If any investor had then possessed a crystal ball which would have shown him what corporate earnings were to be a year later, he could only have concluded that stock prices would be considerably higher. Instead, they were substantially lower in the face of record earnings and dividends.

There was nothing in the "fundamentals"—either in 1946 or 1947—to explain why prices had collapsed in the meantime. But there was considerable evidence of a weak *technical* situation in the market beforehand. . . . The investor who acted on technical grounds did not need to concern himself with *why* the market should seem to be acting irrationally, whereas the analyst of business facts and probabilities—unable to find a "reason"—was forced to conclude that the market could not do what it actually did.

---

[19]*Ibid.*, p. 719.
[20]Granville, *New Keys to Stock Market Profits, op. cit.*, p. 21.
[21]"Statistical Section," *Barron's*, XLVI, No. 24 (June 13, 1966), p. 57.
[22]Graham, Dodd and Cottle, *op. cit.*, p. 418.
[23]*Ibid.*, p. 421.

. . . .

In a broad sense, the experience of the past ten years has very clearly demonstrated that the price-to-earnings ratio is a much more important factor than the actual level and/or trend of earnings themselves. Since the ratio is determined by investment psychology, the study of technical market action has, on the whole, been more fruitful than fundamental analysis.[24]

MAJOR CRITICISMS OF TECHNICAL ANALYSIS

There are at least four major criticisms of technical analysis. The first three are closely interrelated. First, it is contended that the behavior of the stock market in the past may not be indicative of its behavior in the years to come. That is to say, even assuming that technical analysis would have been successful over the last decade, there is no guarantee that it will be successful over the next decade. Typical of the response to this criticism is the following denial by Edwards and Magee.

. . . all the new controls and regulations of the past several years, the new taxes which have placed a heavy handicap on successful investors, the greatly augmented and improved facilities for acquiring dependable information on securities, even the quite radical changes in certain portions of our basic economy, have not much altered the "pattern" of the stock market.[25]

The second contention of the critics is that technical traders acting on the results of their studies tend to create the very patterns and trends which they claim have predictive significance. In other words, the market action may be a reflection of the chart action instead of the reverse. Technicians recognize that this possibility exists. However, they argue that the habits and evaluative methods of individuals are so deeply ingrained that the same kinds of events continually produce the same kinds of market responses. Since these habits and methods are extremely durable, and since fundamental analysts greatly outnumber the technicians, it is unlikely that technical trading alters the response of the fundamentalists to external factors; and hence the actions of technicians probably do not have a major influence on the behavior of a competitive market.[26]

This second criticism inevitably leads to a third—that, if technical analysis is continually successful, an influx of technical traders will neutralize whatever profit potential exists. An analogy can be offered in the field of horse racing. If

---

[24]Drew, *op. cit.*, pp. 242-44.
[25]Edwards and Magee, *op. cit.*, p. 1.
[26]*Ibid.*, pp. 391-92.

someone were to perfect a system of wagering on horses, and if he were to publicize this system so as to make it available for everyone's use, the amount of betting on the highest-rated horses would change the odds sufficiently to offset the profitability of the system. There are several reasons why this criticism is not fatal to the art of technical analysis. First, it is quite possible that extremely successful technical "systems" have been developed but, for this very reason, have not been publicized or made available for general use. Second, it is likely that those who are not engaged in technical analysis would be reluctant to believe the claims of successful technicians. Third, to the extent that technical analysis may depend in part upon the use of electronic computers and sophisticated mathematical techniques, both the expense and the requisite training and knowledge will prevent its exploitation by the majority of the investing public. Fourth, and most important, is the following argument given by Granville:

> There is no danger that the revelation of new techniques will so enlighten the masses as to render them (the techniques) useless. The application of such things requires time and work, and human nature is such that most people will neither have the time, patience or desire to do the work necessary to achieve the results which might be had when these things are done.[27]

Finally, the fourth major criticism of technical analysis is its subjectivity. Advocates of the technical school contend that their methods preclude the somewhat arbitrary determinations which accompany fundamental analysis (e.g., selection of a capitalization rate). Critics, however, maintain that the technician's favorite tool, the chart of stock price movements, is subject to a wide variety of interpretations. Without debating the validity of this criticism, it may be noted that the recent use of the computer for purposes of analyzing price and volume movements would tend to reduce the subjectivity which might otherwise be inherent in technical analysis.

IMPLICATIONS OF THE RANDOM WALK THEORY

The most critical indictment of technical analysis, thereby giving indirect support to the fundamentalists' side of the debate, is the random walk theory. This theory restates the above-mentioned criticisms in slightly different context. It argues that the activities of chart readers, if successful, would help to produce the independence of successive stock price changes. But this independence, once established, renders chart reading an unprofitable activity.

---

[27]Granville, *New Key to Stock Market Profits, op. cit.,* p. 11.

On the other hand, fundamentalists who consistently evaluate the effect of new information on intrinsic values will be able to realize larger profits than those who can not.[28]

> There is nothing . . . which suggests that superior fundamental or intrinsic value analysis is useless in a random walk-efficient market. In fact the analyst will do better than the investor who follows a simple buy-and-hold policy as long as he can more quickly identify situations where there are non-negligible discrepancies between actual price and intrinsic values than other analysts and investors, and if he is better able to predict the occurrence of important events and evaluate their effects on intrinsic values.
> If there are many analysts who are pretty good at this sort of thing, however, and if they have considerable resources at their disposal, they help narrow discrepancies between actual prices and intrinsic values and cause actual prices, on the average, to adjust "instantaneously" to changes in intrinsic values.[29]

The random walk theory, while refuting the concepts of technical analysis and neither proving nor disproving those of fundamental analysis, presents an empirical challenge to both schools of thought. The challenge to the technician is a direct one. If the random walk model is valid, as suggested by empirical evidence to date, then future price movements cannot be predicted by studying the history of past price movements alone. Consequently, the work of the chartist may be useless. To vindicate himself, the technician should not restrict himself to verbalizing about trends and patterns; rather, he should demonstrate their predictive significance empirically. The challenge to the fundamentalist, while still empirical, is indirect. The random walk theory is based on the premise of an "efficient" market where actual stock prices at any given time are likely to be close approximations of intrinsic values. The fundamental analyst must therefore demonstrate that his methods consistently result in the detection of discrepancies between actual prices and intrinsic values when these discrepancies exist.[30]

CONCLUSIONS

The analysis of financial and economic fundamentals must ultimately be the underlying foundation for security appraisal. Market prices will, in the long run, tend to move toward intrinsic values. Thus, the

---

[28]Eugene F. Fama, "The Behavior of Stock Market Prices," *The Journal of Business,* XXXVIII, No. 1 (January 1965), p. 39.
[29]Fama, "Random Walks in Stock Market Prices," *op. cit.,* p. 58.
[30]*Ibid.,* p. 59.

determination of value is the critical factor in investment selection. The criticisms of fundamental analysis presented in this paper are directed at practicability rather than theory. It is the inability of most investors to *properly apply* fundamental techniques which is the basis for skepticism. As the art of fundamental analysis is further developed and properly applied, it will provide a sounder basis for investment evaluation.

Nevertheless, there is conceptual justification for contending that, except for the most sophisticated of the professional analysts, technical stock analysis may be as satisfactory, or perhaps more satisfactory, than fundamental analysis. Moreover, there is conceptual support for recommending technical analysis as a supplement to fundamental analysis for even the top professionals.

However, conceptual reasoning is not enough. There is a vast amount of empirical evidence which supports the random walk model of stock market behavior and thus denies the value of technical analysis. In order to attain recognition from serious students of the stock market, technicians must combine existing conceptual support with empirical evidence which has been heretofore lacking.

24
CHANGING INTEREST RATES AND THE INVESTMENT PORTFOLIO*

HARRY C. SAUVAIN is a member of the faculty of Indiana University.

Last summer there was some unusual excitement in Wall Street and in the financial community. The cause of the disturbance was not the behavior of stock prices, as is usually the case, but rather the fluctuation of market prices

---

*From *Journal of Finance,* Vol. XIV, No. 2 (May 1959), pp. 230-44. Reprinted by permission.

in the ordinarily unexciting bond market. There were days last July when prices for some Treasury bonds fluctuated more than prices for some leading common stocks. In a period of three months, from mid-June to mid-September, 1958, prices for several long-term Treasury issues declined 9-11 points, and the price of the new Treasury bond offered on June 15, 1958, dropped 6 points. These were rather sensational developments in the market for the highest-grade securities in the country. Some speculators in government bonds realized heavy losses, and a lot of people who thought of government bonds as the safest and most conservative media for investment of money to be found anywhere in the world were deeply shocked.

One of the important implications of developments in the bond market during 1958 is that changes in the level of interest rates prevailing in the market may have serious consequences for bond investors and that there is a need for further study and more precise delineation of that hazard that has come to be known as "interest-rate risk."

GREATER IMPORTANCE OF INTEREST-RATE RISK RELATIVE TO FINANCIAL RISK

Two or three decades ago the main concern of the conservative investor, and sometimes his sole concern, was to obtain "safety of principal." I put that term in quotation marks because it had a particular meaning. It meant safety of principal as far as the ability to pay of bond issuers was concerned. It meant little risk that an issuer would fail to make payments of principal and interest in dollars, in full and precisely when due. It also meant little fluctuation in market prices for "safe" securities due to uncertainties about future payment of principal and interest.

Investors have known for a long time that market prices for the better grades of bonds are affected by changes in interest rates. Investments textbooks written in the 1920's sometimes refer to high-grade bonds as "money-rate" bonds and observe that their market prices fluctuate with changes in interest rates. But changes in prices for such securities due to interest-rate changes have not been considered very important even in some fairly recent writings. Graham and Dodd in their excellent book on security analysis, which has been virtually a bible for many of us, say that in the field of high-grade bonds the security analyst does not ordinarily concern himself with price fluctuations. "He knows from experience," they say, "that, while price fluctuations do occur, they are only rarely so wide as to affect the finances or confidence of those holding this type of security."[1]

---

[1] Benjamin Graham and David L. Dodd, *Security Analysis* (3d ed.; New York: McGraw-Hill Book Co., Inc., 1951), p. 24.

I submit that in this era of the 1950's security analysts or investment managers *must* concern themselves with market-price fluctuations even in the field of high-grade bonds because *they are often* so wide as to affect the finances of investors. When government bonds drop 10 points in a few months and when high-grade corporate bonds lose one-fourth of their market value in the course of a few years because of change in interest rates, the finances of those holding such securities are likely to be very much affected. I suggest that investors in high-grade securities should be even more concerned with interest rate than with financial risk. There is, of course, the important problem of classifying securities as to grade; but when a bond qualifies as high-grade, it is protected by such large margins of earnings and assets that the usual fluctuations in the financial condition of issuers accompanying cyclical movements in business have little influence upon market price. On the other hand, the market prices of such securities and the yields at which they may be purchased from time to time are very much affected by cyclical changes in interest rates.

We have always had fluctuations in interest rates and corresponding changes in market prices and rates of yield on high-grade securities, but it seems to me that interest-rate risk has become more important in recent years. For one thing, there has been a great increase in the amount of high-grade and medium-grade bonds in the hands of investors over the past decade or two. The amount of United States government marketable securities outstanding has grown from $42 billion at the end of 1941 to about $172 billion at the end of last October; the amount of corporate long-term debt has increased about two and one-half times since 1946 and currently stands at a figure somewhat in excess of $100 billion. There has been a similar expansion in the total amount of state and municipal obligations to a current figure of more than $50 billion. In addition, there are some foreign dollar bonds and some preferred stocks that qualify as high grade. The fact is that investors now hold somewhere in the neighborhood of $325 billions of securities mostly of the grade that fluctuates in market price with changes in interest rates.

A second development that makes interest-rate risk more important is an apparent increase in the amplitude of cyclical fluctuation in interest rates. I make this observation rather tentatively because it is difficult to measure a trend in the amplitude of such fluctuations over a long period of years and because the experience of the 1950's may not be indicative of basic change in the stability of long-term interest rates. But if you examine the record of yields on government securities over the last forty years as shown in the *Federal Reserve Chart Book* (Historical Supplement), you must be impressed by the relative steepness of the decline in rates for all maturities in the recession of 1953-54 and again in the recession of 1957-58. Similarly, the rise in rates between about the middle of 1954 and the middle of 1957 was very marked. The Treasury bill rate rose from a fraction of 1 per cent to more than 3½ per cent in that period of about three years, and the average yield on long-term Treasury bonds rose from 2½ to about 3¾ per cent. This is an increase of 50 per cent in the long-term rate. The magnitude of these fluctuations is particularly remarkable because the period of the 1950's has been one of relatively mild cyclical fluctuations. If we expect certain periods of great financial crisis, such as 1920-21 and 1931-32, the amplitude of fluctuations in interest rates in the 1950's has been greater than in any similar period of time since World War I.

These developments of recent years support the idea that we need to examine more closely the manner in which changes in interest rates affect market prices and rates of yield for securities and to generalize more accurately the cause-and-effect relationships.

GRADES OF SECURITIES INFLUENCED PARTICULARLY BY INTEREST RATES

We may very well begin the present effort to examine further the influence of interest-rate changes on security investments by consideration of the elementary generalization that prices of high-grade bonds fluctuate inversely with changes in interest rates. This principle is a product of the simple arithmetic of bond-yield computation. When interest rates rise so that bonds must be sold to provide a higher yield than formerly, the increase in yield is accomplished by a downward adjustment of market price. When interest rates in the market change in such a manner that a bond may be sold at a lower yield than formerly, market price is adjusted upward.

But is it sufficient to say that changes in interest rates are important only for high-grade securities? Most of us think of high-grade bonds as comprising governments and corporates and municipals in the first two rating categories. Experience of recent years indicates that this concept is not broad enough. If you compare the average yields on the highest-grade corporate bonds, those rated triple A, and average yields on medium-grade corporate bonds, those rated triple B, over the last ten years, you find that they have fluctuated in much the same pattern. I have worked out the correlation between Standard & Poor's average yields on triple A and triple B bonds, using end-of-month data, for the period from January, 1948, to September, 1958. The coefficient of correlation is 0.957 per cent; R^2 is 91.6 per cent. This is a surprisingly high correlation.

The differential in yield between the two series tends to vary both ways from about 75 yield basis points. In periods of economic improvement when investor confidence is high, the differential declines about 50 basis points. In periods of recession investors seem to have less confidence in triple B bonds, and the differential rises to somewhat more than 100 basis points. In the last ten years the greatest aberration from the pattern of correlation occurred during the sharp decline in business activity from August, 1957, to January, 1958. In these months the yield differential between triple A and triple B bonds increased from about 75 basis points to about 125 basis points. In spite of these variations, the relatively high degree of correlation between the two series over a period of a little more than ten years indicates that changes in interest rates are a major influence upon yields and prices for medium-grade bonds.

It is interesting to observe, too, the close correlation between yields on triple A corporate bonds and yields on a group of high-grade preferred stocks. The coefficient of correlation for these two series as published by Standard & Poor for the period January, 1948, to September, 1958, was 0.931 per cent, and R^2 was 86.7 per cent. This, too, is a high coefficient of correlation, and it would be higher but for the long-term shrinkage in the size of the yield differential between triple A corporate bonds and the group of high-grade preferred stocks. Thus inclusion of high-grade preferred stocks and probably some that are not quite so high grade further enlarges the area of security investment in which interest rates appear to be the major influence upon price changes.

The increase in the importance of interest-rate risk relative to financial risk for these classes of fixed-income securities below the top grade is due not only to the greater amplitude of fluctuation in interest rates but also to the lesser amplitude of fluctuation in the business cycle. In the past decade business recessions have caused little impairment generally in the ability of corporate issuers to make payments of interest and preferred dividends and have not been so severe as to shake seriously the confidence of investors in their continued ability to do so. Many economists think that evolutionary changes in our economic system have brought about this stability and that it will continue in the future. Perhaps it is too soon to be sure about this, but I think that a recurrence of conditions such as those of the 1930's, which sent yields on medium-grade bonds soaring to 10 or 11 per cent, is very unlikely.

It is possible to go further with this kind of analysis and to show that prices for lower-grade bonds and preferred stocks and even for common stocks are affected in some degree by changes in the level of interest rates prevailing in the market. However, casual observation of the behavior of the market prices indicates that as the degree of financial risk in securities increases, considerations of financial risk become increasingly important as an influence upon price and that, in the general category of common stocks, changes in earnings and dividends and changes in investors' expectations concerning earnings and dividends far outweigh the effect of changes in interest rates as an influence upon market prices.

Therefore, I am satisfied to stop with the proposition that the area of security investment in which interest-rate changes are of major importance consists of those grades of securities down to and including the grade represented by the triple B rating. I think that this is a significant enlargement of the usual concept of the investment area affected by interest-rate risk and that it has some important implications for investment policy.

INTEREST-RATE RISK AND THE LENGTH OF MATURITY

Moving further into the relationship between market prices for money-rate securities and changes in interest rates, we come to the generalization that the amplitude of fluctuation in prices with changes in interest rates varies with the length of the period to maturity of securities. In other words, the greater the length of maturity, the greater is the fluctuation of price with a given change in interest rates. Developments in the bond markets recently suggest the need for more careful examination of variation in the amplitude of price fluctuations with differences in length of maturity.

The amplitude of price fluctuations for securities of different maturities with fluctuations in interest rates is governed by two variables. One is difference in the length of maturity of securities. The other is variation in the size of fluctuations in interest rates, or market rates of yield, for securities of different maturities. For the present discussion we assume that changes in interest rates are the sole influence upon market prices for money-rate type securities.

Length of Maturity As the Sole Variable.   The second variable, difference in the size of fluctuation of rates for different maturities, can be held constant by assuming that change in rates of yield required by the market from one time to another is proportionately the same for all maturities. Then the effect of changes in interest rates upon market prices is solely a function of difference in length of maturities. In order to observe the effect of a change of interest rates of the same proportion for all maturities, I assumed that a number of securities with different maturities from one to fifty years, all bearing 3 per cent coupons, were all selling on a 3 per cent yield basis and thus were priced at par. Then I examined the effect upon market price of shifting all maturities to a 3½ per cent yield basis. Thus the increase in rate of yield was 16 2/3 per cent for all maturities.

The effect of this change in interest rates upon prices is shown by the lower curve in Chart I, which is a line drawn through the market prices that would prevail for securities of the different maturities on a 3½ per cent yield basis. The line forms a curve declining at a decreasing rate from the shorter to the longer maturities. Next I assumed that securities of all maturities in this group were selling on a 2½ per cent yield basis and determined their market prices on this basis. The upper curve in Chart I is a line drawn through the market prices that would prevail for all maturities after such a decline in interest rates. The line forms a curve rising at a decreasing rate from the shorter to the longer maturities.

The important idea that emerges from these observations is that the size of price changes with a uniform change in interest rates for all maturities does not increase in proportions varying directly with increase in length of maturity but

Chart I. The Change in Market Prices for Securities of Different Maturities with a Proportionate Change in Interest Rates

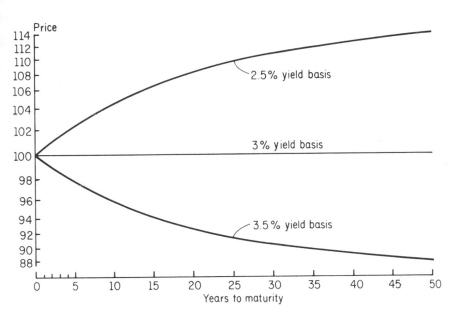

that the size of price changes increases in proportions that decrease with each period of time added to length of maturity.

The detail of this change in price at a decreasing rate with increase in length of maturity can be seen clearly in the data from which Chart I was prepared. They show that when an obligation bearing a 3 per cent coupon and due in 5 years is shifted from a 3 to 3½ per cent basis, there is a price decline of 2.28 per cent. When a similar obligation due in 10 years is priced on a 3½ per cent yield basis, the further decline in price beyond that of the 5-year maturity is 1.95 per cent of the price of the 5-year maturity. When a 3 per cent obligation due in 15 years is priced on a 3½ per cent yield basis, the further decline in price beyond that of the 10-year maturity is 1.61 per cent of the price of the 10 year maturity. This illustration could be continued by 5-year intervals to the point where the price of a 50-year maturity declines only 0.48 per cent more than the price of a 45-year maturity. This is how price declines at a decreasing rate.

The explanation for the increase in size of price change at a decreasing rate with addition of units of time to maturity is to be found in the arithmetic of bond-yield calculations. The annual rate of discount created by a decline in market price below par is the total discount divided by the number of years to maturity. The addition of each year to maturity requires a larger total discount to achieve a given annual rate of discount. However, as years are added to the length of the period to maturity, each year is a smaller proportion of the total number of years to maturity over which the total discount must be spread. Thus the addition of proportionately smaller units of time requires relatively smaller increases in the size of the total discount required to achieve a given increase in rate of yield to maturity.

You may notice that the upper curve in Chart I moves farther away from par than the lower curve. Thus the price of a 3 per cent bond due in 50 years rises 14.23 percentage points above par when it is priced on a 2½ per cent yield basis. But the price of a 50-year, 3 per cent bond priced on a 3½ per cent yield basis declines only 11.77 percentage points below par. This is due to the fact that, as price declines, yield is computed on a smaller cost price; while as price rises, yield is computed on a larger cost price.

Difference in Size of Rate Fluctuation for Different Maturities. If we stopped here, we would have an unrealistic conclusion about the effect of changes in market rates of interest upon prices for securities of different maturities because even casual observation of the behavior of interest rates in the market shows that short-term interest rates fluctuate much more widely than do long-term rates. To cite an extreme instance, the market rate of yield on 3 months' Treasury bills increased from 0.58 per cent on May 31, 1958, to 2.23 per cent on August 30, 1958. In the same period the average yield on Treasury bonds maturing or callable in 10 years or more increased only from 3.13 to 3.67 per cent. The greater amplitude of fluctuation in short-term rates relative to long-term rates would, except for differences in length of maturity, cause wider fluctuations in prices for the shorter maturities as interest rates changed. In the market this relative instability of short-term rates operates in direct opposition to the stabilizing influence of shortness of maturity. The balance of the two influences determines the amplitude of market-price fluctuations for securities of different maturities.

In order to observe variation in size of change in interest rates for securities of different maturities in a period of rising interest rates, I have prepared a schedule of the yields at which eleven Treasury obligations of different maturities ranging from 8 months to about 37 years were selling on June 13, 1958, and a similar schedule of the yields at which these same issues were selling on September 12, 1958. The time interval between dates is 3 months. Then I expressed the yield for each issue on September 12 as a percentage of its yield on June 13. The result is shown in Chart II.

The increase in yields was very much greater for the short maturities than for the longer issues. For example, the shortest maturity in this schedule is the Treasury 1 7/8 per cent note due February 15, 1959. The interval to maturity was approximately 8 months on June 13 and 5 months on September 12, 1958. On June 13 it was selling on a 0.97 per cent yield basis and on September 12 it was selling on a 2.86 per cent yield basis. The yield on the latter date was 295

Chart II. The Change in Market Rates of Yield on Treasury Securities from June 13, 1958, to September 12, 1958

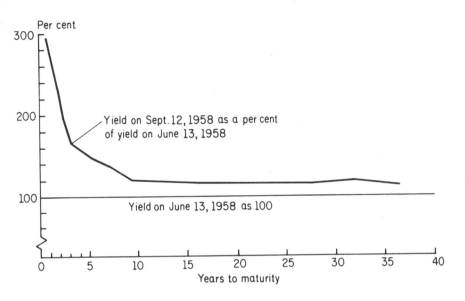

per cent of the yield on June 13. By contrast, the longest maturity in the schedule is the Treasury 3 per cent bond due February 15, 1995, with a time interval to maturity on June 13 of 36 years and 8 months. On June 13 it was selling on a 3.12 per cent yield basis, and on September 12 it was priced to yield 3.55 per cent. Its yield on the latter date was about 114 per cent of its yield on June 13. Chart II shows that the relative size of the increase in yield declined sharply as the interval to maturity increased from 8 months to about 3 years, then declined more moderately for maturities from 3 to 10 years, and that the size of increase was about the same for maturities beyond 10 years. In some other period of rising interest rates, the size of change in yields on securities of varying maturities may be different from that in the period I have examined, but this period is a good test of the effect on market prices of a much steeper rise in short-term than in long-term rates.

Now how did the proportionately much greater rise in short-term rates affect the magnitude of change in market prices for these Treasury securities of widely varying maturities? I have taken the market price on September 12, 1958, for each of the issues included in this study and expressed it as a percentage of its market price on June 13. These percentages measure the relative size of the decline in market prices for the different maturities. Chart III shows clearly that the much greater changes in market rates of yield for the shorter maturities had less effect on market prices than did the much smaller

Chart III.   The Change in Market Prices for Treasury Securities from June 13, 1958, to September 12, 1958

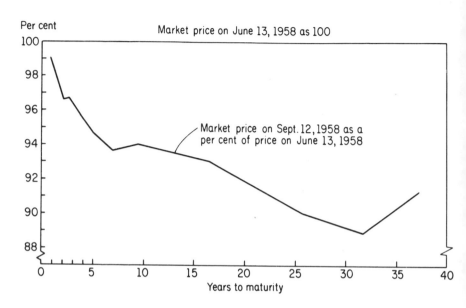

changes in market rates of yield for the longer maturities. In general, the line connecting the September 12 price percentages declined steeply from the shortest maturity to the maturity in about 7 years and then declined more slowly, and with some irregularity, to the longest maturities.

If the irregularities in the curve of Chart III were smoothed out, we would have a curve somewhat like the lower curve in Chart I. This leads me to the conclusion that length of maturity is the dominant influence upon the magnitude of fluctuations in market price as interest rates change, in spite of the much greater fluctuations in short-term than in long term rates. The conclusion may be generalized by saying that, as interest rates in the market change, the magnitude of fluctuation in market prices for securities of different maturities tends to increase with increase in length of maturity but at a decreasing rate of increase. This generalization has significance for investors who seek relative stability of price in money-rate type obligations. It means that a high degree of price stability may be obtained only in relatively short maturities, say, maturities of less than 1 year, and that price instability increases markedly as maturities are extended from 1 to about 7 years. It also means that there is no great difference in price instability for maturities longer than 20 or 25 years. Obviously, the pattern of price change would vary in different periods according to the magnitude of the change in shorter-term rates relative to longer-term rates.

INTEREST-RATE RISK AND THE SIZE OF INVESTMENT INCOME

The phenomenon of change in rates of interest prevailing in the market for money-rate type securities affects not only the market prices for these securities but also the size of income obtainable at any particular time and from time to time by investment or reinvestment in money-rate type securities.

We have first the general proposition that at any particular time yields on securities of different maturities tend to be higher as the length of maturity increases. Thus, generally, the longer the maturities selected for investment, the larger is the rate of yield. When the structure of yields in the market follows this pattern, it is said to form an upsloping yield curve. The pattern of yields on government obligations of different maturities that prevailed on June 13, 1958, as shown by Chart IV, is an example of a markedly upsloping yield curve for maturities up to about 10 years. This chart is constructed from yield data for the same eleven issues used in the two preceding charts.

Chart IV. Yield Curves on Recent Dates

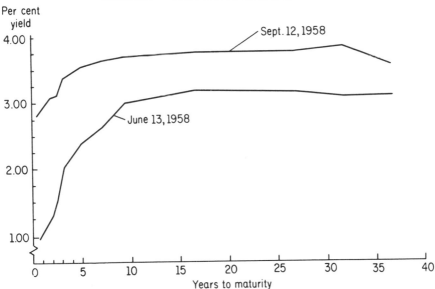

However, the pattern of the yield curve changes at times. Sometimes it is much less upsloping and thus flatter. Chart IV also shows the yield curve on September 12, 1958, which was only moderately upsloping. The data are for the same issues. There have, in fact, been times when the yield curve was somewhat downsloping, with yields on the shortest maturities higher than those on longer maturities. The fact that the yield curve does become relatively flat at times, and even assumes odd shapes with a "hump" toward the middle, raises the question of whether there is any basic tendency for the curve to be upsloping. I submit that there is such a tendency.

The Tendency for Yield Curve to Be Upsloping. We have seen that, as interest rates change, the size of market price fluctuations is greater for longer maturities of securities than for short-term obligations. Thus there is more risk of loss of principal inherent in the longer maturities in the event that they have to be liquidated at market prices. Investors in money-rate type securites generally like to minimize this risk, although the intensity of their effort to do so varies considerably among the different types of investors. Thus there is a preference for the shorter-term and less risky issues. Because investors prefer the less risky issues, they are generally willing to buy them at lower rates of yield than the rates at which they are willing to buy the longer-term and more risky issues. This preference for liquidity is the reason why there is a tendency for the yield curve to be upsloping. The upsloping curve is perfectly logical, in that it provides smaller returns to those who demand the more advantageous terms of investment and provides the larger returns to those who are willing and able to assume the risk of greater fluctuations in market price. In brief, it provides a premium for assuming interest-rate risk.

The yield curve is most steeply upsloping when conditions in the money market are "easy," that is, when there is a relative abundance of funds seeking investment in money-rate type securities. At such times a considerable amount of money comes into the market for more or less temporary investment, pending some other use at some other time. Then the competition of investors for investment media with small financial risk and small interest-rate risk results in a bidding-down of yields on the shorter maturities of high-grade obligations relative to yields on longer maturities.

However, there are times when conditions in the money market become "tight." Demand for money increases, and the demand for short-term money increases more than the demand for long-term money. Under these conditions yields on the shorter maturities rise to a much greater extent than yields on longer maturities. This is not because the shorter maturities have become less desirable from the investors' standpoint but because the stronger demand for short-term money relative to supply has caused a bidding-up of money rates. Investors still prefer short maturities to long maturities, but they are not obliged to accept the smaller returns at the short end of the maturity schedule that prevailed when their preferences dominated the structure of interest rates. With users of money offering higher rates, they happily accept the higher rates.

In the last analysis, the question whether an upsloping yield curve is normal, or usually to be expected, depends upon the question whether relatively easy-money market conditions are normal. I think that in the kind of economy we have now, with the federal government committed to responsibility for economic growth and full employment, a condition of relatively easy money is much more often to be expected than a condition of tight money.

The Instability of Income on Short-Term Investment. Regardless of the shape of the yield curve at any particular time, the fluctuations of interest rates cause changes in the amount of income realized from a given amount of principal invested and reinvested in money-rate type obligations. When principal is invested, a rate of yield is obtained. If securities are held to maturity and the proceeds reinvested, the new rate is the yield prevailing in the market at the time of reinvestment. Except by coincidence, the new rate is different from the old rate. And insofar as it is different, the amount of income from a given amount of principal increases or decreases.

There is fluctuation of income upon reinvestment caused by changes in interest rates for securities of all maturities because rates for all maturities change from time to time. However, the fluctuation is greater for short-term obligations than for those of long maturity. In general, stability of income from funds invested and reinvested varies inversely with length of maturity.

The relative instability of income from short-term obligations is due to two conditions. One is the much greater amplitude of fluctuation in short-term rates. We have observed in Chart II the much greater rise in yields on short maturities than on long-term issues in the period from June 13 to September 12, 1958. Inspection of the chart of interest rates in the *Federal Reserve Chart Book* (Historical Supplement) covering the last forty years shows that relatively wide swings in short-term rates have been characteristic of the money markets. It follows, therefore, that when short-term obligations mature, the rate obtainable upon reinvestment in short-term issues may vary widely from the rate obtained on the original investment. Since long-term rates fluctuate in a narrower range, the yield obtained upon reinvestment of long-term funds is likely to vary to a smaller extent from the original rate.

The other condition is simply the length of the period of investment. Funds invested in short maturities and reinvested in similar obligations come back into the market in a relatively short period of time. Whatever change has occurred in short-term rates in the interval is realized in terms of income. Thus, if funds are invested and reinvested in obligations maturing in one year, there would be a different rate of yield and a different amount of income each year. In recent years the income from a given amount of principal invested and reinvested in one-year maturities of government obligations would have fluctuated much more than the income from a diversified group of good common stocks.

By contrast, reinvestment of funds invested in long maturities occurs only at long intervals, if bonds are held to maturity. Income is stable during the period to maturity and changes only when reinvestment occurs after a considerable period of years. Over a long time there may be secular changes in long-term rates that cause the difference in yields from one time to another to be greater than the normally small cyclical fluctuation in long-term rates. This modifies, but does not invalidate, the general proposition that the stability of income upon investment and reinvestment in long-term issues is greater than that obtained by investment and reinvestment in short maturities.

Thus we have a sort of paradox. Market prices of short-term issues fluctuate much less than prices of long-term issues with changes in interest rates. But the stability of income from long-term issues is much greater than that from short-term issues upon investment and reinvestment at maturity. Clearly, the manager of a portfolio of money-rate type securities must decide whether stability of income or stability of principal is the more important in his particular circumstances.

25

PRICE-LEVEL VARIATIONS AND THE TENETS OF HIGH-GRADE INVESTMENT*

JOHN C. CLENDENIN is a member of the faculty of the University of California at Los Angeles.

The topic assigned to us for discussion at this meeting clearly implies that there may be price-level variations in this country in the future and that they may be of sufficient moment to require appropriate investment policies. It would therefore be reasonable to debate either the outlook for price levels over the longer term or the nature of conservative investment policies which would best meet the probable situation. However, it has been officially suggested to me

*From *Journal of Finance*, Vol. XIV, No. 2 (May-1959), pp. 245-62. Reprinted by permission. The Bureau of Business and Economic Research, University of California, Los Angeles, assisted the author in data collection, computations, and in other ways.

that we might focus attention on the suitability of common stocks, especially the variety known as "growth stocks," as high-grade investment vehicles in a period of price-level instability. This is my purpose; and in discussing stocks I shall mean those of competitive industrial and commercial companies only.

Although it is not my intention to involve this meeting in attempts to predict the long-range economic future of the country, it seem idle to discuss investment dispositions without noting the general nature of the situations for which we must be prepared. Obviously, we would not all agree on the details of the economic road ahead, but I suspect that most of us expect a continuation of welfare-minded monetary and public budget interventionism, major emphasis on full-employment objectives, a secondary hope for price stability and a balanced budget, large-scale public expenditures, and extensive research and development efforts by both public and private agencies. Conceding that all quantitative estimates must be liberally sprinkled with plus-and-minus signs, it would appear that a middle-of-the-road investment planner might reasonably visualize the coming decade as follows:

1. General characteristics of high-level and growing output, moderate cycles of buoyancy and recession greatly influenced by monetary and public budget manipulation, long-term money rates swinging widely in and about the 1958 range, and an intermittent price-level inflation averaging about 1 per cent per annum, firmly underwritten by habitual cost-push pressures.

2. *Possibility* of occasional short booms or depressions which may make sharp temporary impression on the stock market but relatively little permanent impression on either commodity or stock-market price trends.

3. Rapid technological and competitive change, in which products and enterprises are capable of great development or obsolescence in short time.

4. Continuation of heavy taxes.

5. Possibility of war, which would surely distort profit results and dividend rates temporarily and the price level permanently.

The foregoing propositions definitely do not imply that conventional fixed-dollar-amount investments are about to become obsolete or unproductive. On the contrary, they assume that high-grade bond yields of 3½-5 per cent will clearly exceed an inflation-born loss of 1 per cent per year on the principal, even after allowing for the attrition of taxes. The 1 per cent per year inflationary trend is a guess based on evidences of increasing financial sobriety in Washington and relatively greater desire to couple price stability with full employment. If this hopeful projection works out, taxpaying investors may continue to use taxable senior securities and obtain at least a small amount of real net income from them.

Yet the fact remains that inflationary trends impair the real-income productivity of fixed-income investment, while presumably not adversely affecting typically diversified equity positions. Furthermore, public intervention to prevent recession or depression would appear to be a potent insurer of the safety and stability of a diversified equity position. If these things be true, then there may be occasion to indorse the principle of common-stock investment for conservative funds and even to advocate adapting some of our traditional institutions to make better use of common stocks.

At this point we begin to encounter some arguable questions of fact. The first of these is: After a quarter-century of mounting taxes, labor law, and government intervention in business, do the common stocks of leading corporations retain their profitableness and sturdiness and general good prospects?

EVIDENCE ON QUALITY

Since evidence on the trend of stock quality provides only relative data, it is desirable to recall at the outset some of the well-known absolute findings of prior decades. Most famous of these is Edgar L. Smith's *Common Stocks as Long-Term Investments,* which compares the performances of hypothetical good-quality common-stock and bond portfolios over 17- to 22-year spans in the period 1866-1922. The results, you will recall, strongly favored the stock portfolios. Many subsequent studies point, on balance, to the same conclusion, especially in periods when the general trend of commodity prices is level or upward.[1] The first concern of the present inquiry is, therefore, to ascertain whether the corporate strength which made these records possible is still with us. Pertinent evidence is afforded in the accompanying Charts I-III.

Chart I reports in line-graph form the net-profit results of leading manufacturing corporations since 1926. The upper line shows profits as a percentage of net worth, the lower one profits as a percentage of sales. These figures are collected by the First National City Bank of New York, mostly by adding figures available in published annual reports. Only large and fairly large concerns are included, and the list of corporations is obviously not uniform through the years, though the large number included—about 1,800 in recent years—give the series impressive validity. The significant facts to be drawn from Chart I are these: First, the percentages earned on net worth in 1953-57 are as good as, or a little better than, those earned in profitable periods in the past—for

---

[1] E. L. Smith, *Common Stocks as Long Term Investments* (New York: Macmillan Co., 1924); C. C. Bosland, *Common Stock Investment* (New York: Ronald Press Co., 1937); K. S. vanStrum, *Investing in Purchasing Power* (New York: Barron's 1926); D. C. Rose, *A Scientific Approach to Investment Management* (New York: Harper & Bros., 1928); W. J. Eiteman and F. P. Smith, *Common Stock Values and Yields* (Ann Arbor: University of Michigan Press, 1953); W. C. Greenough, *A New Approach to Retirement Income* (T.I.A.A., 1951); P. L. Howell, "Common Stocks and Pension Fund Investing," *Harvard Business Review,* November-December 1958.

example, 1940-41, 1936-37, and 1926-29. Labor costs and the corporate income tax have not eroded earning capacity here. Second, there appears to have been a slight decline in the percentage of net profit to the sales of these companies; 1953-57 is a little below 1940-41, and the latter is, in turn, a little below 1936-37. The disparity between the two trends shown on the chart obviously reflects an increase in the ratio of sales to net worth. Economic logic suggests that the earnings rate on net worth has been a dominant criterion in competitive pricing decisions and that the profit percentage on sales has been cut because a lower percentage would still permit a generous return on invested capital.

Chart I.   Profits of Large Manufacturing Corporations As Percentages of Net Worth and of Sales. (Source: First National City Bank; 1958 Estimated.)

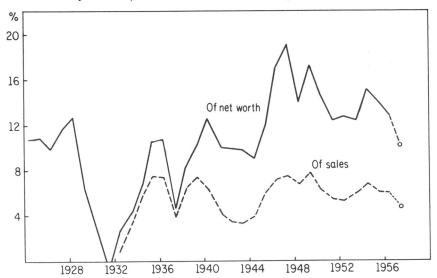

Chart II presents data drawn from *Statistics of Income,* as compiled by the Internal Revenue Service. The year 1957 is estimated. The bars represent the percentages earned by all manufacturing corporations in the country on their book net worths and sales, before and after income taxes. The pretax earnings are shown by the total heights of the bars, the posttax net by the solid portions. It will be noted that the net profit margins earned by manufacturing corporations in the aggregate are not nearly so large as those earned by the large corporations canvassed in the First National City series but that the trends over time are similar. The earnings rates on net worth are firmly maintained, while those on sales have declined since the war. However, this chart has two more significant messages. First, it is clear that the heavy corporate income taxes imposed during the last 25 years—as represented on the chart by the unshaded segments at the tops of the bars—have been paid by widening the pretax profit margin, presumably at the expense of the consumer, and not by impairing the stockholders' profit margins on net worth. Second, it appears that the pretax profit margins on sales—as shown by the total height of the sales percentage bars—are actually a little larger in recent years than they were in the 1920's and 1930's. There is thus a little wider margin of safety between normal operations and red-ink deficits that we had before income taxes climbed to their present levels.

Chart II.   Profits of All American Manufacturing Corporations As Percentages of Net Worth and of Sales. (Source: Statistics of Income; 1957 Estimated.)

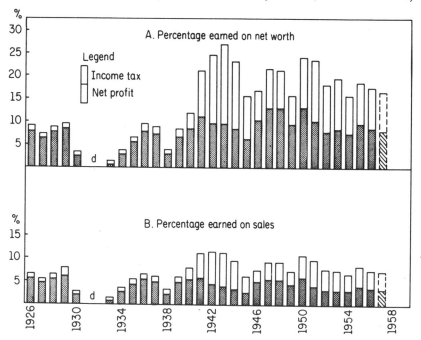

Chart III is similar to Chart II, except that it presents the combined record of all American trade corporations instead of manufacturing concerns. The trends are very similar, though it is apparent that the profit margins of trade corporations are not so high as those of manufacturers. It will also be noted that economic conditions plus inventory and depreciation accounting methods produced almost fantastic profit records for trade corporations in the years 1946-50. These are clearly abnormal and are as little descriptive of earnings trends as are the war years or the years 1931-34.

But reference to depreciation accounting and inventory accounting methods suggests that other accounting devices may be distorting Charts II and III. What of the undervaluation of prewar fixed assets and the consequent

Chart III.   *Profits of All American Retail and Wholesale Trade Corporations As Percentages of Net Worth and of Sales. (Source: Statistics of Income; 1957 Estimated.)*

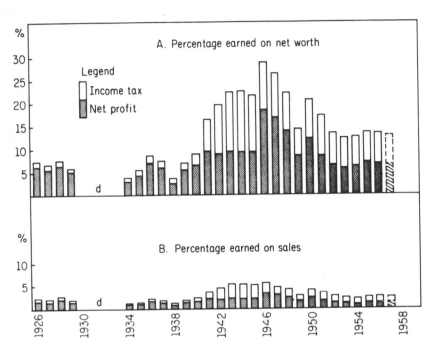

understatement of net worth? What of accelerated amortization? Time does not permit an extended review here, but it is possible to cite a study by the Machinery and Allied Products Institute in which a careful attempt is made to measure the ratio of corrected earnings to corrected net worth, the corrections being designed to state both earnings and net worth on an economic replacement-cost basis for each year. The MAPI results indicate that, on a corrected basis, the net profits of all American corporations in 1923-29 and in 1947-56 averaged almost the same percentage on net worth, about 5 2/3 per cent.[2] The profit level thus defined is appreciably lower than that shown in Charts I, II, and III; this appears to result both from the revision of profit and net worth figures and from the inclusion of all corporations, especially financial and transportation, in the data—but the absence of any downward trend in the ratio of net earnings to net worth is notable here also.

The data on profit margins thus support the proposition that corporations

---

[2]George Terborgh, *Corporate Profit in the Decade 1947-56 (New York: Machinery & Allied Products Institute, 1957).*

are retaining their financial strength rather well. Most other aspects of corporate finance corroborate this finding. For example, operating losses seem to be less frequent; in the years 1926-29 corporations operating at a loss had 18 per cent of the gross sales of all corporations in the nation, and their losses amounted to 17 per cent of the pretax earnings of the profitable corporations; but in 1952-56 the losers' sales were less than 10 per cent of the total and their losses less than 6 per cent of the others' profits. Other measures show manufactuers' net worth to be about 65 per cent of total assets in 1956 as compared to 75 per cent in 1928, but the working capital position is about the same and times interest earned coverage and cash flow are substantially improved.

STOCKS AS A PRICE-LEVEL HEDGE

A second issue of fact which must be noted is the matter of the effectiveness of common stocks as price-level hedges or counterweights. This has been so interminably discussed that one must apologize for raising it—yet this problem is the real reason for the topic we are discussing.

It must be conceded at the outset that public policy, expressed in such media as price controls, excess-profits taxes, credit controls, or public competition with private enterprise, could be the definitive answer to the question at hand. Such public policy has been the answer in certain foreign countries and was partly so in this country during our periods of price controls and excess-profits taxes. However, it seems reasonable to assume that the political hazards to capital in the United States are no greater now than they were in the 1930's. It is therefore pertinent to look at the historical data of the period 1926-57 for generalized indications of the impact of the price level on common-stock investment performance.

Chart IV presents a 32-year study of the earnings per share and the dividends per share applicable to the Standard and Poor's 50-Stock Industrial Stock Price Index. This index is used because its component stocks are those of large companies, mostly good-quality issues of the type considered for long-term investment. The earnings and dividend figures on the chart have been divided through by the GNP deflator index in order to show the data in terms of the prices which presumably affect them.

Inspection of Chart IV brings out clearly four significant points: (1) Over a span of 32 years the earnings and dividends available on a portfolio of good-grade big-company stocks have risen more than the price level. Their net upward trend has averaged between 1½ and 2 per cent per year, compounded. (2) In periods of price-level gain, the earnings may lag behind the price-level upswings, and the dividends will definitely lag behind the earnings. This observation is not too clear on the chart because of the complications of depression, war, controls, and taxes, but financial common sense adds credence to the rough indications. (3) Depressions, wars, price controls, and excess-profits taxes are contingencies which may depress per share earnings and dividends for considerable periods, at least in terms of purchasing power; and the chart does not show compensating long periods of very large earnings. (4) The data on this chart are of dubious quality in certain years, notably 1947-50, when strong earnings data are in part the product of non-economic inventory and depreciation accounting methods.

The major indication of Chart IV is, obviously, the finding that the earnings and dividends on this group of industrials over a generation have outclimbed price-level growth and gained an average of nearly 2 per cent per year in real purchasing power. This, of course, means a substantial capital gain in addition to the mounting tide of dividend income. However, it should be noted that the dividend income itself fell by half during the great depression, and, after recovering in part, declined again during the war. It was not until 1947 that the dollar level of dividend payments permanently surpassed the 1927-29 payments. During the interim, the stockholders got less than a fixed-income investment purchased in the 1920's would have brought them and, in addition, had to bear a painful, if temporary, shrinkage in stock prices. This could happen again.

Chart IV.   Growth of Earnings and Dividends per Share, Standard and Poor's Index of Fifty Industrials. (Real Terms, Adjusted for Price Level.) Indicated Growth Rate 2 Per Cent per Annum.

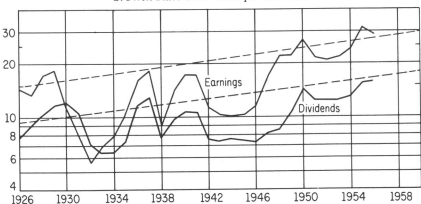

Chart V is in all respects similar to Chart IV, except that it shows only dividend records, not earnings, and compares the performances of a list of 9 growth stocks and 10 non-growth stocks. Data for certain abnormal depression and war years are not shown. This chart has been constructed with the advantage of hindsight; it was prepared in order to compare *ex post facto* the performance of typical high-grade growth stocks with that of high-grade non-growth stocks. The upper line shows the record of the non-growth stocks; their dividends declined less than the price level during the depression years but failed by far to keep pace during the war and early postwar years. By 1948, the buying-power level of the 1920's had been regained, and these stocks have since increased their dividends enough to compensate for further increases in the price level, though they have not made up the deficiencies of 1940-48. *They have at no time shown net real-income growth, despite the fact that undistributed profits have been reinvested in the businesses in most years over more than three decades!*

The lower line on Chart V shows the record of 9 major growth stocks. Over a 32-year term, these stocks have increased their earnings and dividends *in real terms* by an average of about 3 per cent per annum. Their depression-time payments declined below the 1920's in dollars but not in purchasing power, but at no time since has a significant shrinkage occurred. Obviously, the capital appreciation on these stocks has been very great. Whether their growth can continue or whether investors seeking to enjoy such growth in the future can select stocks capable of this performance are open questions.

However, one thing is pretty obvious; the average rise of 1½-2 per cent per year *in real terms* shown by the dividends on the Standard and Poor's 50-stock average must be ascribed to the fact that the average contains an assortment of growth and non-growth stocks. The growth stocks have supplied the vital thrust which makes industrial stocks per se appear to outpace an advancing price level. The ten high-grade non-growth stocks depicted on Chart V have caught up, on the average, but the laggards among them have not; and we all know that there are many lesser stocks and lagging industries which were once vigorous leaders.[3]

Chart V.   Growth of Dividend Rates in "Real" Terms (Adjusted for Price Level). Indicated Growth Rates 0 and 3.2 Per Cent per Annum.

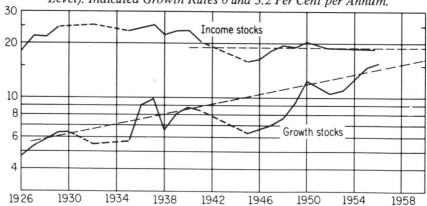

Generalizations at this point are perhaps gratuitous, but the facts suggest that a strong and smartly selected industrial stock portfolio might reasonably be

[3]Cf. E. S. Mead and Julius Grodinsky, *The Ebb and Flow of Investment Values* (New York: Appleton-Century, 1939).

expected to advance its dividend production, earnings, and capital values a little faster than the price level advances, even though earnings and dividend production may be somewhat irregular and prone to gaps. Capital appreciation accompanying earnings and dividend growth will in a sense compensate for inadequate dividends during inclement economic periods. However, our economy is subject to political, technological, and economic change. These are forces which can interrupt income and reverse trends, at least so far as individual corporations and industries are concerned. It is therefore reasonable to inquire whether, over a period of diverse economic trends, reasonably competent investment managements have been able to avail themselves in full measure of the opportunities which seem to be available.

SOME PERFORMANCE RECORDS

For a hasty test of the results of actual common-stock portfolios, the records of major open-end investment companies are most readily available. Accordingly, Table 1 presents some investment company performance data, with performance conventionally measured as the percentage excess of this year's closing asset value plus this year's dividend over last year's closing asset value.

For present purposes, the lessons of Table 1 are two in number. First, the common-stock investment companies do not usually surpass the performance of the market averages. True, they bear a measurable handicap in the form of operating expenses, an unproductive cash position, and a compulsion to diversify, but the fact is that their net performance often does not quite equal that of the averages, despite an enviable opportunity. The only reasonable conclusion is that the imponderables in individual stock situations are so great that good work in times like these parallels the averages, assures against falling far below them, but does not far exceed them. The great similarity in the performance of different funds lends credence to this view. The second lesson from Table 1 has to do with investment objectives. Six of the funds in the table announce as objectives the obtaining of income and appreciation. The other four announce that appreciation is their primary objective, with income incidental. The total performance of the two groups is almost identical. Granted that each group is compelled to diversification and that the income-and-appreciation group will seek appreciation avidly when they see a chance to get it, the record still says that stock-market forecasting is an imperfect art and that a competent and conservative analyst will not dependably improve his total score by stressing a search for market gains.

As a further test of the thesis that foresight is a scarce commodity, Table 2 lists the performance records of 22 stocks which constituted the largest stockholdings of one of our major investment companies in 1946 and 1947. These stocks were not all held throughout both years, but most of them were.

*Table 1.   Performance Records
of Common-Stock Funds and Certain Indexes*

*Performance = (Asset Value End of Year + Dividend
During Year) ÷ Asset Value End of Prior Year, Minus 100 Per Cent*

Funds and Indexes	1948	1949	1953	1954	1956	1957	Average 1948–57	Average 1940–57
S & P 50 Industrial	6	17	− 2	56	7	−11	18	14
S & P 20 Utilities	6	31	8	24	5	6	8	12
S & P 20 Rails	4	8	−12	57	− 3	−28	11	13
S & P 90 Stocks	6	18	− 1	51	7	−10	17	14
General-Purpose Fund No. 2	−1	17	2	43	9	− 4	15	14
General-Purpose Fund No. 3	1	18	0	37	7	− 5	13	11
General-Purpose Fund No. 4	2	19	− 3	52	13	−14	15	14
General-Purpose Fund No. 5	−2	19	− 5	58	12	−22	16	15
General-Purpose Fund No. 6	1	20	0	51	11	−11	16	13
Growth Fund No. 1	−1	16	− 1	48	10	−12	13	NA
Growth Fund No. 2	1	18	− 3	55	19	−12	17	14
Growth Fund No. 3	4	22	− 1	34	8	−12	13	12
Growth Fund No. 4	−3	16	1	63	14	−15	16	NA
Consumer Price Index per cent increase plus 5 per cent	8	3	5	4	7	7	7	10

Unquestionably the poorer performers among these stocks were bought and held in the expectation of good results in each individual case, and beyond doubt a larger quantity of the more successful holdings could have been carried had their success been anticipated. The table looks at first glance as though the selections were made by guess. However, this is a successful fund, whose total performance ranks high and whose management is deemed astute. Table 2 does not record good and bad luck; it records the process by which good results are achieved with reasonable certainty in a very unstable area.

These last two exhibits seem to justify the conclusion that secure and

Table 2. *Performance Records
of Leading Stocks Held by Fund Portfolio in 1946–47*

*Performance = (Median Price in Stated Year + Dividend of
Stated Year) ÷ Median Price of Prior Years, Minus 100 Per Cent*

Stock	1946	1947	1948	Average 1948–1952	Average 1953–1957
Allied Chemical	10	9	6	15	8
Atchison T. & S.F	12	−11	37	26	12
Amerada	17	19	21	40	7
Chrysler	−4	6	13	20	5
du Pont	16	−1	1	21	22
Eastman Kodak	19	2	−6	10	25
General Electric	1	−12	8	17	32
General Motors	−5	0	5	27	24
Gulf Oil	25	4	8	15	31
Int'l Harvester	−2	3	15	11	6
Loew's	11	−27	−18	1	9
Montgomery Ward	33	−18	4	7	9
J. C. Penney	20	−8	7	15	8
Sears, Roebuck	20	−15	19	17	12
Standard Oil, N.J.	17	8	18	28	24
Southern Pacific	15	−14	36	25	4
Texas Company	13	7	4	22	25
20th Century–Fox	43	−30	−25	−2	22
American Telephone	6	5	0	6	7
Commonwealth Edison	8	43	-3	8	12
Swift & Company	8	1	2	6	9
Ligget & Myers	8	2	5	1	6
Consumer Price Index per cent increase +5 per cent	25	14	8	7	6

dependable results with common stocks require both selection and diversification. The very high probability of successful workout which characterizes individual good bonds apparently does not exist to the same extent in stocks, and a diversified position which balances fortuitous gains against unforeseeable losses is an indispensable procedure in a conservative stock account.[4]

---

[4]For bond performance see W. B. Hickman, *Corporate Bond Quality and Investor Experience* (New York: NBER, 1958).

SOME OBSERVATIONS ON PRICE

The final point of statistical inquiry before us has to do with price. Stocks are non-reproducible goods; they provide a somewhat irregular income and have no maturity date; the eagerness with which the community desires them varies with popular thought and with the political and economic climate; and the demand for them is also affected by the incomes of stock-buying individuals and institutions and the other uses such buyers have for their money. Even in the absence of emergency conditions, stock prices are stubbornly variable; during the middle 1920's stock yields were very close to those of high-grade bonds; in the late 1940's stocks yielded almost twice as much as bonds; and now they yield considerably less than bonds. There is thus no stable and enduring yield basis for stock valuation, yet the absence of maturity places extreme emphasis on capitalization rate in arriving at a value estimate. It is probably inherent in the nature of things that stock prices and price-earnings ratios and yields should move through wide ranges both at short term and over long but irregular cycles.

The quantitative extent of these price cycles is normally not great enough to do unbearable damage to well-diversified common-stock positions which can be held for long periods, particularly if accumulation and liquidation can be advantageously timed or spread over a span of years. This is demonstrated by the studies previously cited. However, we must admit that a wide potential range of stock prices makes an accurate projection of medium-term investment performance almost impossible. Five or even ten years' income plus growth could be heavily impaired by adverse stock-price trends or by adverse liquidating prices. This is not a contingency to be lightly regarded, even in an inflationary era, by any portfolio which must make large distributions or stand ready to do so.[5]

The problem of price may be illustrated by current figures. The immediate dividend yields on the Standard and Poor's 50 stock index, my growth stock index, and my non-growth stock index approximate 3.5 per cent, 2.9 per cent, and 4.5 per cent, respectively. If we make allowance for continued growth and 1 per cent per year of inflation over the next 20 years and assume indefinite retention of holdings, the dividends on each of these groups should over 70 or 80 years amortize today's dollar cost and provide an average income yield of about 5 per cent. But 5 per cent is not an attractive long-term total return by past standards, and principal invested at this level is clearly subject to drastic impairment if the markets revert to a more conservative yield basis.

---

[5] W. A. Berridge, "Economic Facts Bearing on Some Variable Annuity Arguments," *Journal of Insurance,* November 1957.

It is difficult to escape the conclusion that industrial stocks are suitable for conservative investment when the object is the purchase of a very long-term annuity which needs to compensate for price-level changes, but that stocks may be troublesome if the portfolio is subject to market-value solvency tests or liquidation.

TENETS OF INVESTMENT IN STOCKS

This cursory review of fact and fancy has been intended to serve as justification for a statement of "The Tenets of High-Grade Investment" in a period of buoyant price levels. A tenet is a principle or a doctrine and, as such, may state either a fact or a way of life. This review has not covered all phases of investment activity, hence will not attempt to phrase a whole creed of investment, but the following tenets certainly would seem to belong in the creed:

1. The corporate institution is as sturdy and vigorous as it was 30 years ago, and a managed cross-section of the better common-stock equities may be regarded as productive and safe for the very long term.

2. Diversification is indispensable.

3. Both stable-income and growth industrial company stocks seem to earn and pay more dollars after an inflation takes place, but decadent industries or companies may not do so.

4. Price-level protection in an era in which the cost of living may rise drastically justifies the investment of relatively large amounts in stocks, by individuals and by institutions whose liabilities may have to be discharged in future years in large amounts of depreciated dollars.

5. Common-stock dividends, earnings, and prices may decline or lag during depressions, wars, periods of price control, and periods of rapid inflation.

6. Extensive common-stock price fluctuations appear likely in the foreseeable future. This seems to require that accounts subject to continuous dollar-value solvency tests or demand withdrawals use stocks only in modest degree and that those partially obligated make provision for liquid payment-reserve funds, deferred payments, or other ameliorative devices.

7. Finally, it is necessary to admit that we are without any effective capacity to estimate "normal" future prices for stocks or stock groups, even if we believe that we can "guesstimate" their probable future earnings and dividends. We have the price-earnings and yield data of the past, but these are not good benchmarks for judging stock prices in an era when both individuals and institutions fear the value of the dollar and are becoming increasingly uninhibited in their investment policies.

A CONCLUDING DIGRESSION

The foregoing are conventional and unsurprising conclusions. They assume mainly a continuation of existing economic trends and no major institutional changes. However, we are not exempt from rather significant institutional changes which may come about as much because of popular beliefs and fears as because of solid economic fact.

There is abroad among us the conviction that the cost of living will continue to trend upward, probably slowly but possibly rapidly. This has seemingly fostered a "flight into stocks" which has already developed stock-price repercussions and stock-price logic reminiscent of the unlamented New Era. Our new New Era has powerful institutional support in the investment company and the pension trust, among trusts and endowments generally, and may soon have the appealing variable annuity on a substantial scale. It is not unlikely that the entire situation may create a more or less permanent shift in the relative prices and immediate yields of stocks and bonds, with equal or lesser immediate yields on the stocks expected to be compensated by increases due to inflation and growth. This kind of stock-bond price relationship, with the stocks yielding less than bonds, already exists in the case of growth stocks.

No real business damage would of necessity result from this stock-bond pricing situation; financial practices could adjust to a case in which bond and mortgage rates remained above high-grade stock yields. Yet it would be unfortunate if, in hedging against an alleged inflationary drift, individuals and institutions were compelled to abandon too completely the security and liquidity of a senior and guaranteed position. It would be safer public policy to induce debtors and creditors to make some of their bond contracts on a purchasing-power basis, with the bond maturity sums and possibly the coupons adjusted up or down in proportion to changes in the price level. In fact, I am confident that several billions of long-term federal purchasing-power bonds could be sold over a few months' time to people and institutions who are now reluctantly turning to stocks, at an interest rate well below the market rate for straight bonds. Quite possibly the savings on interest rate would finance the excess payments required by our slow inflation. In any event, a successful step in this direction might help to solve several pressing economic needs,[6] including that of holding our second New Era stock market somewhere near the bounds of common sense.

---

[6]Nearly a third of the 11 million employees now covered by trusteed pension plans enjoy protective clauses which to some extent adjust pension expectations to final pay rates or similar measures. Many of the others obtain revisions of plan as economic elements change (see New York State Banking Department, *Pension and Other Employee Welfare Plans* [1955]).

26
ANALYSIS OF INTERNAL RISK
IN THE INDIVIDUAL FIRM*

*ROBERT W. MAYER is professor of finance at
the University of Illinois; he is in charge of the
courses in Investment and Securities Analysis.*

What is the nature and degree of risk in the individual firm? The question can have no general answer, of course, but to the financial or investment manager it is so fundamental that he must try to find some kind of answer in each particular case. As Dewing succinctly puts the matter,

> Under our competitive system of economic values, ... the rate at which (the earnings of) a business shall be capitalized, to obtain its value, will depend on the confidence the buyer may feel in the continuation of the earnings.
>
> This is the relative risk. The greater risk, the greater the doubt of continued earnings, the lower is the capitalized value of those earnings; and, conversely, the lower the risk, the greater the value. Consequently, to proceed further with a study of the rate of capitalization we must analyze the risk of the business as an instrument for producing earnings.[1]

Discussion of risk in connection with business finance and investment has a long and distinguished history.[2] There are two respects, however, in which the

---

*From *Analysts Journal*, Vol. XV, No. 6 (November 1959), pp. 91-95. Reprinted by permission.

[1]A. S. Dewing, "The Financial Policy of Corporations" (New York: Ronald Press Co., 5th Ed., 1953), p. 288.

[2]See, e.g., Alfred Marshall, "Principles of Economics" (London Macmillan and Co., 1890), pp. 525, 622; W. H. Lyon, "Capitalization: A Book on Corporation Finance" (Boston: Houghton Mifflin Co., 1912), pp. 54-55; F. H. Knight, "Risk, Uncertainty and Profit" (Boston: Hougton Mifflin Co., 1921), pp. 197-232; C. O. Hardy, "Risk and Risk Bearing" (Chicago: University of Chicago Press, 1931), pp. 1-8; A. S. Dewing, "The Financial Policy of Corporations" (New York: Ronald Press Co., 3d Rev. ed., 1934), p. 145; J. M. Keynes, "The General Theory of Employment, Interest and Money" (New York: Harcourt Brace and Co., 1936), pp. 144-45; H. H. Evans and G. E. Barnett, "Principles of Investment" (Boston: Houghton Mifflin Co., 1940), pp. 49-76; G. W. Dowrie and D. R. Fuller,

literature is disappointing. In the first place, the analysis often undertakes to differentiate and classify various types of risk with familiar words used by different authors in senses which are inconsistent to the point of contradiction.[3] In the second place, little use is made of certain analytical techniques which are now familiar to financial analysts and which lend at least some precision to the argument. It is not the purpose of this paper to attempt a settlement of all the conceptual questions, but only to treat one phase of the problem of risk and to show how certain well-known quantitative methods can be applied to analysis of that phase. Even this limited objective, however, requires the adoption (and brief explanation, if not defense) of certain concepts necessary to communication on the subject.

Fundamentally, the financial or investment manager's concern about the individual firm is in respect to its prospective earnings (E), its risk (R), and its value (V). This concern may take the form of an explicit or implicit transformation of the prospective earnings into a capital value $(V = E/R)$—the concept referred to by Dewing in the passage quoted in the opening paragraph above—with a view, say, to passing judgment upon the propriety of the aggregate nominal value of the firm's securities (capitalization), or upon the reasonableness of their aggregate market value. Or, it may take the form of a determination of the rate of earning on the firm's aggregate book or market value $(R = E/V)$ with a view to judging whether it adequately compensates for risk. The value theory on which this interrelation is based applies only to firms in unregulated, competitive industries. In the public utility and other regulated industries there are important institutional limitations on the interdependence of value, prospective earnings, and risk. This analysis, therefore, deals only with firms in the unregulated industries.

Risk is taken to mean the probability, expressed as a fraction not exceeding unity, that the firm will fail. There are many meanings of "fail," of course, some highly legalistic, some purely economic or financial; but they all reflect, as cause or effect, cessation of the prospect of productivity. To the

---

"Investments" (New York: John Wiley & Sons Co., 1941), pp. 139-197; B. B. Howard and Miller Upton, "Introduction to Business Finance" (New York: McGraw-Hill Book Co., 1953), pp. 19-23; H. C. Sauvain, "Investment Management" (New York: Prentice-Hall, Inc., 1953), pp. 98-158.

[3]*Cf.,* e.g., the varying uses of "business risk" and "financial risk" in Marshall, *op. cit.,* p. 525; Lyon, *op. cit.,* pp. 54-55; Hardy, *op. cit.,* pp. 1-8; Dowrie and Fuller, *op. cit.,* p. 143; J. O. Kamm, "Economics of Investment" (New York: American Book Co., 1951), p. 205; Howard and Upton, *op. cit.,* pp. 19, 23; Sauvain, *op. cit.,* p. 98; and J. C. Clendenin, "Introduction to Investments" (New York: McGraw-Hill Book Co., 2nd ed., 1955), pp. 4-6; the varying uses of "internal risk" and "external risk" in Evans and Barnett, *op. cit.,* pp. 59-60; Dowrie and Fuller, *op. cit.* (2nd ed., 1950), pp. 109-113; and R. R. Pickett and M. D. Ketchum, "Investment Principles and Policy" (New York: Harper and Bros., 1954), pp. 262-64; and the identity of "personal risk" as used in Marshall, *op. cit.,* p. 622, and "lender's risk" as used in Keynes, *op. cit.,* p. 144, with "financial risk" as used in Lyon, *op. cit.,* pp. 54-55.

financial or investment manager this[4] is the essential meaning of failure, and it is therefore the one adopted here.

REASONS FOR CORPORATE FAILURES

It is usually considered desirable to distinguish, if possible, between *internal* and *external* risks, for the reason that in the former case most of the evidence to be analyzed in evaluating the risk can be found within the firm, while in the latter case it must be sought outside. The distinction, however, is not so easy to make as might at first be supposed. Of the various kinds of risk commonly considered in the context of financial investment, some—e.g., the risks of operating inefficiency, of exhaustion of mineral deposits, and of imprudent financing—seem clearly internal as to both cause and effect. Other kinds—e.g., the money rate risk, the purchasing power risk, and the price (or market) risk—seem obviously external since their causes lie outside the firm and since they do not have differential impact on the productivity of individual firms, per se.

Still other kinds—e.g., the risks brought on by growth of the economy and by technological change—are external as to cause but may be internal as to effect. Since the focus of the financial or investment manager evaluating the general risk of the individual firm is on its prospect of productivity, any particular risk which casts a shadow upon that prospect will be regarded here as internal even though part of the evidence concerning it may have to be sought outside the firm.

Business risk is taken to mean the probability, expressed as a fraction not exceeding unity, that the firm's prospective business productivity will cease to be compensatory. Business productivity means the ratio of net income[5] to total capital. It is compensatory when Business Productivity = Pure Interest + Business Risk.

---

[4]Perhaps "normally" should be inserted here. In a period when large numbers of "investors" and, by extension, investment managers, seem to measure the success of their "investment" operations by their realized or unrealized market value appreciation based on inflation fear and game strategy, some may wonder whether the theory of economic productivity as the ultimate basis of investment value has become obsolete. The financial chaos which usually follows such periods, however, has a way of evoking revival of interest in it.

[5]After deducting operating expenses (including capital consumption allowances) but before deducting interest or dividends. Whether income taxes are to be regarded as operating expenses or as distributions of net income is moot. The deductibility of explicit interest on borrowed capital in determining taxable income argues the latter treatment; the non-deductibility of implicit interest on owned capital argues the former. In the theoretical mileu this is a side issue, although as a practical matter the analyst must settle it one way or the other. In the illustrations in this paper, income taxes have been treated as operating expenses; but nothing about the principles discussed in the paper would be changed if they were to be treated as distributions of net income.

Business risk is not affected by the manner in which the firm raises its capital but only by the economic factors which govern the success of the firm as a producing unit. Such factors may be classified, for the sake of analysis, as (a) those which affect the *activity* of the firm's capital and (b) those which affect the *efficiency* of the firm's operation.

The activity of the firm's total capital may be measured by the ratio commonly called its turnover,[6] i.e.,

$$\text{activity} \quad = \quad \frac{\text{sales (or gross revenues)}}{\text{total capital}}$$

Other things being equal, business productivity varies directly with the activity or turnover of the total capital.

The activity of total capital is a composite of the activity of its elements. As a first step of analysis, it is appropriate to examine the elements to determine the relative proportions of fixed (long-lived) assets and current (short-lived) assets. Generally speaking, the larger the proportion of fixed assets—whose value is extracted by the firm's operation only over a long period of years—the less the activity of the total.[7] Any factor, internal or external, giving rise to expectation of an increase in the proportion of fixed assets thus tends to reduce the firm's prospective business productivity, i.e., to increase the business risk. (Such a tendency may be offset, of course, by expectation of an increase in efficiency.) Even within the fixed and current asset categories, shifts in the direction of longer-lived forms reduce the activity of the total capital, so any factors giving rise to expectation of such shifts must be considered to increase the business risk.

Where sales or gross revenues arise from the disposal of different products or services in different markets manifesting substantially unlike demand conditions[8] they may require separate analysis. In this case, the important

[6]Omission of "prospective" from the labels on the components in this and subsequent ratio specifications implies only that as a practical matter historical data very likely will be utilized as the best available guide to the future. The real focus is on the prospective, however, and if better evidence of the future than historical data is available it should by all means be utilized.

[7]Compare, e.g., R. H. Macy & Company, which in 1957 had a fixed (to total) asset ratio of 35% and (total capital) activity of 2.13 times a year, with Corning Glass Works, which had a fixed asset ratio of 50% and activity of 1.11 times, and with Dow Chemical, which had a fixed asset ratio of 66% and activity of only 0.85 times.

[8]See, e.g., Radio Corporation of America, which in 1957 derived 72% of its revenues from the sale of radio and television equipment, the other 28% from broadcasting; General American Transportation Corporation, which derived 53% of its revenues from the sale, the remaining 47% from the rental, of freight and refrigerator cars; and International Business Machines Corporation, which derived 40% of its revenues from the sale, 60% from the rental and servicing, of office machinery.

principle is that the more *indirectly* the demand is derived from some ultimate consumer satisfaction, the more susceptible the revenue to fluctuations from changes of demand. Thus, the greater the proportion of revenues arising from such sources, the greater the business risk. Where the firm's output is sold in a homogeneous market, on the other hand, this phase of analysis mainly involves examination of such factors as may affect the volume of sales without significantly altering the capital investment: changes in demand conditions, price and service policies, sales promotion, and the like. These do not lend themselves easily to ratio analysis, and they may require for their study considerable external evidence; yet they must often be investigated thoroughly as important determinants of prospective productivity and thus of business risk.

The efficiency of the firm's operation may be measured by the complement of the operating ratio, i.e.,

$$\text{efficiency} \quad = \quad 1 \quad \frac{\text{operating expenses}}{\text{sales (or gross revenues)}}$$

Other things being equal, business productivity varies directly with efficiency, that is, with the complement of the operating ratio.[9] Analysis of sales is essential in connection with efficiency, as well as with activity, since any cause which might bring about a decline of sales (without corresponding reduction of operating expenses) forebodes a diminution of efficiency and therefore of prospective business productivity, i.e., increases business risk.

Analysis of operating costs is of course equally important, especially of "indirect" costs[10] which do not vary closely with the volume of sales and which thus produce a kind of "leverage"[11] in the operations of the firm. The greater the proportion of such costs, the greater the hazard to efficiency and to prospective business productivity, i.e., to business risk. Such cost analysis may also necessitate thorough study of conditions in the markets in which the firm must purchase its inputs of goods and services.

---

[9] In the physical sciences efficiency is conceived as the ratio of output to input the values yielded by such calculations (considering the law of conseration of energy and the inevitability of frictional losses in all energy transformations) being less than unity and thus more convenient than reciprocal values ranging to infinity. In financial analysis it has long been customary to measure efficiency by the ratio of input to output, no doubt because the values yielded by such calculations usually (considering the practical necessity of omitting some inputs—such as social costs— in accounting for the firm's net income) fall in the convenient range below unity.

[10] Such as selling, general and administrative expenses; maintenance and repairs; capital consumption allowances (depreciation, depletion and amortization); taxes (except excise and payroll taxes); and rents and royalties. Of Boeing Airplane Company's total operating expenses in 1957 only 8% were indirect, of Coca-Cola Company's nearly 57%, and of International Business Machine Corporation's more than 66%.

[11] See later discussion of financial leverage.

By way of summary at this stage, it may be observed that the factors discussed above in connection with analysis of business productivity are interrelated as follows:

activity	=	sales/capital
efficiency	=	1 $-$ (operating expenses/sales)
net income	=	sales $-$ operating expenses
business productivity	=	net income/capital
	=	activity $\times$ efficiency

That is to say, activity and efficiency, as defined, are the sole determinants of business productivity.

Financial risk is taken to be the probability, expressed as a fraction not exceeding unity, that the firm's financial productivity will cease to be compensatory. Financial productivity means the ratio of owners' earnings (net income minus financial expenses) to owned capital. It is compensatory when Financial Productivity = Pure Interest + Financial Risk.

The firm's financial risk is governed by (a) its business risk and (b) the manner in which it raises its capital, i.e., the degree of financial leverage or "gearing"[12] in its financial structure. The relationship between business risk and financial risk, somewhat over-simplified, may be indicated by

$$\text{financial risk} = \frac{\text{business risk} \times \text{total capital}}{(\text{business risk} \times \text{borrowed capital}) + \text{owned capital}}$$

When there is no financial leverage—that is, when the firm employs only owned capital—financial risk is identical with business risk. Introduction of leverage

---

[12]W. Hastings Lyon introduced the expression "trading on the equity" into American financial literature in his "Capitalization: A Book on Corporation Finance" (1912), p. 50, to denote the policy of utilizing borrowed as well as owned capital in the firm's operation, adopting it from British usage. Except among academic authors, the expression has not found very wide acceptance, however, having been superseded, in the American vernacular, by "leverage" and in the English (at least with respect to investment trusts) by the more modern-sounding "gearing." These picturesque terms evoke a sharp mental image of the effect which borrowing at fixed interest and maturity value has upon the earnings on, and value of, the owned capital – multiplying or magnifying the impact (upon owned capital) of fluctuations in the earnings on, and value of, the total capital. Leverage has always been most common in the financial structures of the railroads and public utilities, but even among industrial firms today practically all have at least a little, and many have a great deal. Weyerhaeuser Timber Company, outstanding as one of the few remaining large firms to maintain almost the "New England Plan of Finance" (no debt at all), in 1957 utilized borrowed capital to the extent of only 7% of its total capital; Aluminum Company of America used 47%; and P. Lorillard Company used 65%.

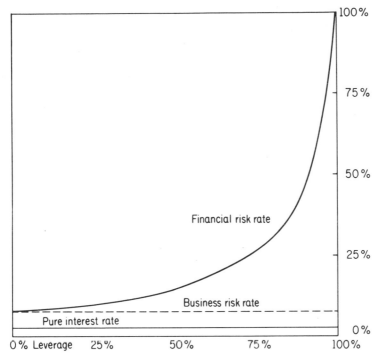

produces a financial risk higher than the business risk; and as leverage is increased to such an extent that owned capital approaches the vanishing point, the financial risk approaches 100% (certainty) as a limit. See accompanying chart.

FINANCIAL PRODUCTIVITY EXAMINED

This description oversimplifies the relationship because the cost of borrowed capital, although relatively constant, is not absolutely invariable and is a determinant, however minor, of financial risk. That is, complete explanation of financial productivity requires analysis of (a) business productivity, (b) financial leverage, and (c) the cost of borrowed capital.

Leverage may be measured by the proportion of borrowed capital in the financial structure, i.e.,

$$\text{leverage} \quad = \quad \frac{\text{borrowed capital}}{\text{total capital}}$$

Analysis of leverage is thus essentially analysis of borrowed capital, and the primary differentiation traditionally observed is that between short term debt and long term debt. The usefulness of this distinction in the study of financial risk rests upon the presumption that if the debt position becomes "unsound" and creditors consider the firm's obligations to them to be in jeopardy, they will take action, in protection of their interests, which may impair the firm's freedom of action and its prospective financial productivity. Soundness of the short term debt position is judged by application of the current, or "bankers" ratio—probably the oldest of all credit tests— and the "acid test," and by comparison of their values with either rule-of-thumb standards generally considered to provide adequate margins of safety or with statistical norms for the industry in question. Doubts about the liquidity of such current assets as inventories and receivables may be resolved by calculating their turnovers and comparing the resulting values either with production cycles and credit terms or, again, with statistical norms for the industry in question.

Soundness of the long term debt[13] position is best judged by two types of tests: (a) those relating the debt to the book value of the long-lived assets which, presumably, the long term debt was incurred to finance and which, directly or indirectly, constitute the security for its discharge; and (b) those relating the earnings available for financial expenses to the financial expenses, commonly called "coverage" tests.[14] Values derived from such tests usually are compared, not with statistical norms for the particular industry in question, but with pragmatic rule-of-thumb standards which are presumed to be rather broad in their applicability. Individual analysts differ in detail as to the manner of applying the tests and as to the standards of comparison; but since the publication of Graham and Dodd's book on *Security Analysis* there has been very general agreement, at least in principle, among academic and professional analysts alike, with the views expressed therein.[15]

For analyzing the determinants of financial productivity, it is more significant to differentiate the elements of debt by their costs. In the aggregates

$$\text{cost of borrowed capital} = \frac{\text{financial expenses}}{\text{borrowed capital}}$$

---

[13]Where preferred stock is cumulative and non-participating, as generally is the case today, its financial risk character (although not its legal character, to be sure) is more nearly that of borrowed, rather than owned, capital. It is therefore regarded as long term debt and its dividend requirements as financial expenses.

[14]Invalidity of the "prior deductions" method of computing coverage—in which the financial expenses attributable to senior issues are deducted in arriving at the base for computing coverage of the financial expenses attributable to a junior issue—is now so widely recognized that it has virtually disappeared except in the short cut method commonly (and implicitly) employed when one mentally computes the coverage of preferred dividends by dividing the per share dividends into the per share earnings.

[15]Benjamin Graham and D. L. Dodd, "Security Analysis" (New York: McGraw-Hill Book Co., 3d Ed., 1951), pp. 316-384. The first edition was published in 1934.

but this, of course, is a composite of the costs of the elements. In the typical industrial firm today most of the debts which are of short maturity are also non-interest bearing. More precisely, they bear no *explicit* interest, and it is usually considered not to be practically feasible to impute to them their *implicit* interest cost. These debt elements—e.g., open accounts and accrued expenses—are usually incurred under circumstances in which the cost of borrowing does not play a very significant part. They are not to be ignored as a leverage factor, however, since they constitute a source of borrowed capital which has the effect of magnifying fluctuations in financial productivity and also of magnifying the financial risk—if not by occasioning a fixed financial expense charge, at least by imposing a (potential) threat to the soundness of the current position.

The case of long term debts is more obvious since they nearly always occasion fixed financial expense charges which are quite explicit and therefore clearly magnify changes in financial productivity and financial risk. Whether in a particular firm the leverage policy is "profitable" may be judged at a glance by comparing business productivity either with the cost of borrowed capital or with financial productivity.[16] This concept must be used with caution, however, because a next step which might superficially appear to be logical —comparison of the rates on particular debt issues with over-all business productivity—is not valid. Even in theory, the proper analytical comparison would be between the costs of the increments of debt and *the marginal productivity of the resulting increments of assets;* but this meticulous refinement is feasible only in rare instances.

The factors discussed above in connection with analysis of financial productivity are interrelated as follows:

business productivity = net income / total capital
leverage = borrowed capital / total capital
cost of borrowed capital = financial expenses / borrowed capital
financial productivity = owners' earnings/ owned capital

$$= \frac{\text{business productivity} - (\text{cost of borrowed capital} \times \text{leverage})}{1 - \text{leverage}}$$

---

[16]Aluminum Company of America in 1957 enjoyed business productivity of 6.9%, while its cost of borrowed capital was only 2.8%, the difference of 4.1% representing the "profit" on the 46% of total capital which was borrowed. Alternatively, the business productivity of 6.9% might be compared with the financial productivity of 10.4%, the difference of 3.5% representing the rate by which leverage "profit" added to the return on the 54% of the total capital which was provided by the owners.

That is to say, business productivity, leverage, and cost of borrowed capital, as defined, are the sole determinants of financial productivity.

Analysis of risk in the individual firm is important to the financial or investment manager because of the key role which risk plays in deriving value from prospective earnings. Business risk, the probability that business productivity will cease to be compensatory, is governed by the factors which govern business productivity, namely: activity of capital and efficiency of operation. These factors may be analyzed by differentiating asset componenets with respect to their anticipated useful lives, of revenues with respect to the derivation of demand in their sources, and of operating expenses with respect to the directness of their relation to the volume of business.

Financial risk, the probability that financial productivity will cease to be compensatory, is governed by the factors which govern financial productivity; namely, business productivity, leverage, and the cost of borrowed capital. The latter two factors may be analyzed by differentiating debt components with respect to their costs. All of these analytical operations may be carried out with data which are conveniently available and techniques which are familiar. It has been the purpose of this paper merely to show their interrelation by reference to the risk theory on which the analysis is based.

G 758